# Foster Care in America

Recent Titles in the
# CONTEMPORARY WORLD ISSUES
## Series

Books in the **Contemporary World Issues** series address vital issues in today's society such as genetic engineering, pollution, and biodiversity. Written by professional writers, scholars, and nonacademic experts, these books are authoritative, clearly written, up-to-date, and objective. They provide a good starting point for research by high school and college students, scholars, and general readers as well as by legislators, businesspeople, activists, and others.

Each book, carefully organized and easy to use, contains an overview of the subject, a detailed chronology, biographical sketches, facts and data and/or documents and other primary source material, a forum of authoritative perspective essays, annotated lists of print and nonprint resources, and an index.

Readers of books in the Contemporary World Issues series will find the information they need in order to have a better understanding of the social, political, environmental, and economic issues facing the world today.

CONTEMPORARY WORLD ISSUES

# Foster Care in America

## A REFERENCE HANDBOOK

Christina G. Villegas

An Imprint of ABC-CLIO, LLC
Santa Barbara, California • Denver, Colorado

**Library of Congress Cataloging-in-Publication Data**

Names: Villegas, Christina G., author.
Title: Foster care in America : a reference handbook / Christina G.
   Villegas.
Description: Santa Barbara, California : ABC-CLIO, [2022] |
   Series: Contemporary world issues | Includes bibliographical
   references and index.
Identifiers: LCCN 2021058135 (print) | LCCN 2021058136
   (ebook) | ISBN 9781440874291 (hardcover) |
   ISBN 9781440874307 (ebook)
Subjects: LCSH: Foster home care—United States. | Foster
   children—United States—Social conditions. | Foster children—
   United States—Psychology.
Classification: LCC HV875.55 .V55 2022 (print) | LCC
   HV875.55 (ebook) | DDC 362.73/30973—dc23/eng/20220121
LC record available at https://lccn.loc.gov/2021058135
LC ebook record available at https://lccn.loc.gov/2021058136

ISBN: 978-1-4408-7429-1 (print)
       978-1-4408-7430-7 (ebook)

26 25 24 23 22    1 2 3 4 5

This book is also available as an eBook.

ABC-CLIO
An Imprint of ABC-CLIO, LLC

ABC-CLIO, LLC
147 Castilian Drive
Santa Barbara, California 93117
www.abc-clio.com

This book is printed on acid-free paper ∞

Manufactured in the United States of America

In a 1988 address dedicating May as National Foster Care Month, President Ronald Reagan emphasized that "the family is the indispensable foundation of society; at its best, it performs tasks that no other entity can hope to duplicate." All members of an immediate and extended family are important, but parents are especially essential as they bear the primary responsibility for children's physical, emotional, psychological, and social development. Dedicated parents are instrumental in building confidence, character, and self-sufficiency in adulthood. In fact, social science research over the past several decades has overwhelmingly demonstrated the importance of parental/child relationships and the beneficial influence of a stable family life on children's development and overall well-being and in preventing a variety of social pathologies (Wilcox et al. 2011). Unfortunately, this stability is absent for the large percentage of children who are removed from their family of birth and placed in the foster care system because they have been abused, neglected, abandoned, or are otherwise unable to continue living safely with their original guardians.

According to a 2020 study released by the federal Children's Bureau, more than 400,000 children reside in foster care in the United States on any given day, and nearly 675,000 different children spent at least some time in care in 2019. This number reflects an increase in the need for foster care over the past decade from a variety of factors, one of the most notable being the opioid and substance abuse epidemic plaguing the nation. The social isolation, economic insecurity, and heightened caregiving burden resulting from the COVID-19 pandemic and corresponding shutdowns is also likely to affect the foster care system and the need for care for years to come.

The foster care system—which operates independently in each state under the direction of social service agencies—is meant to provide temporary refuge and care for children while their biological families or original guardians work to create a safe and healthy environment for their return. Once children are placed in foster care, the primary goal of the state social service agencies is to make every attempt to reunify them with their families or, when reunification is not possible, to find them permanent, safe, and loving homes.

More than half of the children who enter care will eventually be reunited with their parents or primary caregivers, and another quarter will be adopted, many by their foster parents. Yet, numerous others languish in the system for years and experience multiple placements rather than the love of a permanent and stable family. Over 20,000 youth leave foster care each year without a permanent home, a trend that without the implementation of major reforms is likely to continue. Although federal and state efforts have expanded to provide independent living services to help youth who have aged out of the system to successfully transition to adulthood, these youth are still at increased risk of poor educational outcomes, unemployment, homelessness, mental and physical illness, and involvement with the criminal justice system. Even those who achieve permanency through adoption prior to aging out frequently suffer from the effects of serious trauma and other harms that come from having experienced abuse and neglect, a disruptive home life, inconsistent education, and separation from their parents, siblings, and other relatives. These outcomes are worse the longer children languish in foster care and are particularly acute for children placed in group homes or congregate care rather than with relatives or foster families.

In light of signs that the U.S. foster care system is failing many of the children who come into it, individuals, faith-based groups, and other public and private organizations across the country are expanding their efforts in new and creative ways to reduce the need for foster care, to improve experiences and outcomes for foster youth, and to increase the likelihood that children placed in care will be raised in healthy environments with a loving family.

*Foster Care in America: A Reference Handbook* is a valuable resource for students and general readers seeking to understand the history and operation of foster care in the United States and to identify the key issues at stake in the foster care system. The book additionally highlights ongoing and proposed efforts to improve the delivery of care and outcomes for foster youth and provides a listing of key actors and resources as a foundation for further research and engagement of the topic.

*Foster Care in America* is organized into seven chapters. Chapter 1, "Background and History," presents an overview of the scope and operation of foster care in the United States. It introduces the historical development of the American foster care system and outlines the various federal laws that have been adopted to govern and influence state foster care practices and systems.

Chapter 2, "Problems, Controversies, and Solutions," outlines common and persistent problems plaguing foster care as well as some of the most prominent controversies related to the delivery of care. Included in this discussion is an examination of the socioeconomic contexts of foster care and the various phenomena that contribute to the abuse, neglect, and other factors that necessitate children's placement in foster care. The chapter explores specific efforts and proposals aimed at improving the experiences and outcomes for children and families who are currently involved with, have been involved with, or are at risk of involvement with the child welfare system. The chapter concludes with a discussion of how the COVID-19 pandemic and corresponding shutdowns have made it more difficult to detect child abuse and neglect in U.S. society. It also discusses how the pandemic has hampered the capacity of foster care systems to provide effective care as well as potential promising reforms.

Chapter 3, "Perspectives," includes seven essays written by authors from a variety of viewpoints and professional and personal backgrounds on a range of topics related to the issue of foster care. These essays are intended to supplement and enrich the presentation laid out in chapters 1 and 2.

Chapter 4, "Profiles," lists and describes key government-sponsored entities, policy and research institutions, faith-based groups, and other private nonprofits dedicated to providing direct services to foster youth, promoting better policy, and recruiting, equipping, and assisting strong, loving foster families.

Chapter 5, "Data and Documents," offers data and primary source documents, including testimonies, speeches, executive orders, and court briefs, to provide readers with firsthand information on the scope and nature of foster care, insights from those who have experienced foster care, controversies over policy, and suggestions for how the system can be improved to better serve foster youth.

Chapter 6, "Resources," provides an annotated list of selected books, articles, and reports on a variety of topics related to foster care in the United States. Several magazines, periodicals, and nonprint sources—including movies and documentaries—are listed and annotated as well.

Chapter 7, "Chronology," offers a timeline of defining moments and major events affecting the U.S. foster care system.

The book concludes with a glossary of key terms related to foster care in America and its various contexts as well as a comprehensive index.

I would like to thank Robin Tutt and Kevin Hillstrom at ABC-CLIO, who assisted me in various stages of this project. Thanks also to Martha Elwell, who reviewed drafts of a few of the chapters. I am additionally thankful to Brian Janiskee, chair of the Political Science Department at California State University, San Bernardino, for his professional support and mentorship and to Marilyn Gareis, the political science administrative support coordinator, for her assistance in various administrative tasks.

In the spring of 2020, I conducted an independent study on the foster care system with several undergraduate political science students at California State University, San Bernardino—Javier Cordova, Jaymie Gonzalez, Alexandra Janiskee, and Keonte Jefferson. I am grateful for the unique insights they each provided in their discussion and research of the topic.

I am forever indebted to Diana Hayes for her invaluable mentorship. She convinced my husband and me to become foster parents, and she offered essential guidance and support as we fostered and eventually adopted our four beautiful children.

Above all, I am grateful to my husband, Manuel, and our children, Alexander, Anna, Izabella, and Sophia, for their support and for the profound joy they bring to my life.

# Foster Care in America

## Introduction

The term *foster care* refers to the juvenile dependency system intended to serve neglected, abused, and abandoned children who need to be either temporarily or permanently removed from their families of origin. Today, the system serves more than 670,000 children a year, and on any given day, over 400,000 of the nation's children are in some form of foster care (Children's Bureau 2020). While the concept of out-of-home care for abandoned or maltreated dependent children has existed in some form since the nation's founding, the provision of that care looked very different in America's early years compared to the complex government-run juvenile dependency system that exists today. This chapter provides a brief overview of the current structure and operation of foster care in America and outlines the historical development of the American foster care system, with a specific focus on the various federal statutes adopted to govern and influence state practices.

## Overview of Current System

Foster care in America has never been and is still not a national system. Under the U.S. Constitution, the federal government

A group of boys being fostered in a juvenile asylum learn how to resole shoes. Foster care in early America often involved the placement of orphan or abandoned children in a family or institutional setting where they would have the opportunity to learn skills that would enable them to live independently once they came of age. (Library of Congress) was given legislative authority over specific areas of policy, and the 10th Amendment left all remaining powers to the states or to the people. These reserved powers, commonly referred to as the *police powers*, cover a wide range of policy areas, including the health, safety, morals, and general welfare of residents. Under this broad policy umbrella, states pass laws governing law enforcement, punishment for civil and criminal offenses, marriages, contracts, education, child welfare policy, and other societal areas. Today, the federal government primarily influences the child welfare system through the provision of technical assistance and funding to states and private agencies. The funding is generally contingent on the states and agencies using the funding in a way that is consistent with federal law. Such federal child welfare policy is generally administered by the Children's Bureau, a branch of the Administration on Children, Youth, and Families (ACYF) within the Department of Health and Human Services (HHS). The federal government has also increasingly governed state policy in an effort to ensure compliance with the U.S. Constitution and civil rights laws.

Despite increased federal involvement and oversight over the past several decades, the states still retain control over the administrative framework for child welfare within their borders. Consequently, the operation and delivery of programs and services vary from state to state and even from locality to locality. At the state level, child welfare services are generally administered in one of three ways (CWIG 2018b). Most states operate a centralized administrative system run by the state government through its health and human services department or by an independent state-level child and family services agency.

Nine states—California, Colorado, Minnesota, New York, North Carolina, North Dakota, Ohio, Pennsylvania, and Virginia—have decentralized county-administered systems. Under such systems, county-level administrators submit a plan for how they will provide services to meet the needs of the region within the bounds of state and federal guidelines. The final form of child welfare service administration utilized by several states is a hybrid system in which the state government directly supervises and finances services, but county governments have significant influence over the funding and implementation of programs.

Under all three administrative systems, a variety of local agencies typically work together to serve those within the system. Public agencies often contract with and rely on private agencies and nonprofit community organizations to provide services related to family preservation; foster family recruitment, training, and support; mentorship for children and families; mental health care; substance abuse treatment; parenting skills classes; employment, housing, and financial assistance; and more. The process of placing children in care and working toward reuniting them with their families or finding a permanent placement for them elsewhere also requires the involvement of the state court system and sometimes local law enforcement.

## Reporting and Investigation of Abuse

The process through which children are placed in foster care is for the most part uniform across the country (CWIG 2020). About a third of children enter foster care because of delinquent behavior or because of the absence of their parents resulting from illness, death, or disability. Some parents voluntarily relinquish their children if they believe they can no longer care for them.

Typically, however, children first become involved with the child welfare system through a report of suspected child maltreatment, which may include abuse, neglect, or abandonment. *Maltreatment* that qualifies as child abuse and neglect is defined in both federal and state laws. The federal government provides guidance to states by setting a minimum standard definition of *child abuse and neglect* that states must adopt to be eligible for federal funding.

The federal Child Abuse Prevention and Treatment Act (CAPTA), as amended in 2010, defines *child abuse and neglect* as "any recent act or failure to act on the part of a parent or caretaker, which results in death, serious physical or emotional harm, sexual abuse or exploitation, or an act or failure to act which presents an imminent risk of serious harm" (CWIG 2019). The 2015 Justice for Victims of Trafficking Act expanded CAPTA's definition *of child abuse and neglect and sexual abuse* to include a child who is identified as a victim of sex trafficking or other severe forms of trafficking in persons.

States can expand on CAPTA's definition of *child maltreatment* in both their criminal and civil laws. Whereas criminal law definitions provide grounds for arrest and prosecution in criminal courts, civil law definitions determine the grounds for the reporting obligations of individuals and the required intervention by state and local child protection services (CPS) agencies and civil courts. Child welfare agencies typically do not intervene in cases of harm caused by acquaintances or strangers because these cases generally involve criminal charges and are handled by law enforcement.

Some states, however, do authorize CPS agencies to respond to both criminal and civil charges of child maltreatment. In cases where a child's parent or guardian is accused of severe abuse, such as sexual abuse or serious physical abuse, CPS agencies will generally call on the police to investigate and file criminal charges against the perpetrator.

Anyone can report suspected child abuse or neglect, but most warnings of possible abuse are made by mandated reporters. The term *mandated reporter* refers to individuals such as teachers, medical care providers, social workers, and the like who are required by state law to report cases of suspected child abuse and neglect. If an allegation of abuse or neglect involves sufficient information to warrant further involvement, a caseworker will be assigned to conduct further investigation.

## Substantiated Cases of Abuse and Neglect

In cases of substantiated abuse or neglect that are determined to be low to moderate risk, a caseworker may work to connect a family with prevention services and community-based resources and support—such as counseling, housing, child-care, job training, substance abuse treatment, and so on—in an effort to avoid having to place children in foster care. If, however, a caseworker or agency determines that removal may be necessary to keep a child safe, the agency will initiate proceedings with a juvenile dependency court (CWIG 2016). Children who are deemed to be in immediate danger may be temporarily moved to a care facility or foster home under a court-issued emergency protection order while the investigation proceeds.

Following a fact-finding hearing or adjudicatory trial to determine whether sufficient evidence of child maltreatment exists, a juvenile dependency court will hold a dispositional hearing to determine whether the child can remain at home or, if not, where the child will live. During this hearing, a judge may place the child in the custody of a child welfare agency for out-of-home placement and will determine a visitation plan for the child's parents or guardians. An assigned caseworker will develop a case plan to outline the services provided and the steps the parents or guardians must take to reunite with their children.

At least every six months, the court will hold a review hearing to determine whether the parents or guardians have made progress or have successfully completed their case plan. If the parents have successfully completed their case plan, they regain custody of their child, and their case is closed. If parents fail to follow the case plan after a certain amount of time (usually one to two years), the court may hold a hearing to terminate parental rights. Parents or guardians may also voluntarily relinquish their parental rights. In most states, a child becomes eligible for adoption directly following the termination of parental rights.

Once children are placed in out-of-home foster care, federal law requires child welfare agencies to design and implement a legal permanency plan within 12 months. The permanency plan usually aims at family reunification, but in certain cases, it may involve permanent placement with a relative or the termination of parental rights and adoption by either a relative caregiver or a nonrelative foster family. The dependency court may schedule frequent hearings to ensure the assigned child welfare agency is actively pursuing permanency and that the children are not languishing in out-of-home care.

Although family reunification is the default permanency plan in almost all cases, in situations where family reunification is less likely, an agency may develop a concurrent permanency plan (CWIG 2018a). Concurrent planning involves the simultaneous pursuit of an alternative permanency plan (such as permanent guardianship with a relative or adoption by a foster family) that can be implemented if parent-child reunification fails. The goal of concurrent planning is to shorten a child's stay in foster care by pursuing more than one plan for permanency.

In the late 1970s, Seattle juvenile court judge David W. Soukup developed the Court Appointed Special Advocate (CASA) model. He designed the CASA model after coming to the realization that he had insufficient information to make life-changing permanency decisions for children who had suffered from child abuse and neglect because the only information available was that provided by the state's Child Protective Services. Under the CASA model, now used throughout the country, courts assign a trained volunteer to children in foster care. This volunteer stays with the assigned child through his or her placement experience and is meant to provide detailed court reports and to serve as a consistent advocate on behalf of the child for the duration of the child's time in foster care.

According to data provided by the Children's Bureau (2020), reunification with birth parents or an original caretaker was the primary case plan goal for about 55 percent of children placed in foster care in 2019. About 47 percent of children exiting the system achieved this goal. A little more than a quarter of children exiting care were adopted by either a relative or their foster family. Another sizeable percentage left foster care through placement with a legal guardian, a person who is given the right to care for and make parental decisions for a child. Legal guardianship, which can be granted to relatives, foster parents, or other adults who have an established relationship with a child, provides a level of stability and permanency without the termination of parental rights.

Over 20,000 youth, however, left foster care when reaching 18 years of age without being reunified with their families, adopted, or placed in a permanent home. Improving the life outcomes of this latter category of foster youth has become a matter of primary concern for state and federal policy makers and nonprofits in recent years.

## Forms of Placement

Today, children in foster care are placed in one of three main types of care: in kinship care, with nonrelative foster parents, or in a group home, which is also known as congregate care.

### Kinship Care

*Kinship care* refers to a situation in which a child does not live with his or her parents but with a biological family member or close family friend who had an established relationship with the child before removal from the family home. Most children enter kinship care through informal arrangements, but a child welfare agency or court can also facilitate placement.

Informal kinship care occurs when a family voluntarily decides that a child will live with a relative or other acquaintance. In such cases, the parents retain legal custody of their children. A caseworker may become involved to provide minimal oversight and supportive services, but a child welfare agency does not assume legal custody or responsibility for the child.

Formal kinship care occurs after a court rules that a child must be separated from his or her parents because of abuse, neglect, abandonment, or other circumstances. The child is placed in the legal custody of a child welfare agency, and the relative caregivers are trained, licensed, and financially compensated. Today, a little over a third of children who enter the foster care system are placed in some form of kinship care (Children's Bureau 2020).

### Nonrelative Foster Parent(s)

*Nonrelative foster parents* are individuals or couples who are licensed, trained, and partially compensated by the state to temporarily provide a safe living environment and food, clothing, transportation, and other care until a child can be reunited with his or her family or is adopted. Foster parents have to balance being a child's de facto parents; loving a child, often alongside their own children; and providing as much normalcy as possible while simultaneously helping prepare a child for a return to his or her birth parents, permanent guardianship, or adoption. In 2019, nearly half of all foster placements were with nonrelative foster parents, and more than half of all children adopted out of foster care were adopted by their foster parents (Children's Bureau 2020).

### Congregate Care

While most children in foster care are placed with relatives or foster families, some are placed in group or residential settings known as *congregate care* that serve larger groups of foster children in a single facility. Congregate care includes the following types of care facilities: group homes, where a group of foster children lives together in a licensed facility operated by staff members who work in shifts and are sometimes called *house parents*; shelters; and therapeutic or psychiatric residential treatment centers that are designed for children who require a higher level of supervision and treatment due to medical, behavioral, or emotional issues. Children are placed in congregate care settings either because they have unique needs or because there is a shortage of qualified foster family homes able or willing to take them in. Congregate care is more frequently used for older children.

## Historical Foundations of Foster Care in America

The provision of care for abandoned and orphaned children in the United States has a history in both the Christian and Jewish religious traditions, both of which feature religious texts that portray caring for dependent children as a duty under law. Early church records show that monetary collections were used to support widows who took in such children (Sabini 2017). The first orphanage was reportedly established in the colonies in 1729 for the child survivors of an Indian massacre near Natchez, Mississippi. Prior to the mid-19th century, however, such institutions were uncommon. Typically, relatives or neighbors took over the care of children who had lost their parents (Warren 1998).

English Poor Laws inspired the first legal provision for the care of dependent children in the United States. These laws, initially adopted in England around 1562, allowed for the placement of poor and neglected children into indentured service until they came of age (Bremner 1970). Beginning in the 17th century, several localities within the American colonies began to codify the English Poor Laws, allowing orphaned, abandoned, and impoverished children to be placed with a family under whose care they would have the opportunity to learn skills that would enable them to live independently once they came of age. Indentured contracts generally required a family to house, feed, clothe, and teach skills to indentured children in exchange for their labor. Prior to the 19th century, many higher-income families likewise made use of skill-based apprenticeship contracts for their own children. By the early 1800s, however, typically only children from low-income families were indentured (Hacsi 1995).

Concentrations of poverty, epidemics of disease, and an increase in drug and alcohol addiction that accompanied rapid immigration and urbanization increased the need for out-of-home care for children during the early decades of the 19th century (Rymph 2017). Many poor children and orphans who lacked a suitable caretaker were housed in almshouses, insane asylums, and even adult prisons. During this period, religious communities began to establish orphanages throughout the country as an alternative to those grim accommodations. Later in the century, as state legislatures started to outlaw the placement of children in almshouses, public funding was provided for the continued expansion of orphanages. By the late 1800s, there were several hundred orphanages in the United States. As these orphan asylums became the predominant method for caring for dependent children, they faced increasing criticism by those who argued that they produced institutionalized children unprepared to function as self-reliant adults (Hacsi 1995). Such advocates instead favored placing children in homes with families.

In 1853, Congregational minister Charles Loring Brace spearheaded the next major development in the American child welfare system. Concerned by the large number of neglected and homeless children living in squalid slums on the streets of New York City, Brace founded the Children's Aid Society (CAS), which included lodging houses and industrial schools to help those children.

Brace also believed that a strong family life was necessary to help children become productive adults. Consequently, a year later, the CAS began a "placing-out" program, known as the *orphan train movement*, in which approximately 200,000 orphaned or abandoned children from eastern cities were sent to live with pioneer families in small towns and rural areas, primarily on farms in the Midwest. Brace recruited families who were willing to provide free homes for these children, either for charitable reasons or because these children could help with chores, by advertising to southern and midwestern communities. Some of these children were assigned to specific families in advance, but most were only placed after being displayed to local families when they arrived at train stops.

In contrast to the previous system of indenture, in which children often maintained close ties with their biological families and communities of origin, the CAS's placing-out system was designed to "protect" children from the urban environment and other dangerous influences by severing all ties between children and their biological families (Hacsi 1995). Unfortunately, advertising and placement agencies rarely maintained contact with or checked in on children after they had been placed. While many children were placed with families who loved and cared for them, a large percentage were mistreated, abused, and treated like hired help rather than children in need of loving families.

By the 1920s, the use of orphan trains and labor-based adoptions began to wane as the need for farm labor in the Midwest declined. States started passing laws prohibiting the placement of children across state lines, and state and local governments became more involved in alleviating the factors that led to children living on the streets. Despite its apparent flaws, however, the CAS's placing-out system prompted public and private local agencies and state governments, beginning with Massachusetts, Pennsylvania, and South Dakota, to become more involved in the support and regulation of foster home placement. Efforts by officials and administrators in these states became the foundation for the foster care system that exists today.

The growth of the American Progressive movement at the turn of the 20th century marked the wider acceptance of the view that childhood is a distinct, important, and vulnerable stage of life deserving greater protection and that the state and federal governments should take a more involved role in promoting the health and welfare of all Americans (Yarrow 2009). Consequently, concerns about the effects of growing up in an orphanage became even more pronounced. Social reformers began to organize orphan asylums as smaller dwelling units partitioned into bedrooms, and they also experimented with alternatives such as promoting adoption, placing children with foster families, and giving "widow's pensions" to mothers to enable them to keep their children at home (Gates 1994).

By the early 1900s, several states had passed laws to prevent child abuse and neglect and had authorized the creation of children's aid societies to represent children's legal interests. State social service agencies also began to place greater weight on children's individual needs when making placements and to inspect foster homes and supervise and compensate foster parents.

In 1909, President Theodore Roosevelt called together the first White House Conference on the Care of Dependent Children in response to concerns about the institutional placement of children. The conferees recommended that measures be taken to prevent the removal of children from their homes, except under extreme circumstances, and to place those children who did have to be removed with other families instead of institutions. The conferees also pressed for the creation of a federal agency with the goal of overseeing state legislation and disseminating data on child welfare.

In response to such recommendations, President William Howard Taft signed the law establishing the Children's Bureau on April 9, 1912. Originally housed in the Department of Labor and now part of the Department of Health and Human Services (HHS), the Children's Bureau was the first federal department devoted to the welfare of children. It was given the responsibility of investigating and reporting on all matters pertaining to infant mortality, the birth rate, orphanages, juvenile courts, dangerous occupations, accidents and diseases of children, and employment.

In 1919, the Children's Bureau published Minimum Standards of Child Welfare, highlighting the importance of keeping children in their own homes whenever possible. It stated that if removal from a home was necessary, offering an environment of "home life" through foster placements was highly desirable. Nevertheless, at the time, the idea of families raising strangers' children was not widely accepted culturally; it was not until the

1950s that it became more common for dependent children to be placed in a foster home rather than an orphanage or other institutional setting.

## The Evolution of Federal Policy

Since the mid-20th century, the foster care system has in large part evolved in response to the passage of specific federal laws and regulations, including standards and stipulations attached to the allocation of grants to the states.

### The Social Security Act of 1935

During the 1930s, under Franklin D. Roosevelt's administration, the Depression-wracked United States witnessed an unprecedented growth of federal regulation and spending in areas such as labor and employment, education, and child welfare. The Social Security Act of 1935, which was primarily implemented to insulate individuals from financial insecurity in old age, also authorized the first federal grants for child welfare services. Specifically, Title IV of the law created the Aid to Dependent Children (ADC) grant program, which was later renamed Aid to Families with Dependent Children (AFDC).

The ADC program aimed to reduce the number of children placed in institutional settings by enabling the states to provide cash assistance payments, in most cases to mothers, for needy children at risk of neglect because of an absent, incapacitated, deceased, or unemployed parent. Though initially minimal in size, these grants became more generous over time, prompting the states to establish child welfare agencies and to develop programs for facilitating child welfare services.

Despite ADC designers' intention to aid mother-headed homes regardless of race or marital status, a provision in the original act authorized assistance only to "suitable homes." This provision effectively reduced the number of eligible children and inhibited coverage of "illegitimate" children—those born out of wedlock (Gordon and Batlan 2011). For the first couple decades of implementation, ADC caseworkers were given discretion to investigate clients and to cut off benefits for those deemed "unsuitable." By the late 1950s, it became apparent that needy children were routinely denied benefits because their unmarried mothers were cohabitating with a man or otherwise did not live in a morally "suitable home."

In 1960, the U.S. Department of Health, Education, and Welfare (DHEW), the department charged with administering ADC, implemented the Flemming Rule. This rule, named for President Eisenhower's DHEW secretary, Arthur Flemming, was passed in response to the "Louisiana Incident," in which Louisiana purged more than 20,000 children from its welfare rolls because their mothers had birthed them out of wedlock. The ruling declared that states cannot deny funding to children simply because they are living in households deemed "unsuitable." Under the ruling, states were required either to provide appropriate services to make the homes suitable or to move children to a suitable placement while continuing to provide financial support for such children. The following year, Congress codified the Flemming Rule and created a foster care component to ADC.

Under ADC-Foster Care, the states were granted federal matching funds for foster care payments made on behalf of children who had received ADC payments prior to removal from an unsuitable home. In 1962, additional amendments were added to the Social Security Act that expanded funding for children removed from homes deemed unsuitable and required state agencies to report troubled families with children identified as candidates for removal to the court system. The availability of federal AFDC funds for foster care helped spur the growth of foster care caseloads, and by 1976, well over 100,000 children were in AFDC-funded foster homes (Hacsi 1995).

In addition to increased federal funding for child welfare, the 1960s also witnessed a nationwide policy campaign to protect children from abuse and neglect. These efforts were a direct response to pediatrician C. Henry Kempe's well-publicized research on maltreated children. In 1962, Kempe and a colleague published a groundbreaking study titled "The Battered Child Syndrome." The study detailed evidence of severe physical abuse of children in their own homes and established a clear diagnostic criterion for battered child syndrome. Public outrage about the findings in Kempe's work put pressure on state legislatures to respond. By the late 1960s, all states had passed some form of a mandatory reporting law. In addition, several states began implementing and expanding policies outlining intervention and protective measures, such as home visitations, temporary guardianship, and termination of parental rights.

### The Child Abuse Prevention and Treatment Act of 1974

During the 1970s, the federal government took on a more active role in creating a policy framework for child welfare practices. Passed in 1974, the Child Abuse Prevention and Treatment Act (CAPTA) was the first major policy initiative at the federal level that attempted to shape the child welfare system. CAPTA was largely responsible for creating the modern process through which state and local agencies receive reports of suspected maltreatment and investigate those reports to determine (1) whether they are valid and (2) whether intervention services or out-of-home placement is necessary.

CAPTA launched the Child Welfare Information Gateway (CWIG), which acts as a national clearinghouse of information related to child maltreatment, and the Office on Child Abuse and Neglect (OCAN). CAPTA additionally established a minimum standard legal definition of *child abuse and neglect* to govern state-imposed mandatory reporting laws and earmarked federal funds to improve states' capacity to prevent, identify, and address child abuse and neglect. To be eligible for CAPTA funds, it required that states adopt mandatory reporting laws, investigate reports of abuse and neglect, educate the public about abuse and neglect, provide a guardian ad litem to every child who had been abused or neglected whose case resulted in a judicial proceeding, and maintain the confidentiality of Child Protective Services records. The law has been reauthorized and amended several times to update the standard definition of *child maltreatment* and to expand services.

CAPTA's establishment of a nationally accepted definition of *child maltreatment* and its support for greater enforcement of mandatory reporting laws, public awareness campaigns, and reporting hotlines contributed to a dramatic rise in the number of reported cases of suspected abuse. On the one hand, this successfully brought the problem of child abuse and neglect out from behind closed doors. On the other hand, by the early 1990s, millions of reports of suspected abuse were being made each year compared to about 100,000 reports a year prior to the passage of CAPTA (Gelles 2017). The increased number of reports grossly exceeded estimates of how many children were actually being maltreated, thereby straining state and local personnel and the financial resources of child welfare agencies. Responders now had to sift through a never-ending deluge of reports to identify and prioritize their investigations, creating a danger that they might not respond quickly enough to the most high-risk cases.

## The Adoption Assistance and Child Welfare Act of 1980

By the late 1970s, family preservation was becoming an increasingly salient issue for policy makers, chiefly due to the social and cultural changes brought about by the sexual revolution and the corresponding rise in divorce and teen pregnancy rates. At the same time, it became apparent that so much attention had been focused on removing children from high-risk situations that too little attention had been paid to what happens to them once they had been placed in foster care.

As the number of children entering foster care had increased over the decade so had their length of stay (O'Neill Murray, and Gesiriech 2004). Many children in foster care drifted from one placement to another without a permanent placement plan. In an effort to recognize and respond to the needs of these children, Congress passed the Adoption Assistance and Child Welfare Act of 1980 (AACWA).

The AACWA, which established a major federal role in the administration and oversight of child welfare services, had three major components. First and foremost, the act mandated that states make "reasonable efforts" to prevent foster care placement or to reunify children with their families as quickly as possible by providing abuse prevention and reunification services. The law, however, did not provide additional funding for such services. Instead, it shifted the financial burden for compliance with child welfare regulations to the states. Furthermore, due to the vague nature of the term, "reasonable effort" was often interpreted by caseworkers and administrators as requiring "every possible effort" (Gelles 2017). These changes effectively shifted the primary goal of state action away from protecting children from the possibility of abuse toward helping biological parents quickly reunify with their children.

Second, the act required that states develop a plan for achieving a permanency goal (e.g., reunification, relative placement, or adoption) within 18 months of a child's placement in out-of-home care. The act additionally mandated periodic court and administrative hearings to review and monitor the agency's progress in finding a permanent home for the child.

Finally, the AACWA created Title IV-E of the Social Security Act and transferred the AFDC-Foster Care grant program to this new title. In addition, the act added a federal adoption assistance program for children with special needs. The goal of this provision was to encourage the adoption of children who might otherwise be hard to place because of the high costs of raising children with ongoing medical and psychological needs.

Following passage and implementation of the AACWA, the number of children entering foster care and the average time spent in care briefly decreased during the early 1980s. Within a few years, however, the size of the country's foster care system had begun to grow again.

### The Influence of Cultural Heritage, Race, and Ethnicity on Child Welfare Policy

From the late 1800s to the 1950s, the federal government had imposed a policy of forcing Native American children to leave their family homes to attend boarding school. This misguided effort had been crafted to promote cultural assimilation of these children into mainstream "white" society. This practice inflicted terrible damage on tribal children, often permanently severing their connection with their family, tribe, and heritage.

In the late 1950s through the late 1960s, the Child Welfare League of America contracted with the Bureau of Indian Affairs to place Indian children with white adoptive families. The intention was to continue to assimilate needy and neglected Native American children into the mainstream culture while providing them a stable family and good upbringing. Tribal advocates, however, argued that, in practice, the program needlessly removed many Indian children from their homes, families, and tribes solely because their families were Native American and poor.

During the 1970s, Congress held a series of hearings confirming that a disproportionate number of Native American children were being removed from their homes and placed in foster care. In some states, 25–35 percent of Native American children were placed in foster care between 1974 and 1978 (Renick 2018). A vast majority of these children were placed outside of their tribes with non-Indian families, thereby threatening tribal survival and Native American culture.

Around the same period, several states overturned laws banning transracial adoption, and the country experienced a rapid increase in the acceptance and practice of adoption across racial lines. Widespread transracial adoption, however, eventually culminated in a backlash against the practice. Over the next couple of decades, two laws with very different provisions regarding cultural heritage, race, and ethnicity were implemented to govern foster care placement and adoption.

### *The Indian Child Welfare Act of 1978*

In 1978, Congress enacted the Indian Child Welfare Act (ICWA), which established new standards for child custody and adoption proceedings for Indian children. Specifically, the ICWA granted tribal courts jurisdiction over Native American children living on reservations who were wards of the state. It also gave tribal governments the right to be notified about—and intervene in—state court proceedings involving the placement of Indian children living off a reservation. The act imposed stricter evidentiary standards for removal in cases of Indian children and gave tribal governments the ability to request a transfer of such cases to a tribal court. The act additionally established the ICWA grant program, which provided funding for a wide array of tribal child welfare services.

### *The Multiethnic Placement Act of 1994 and Interethnic Provisions of 1996*

By the latter half of the 20th century, many American families were adopting children of all backgrounds, which led to many African American children being placed in transracial homes. In the early 1970s, however, various advocacy groups began to raise concerns over the adoption of African American children by white families. They started a campaign against transracial adoption based on the assumption that parents of the same race could best meet the cultural, emotional, social, and psychological needs of a child. In 1972, the National Association of Black Social Workers (NABSW) issued a position statement that took "a vehement stand against the placement of black children in white homes for any reason" and called on agencies to alter their requirements, methods of approach, definitions of a suitable family, and prohibitions against interstate placement to facilitate Black families for Black children (NABSW 1972).

The year following the NABSW resolution, the Child Welfare League of America revised its adoption standards to specify that same-race placements should be preferred in all cases. Social workers increasingly implemented race-matching policies as a result. Such actions led to a rapid decrease in transracial foster care placements, and the number of transracial adoptions dropped by more than 50 percent (Gelles 2017). The decline in transracial placements and adoptions caused by race-matching policies also contributed to longer stays in foster care for minority children and made it less likely that they would be adopted. Such findings, in addition to a growing body of social science research showing no developmental disadvantages or lasting harm among transracially adopted children, led many child welfare advocates to lobby for a "color blind" approach to placement and adoption.

Congress responded to these shifting sentiments and attitudes by passing the Multiethnic Placement Act (MEPA) in 1994. The act aimed to decrease the length of time children wait to be adopted; to eliminate discrimination against prospective foster or adoptive parents when they are of a different race, color, or national origin than the child; and to encourage the increased recruitment and retention of ethnically diverse foster and adoptive parents. To achieve these goals, the act prohibited state agencies and other entities involved in foster care or adoptive placements that receive federal financial assistance from delaying or denying a child's foster care or adoptive placement solely based on the child's or the prospective parents' race, color, or national origin. It also required states to diligently recruit foster and adoptive parents who reflected the racial and ethnic diversity of children in need of foster and adoptive homes.

In the meantime, in light of growing evidence that provisions in MEPA harmed African American and other minority children by implicitly condoning avoidance of transracial placements, Congress passed the Interethnic Provisions of 1996 to address perceived loopholes in the original law. Among other things, these amendments repealed a provision that had allowed states to consider the child's ethnic/cultural background and the prospective parents' ability to meet the child's related ethnic/cultural needs in placement decisions. The provisions instead prohibited any action that delayed or denied placement based on race, color, or national origin and imposed a funding penalty for states that delayed placement on any of those grounds. The law also placed foster care and adoption under the protection of Title IV of the Civil Rights Act of 1964 by creating a right for children, prospective parents, or the federal government to sue state or private foster agencies for delaying or denying placements based on race, color, or national origin.

In 1997 and 1998, HHS issued guidance documents stating that under the law "a child's race, color, or national origin cannot be routinely considered as a relevant factor in assessing the child's best interest." In practice, however, state and local governments have increasingly passed kinship care policies designed to keep children in families with their same racial and ethnic makeup.

### Challenges to the Indian Child Welfare Act

In contrast to MEPA, which sought to restrict the ability of child welfare agencies and courts to take race, color, or national origin into account when making foster care and adoption placement decisions, ICWA specifically requires considerations of race and ethnicity when it comes to children of Native American ancestry. The intention of ICWA was to redress past wrongful actions against tribal children and to prevent state child welfare agencies from removing Indian children from their parents and placing them outside of their communities for reasons of poverty or bigotry. Despite its noble intentions, ICWA has been embroiled in controversy over claims that its provisions have inhibited protection and permanency for Native American children living on and off reservations.

As discussed at greater length in the next chapter, critics have charged that the act has created a separate and unequal child welfare system for Native American children. They assert that ICWA enables courts to violate federal law by denying or delaying adoption cases based solely on the child's race. The law has faced many challenges in court on these grounds. In October 2018, a U.S. district court in Texas ruled in the case of *Brackeen v. Bernhardt* that components of ICWA violate various provisions of the U.S. Constitution. In April 2021, the Fifth Circuit Court of Appeals reached a divided decision in the same case, thereby upholding much of the trial court's ruling. The *Brackeen* case, along with other ICWA-related lower court decisions, is likely to be reviewed by the U.S. Supreme Court soon.

## Permanency Planning and Child Welfare Policy

During the 1980s and 1990s, Americans were increasingly taking advantage of new reproductive technologies and adopting healthy infants and toddlers through open and international adoptions. At the same time, though, adoptable foster children continued to languish in the system, drifting from placement to placement without the prospect of permanency. The longer children remained in care with little chance of reunification, the less likely they were to secure permanency through adoption.

The Adoption Assistance and Child Welfare Act of 1980 (AACWA) had required states to make "reasonable efforts" to keep children in their homes or to reunite them with their biological parents or caregivers as soon as possible. In addition, the Family Preservation and Support Services Program Act of 1993 had authorized additional funding for services to preserve, support, and reunify families in crisis. Despite these laws, however, evidence surfaced demonstrating that up to 40 percent of children reunited with their families of origin returned to foster care within 18 months of reunification (Gelles 2017). In some horrible cases, children who remained in their homes, even following allegations of severe abuse, were killed or permanently disabled by their parents. In other cases, children who were transferred out of foster care to go back to their family homes suffered the same fate.

Significant advocacy efforts on behalf of such children contributed to heightened public concern about child safety, permanency, and removing barriers to adoption. This shift in public sentiment eventually inspired the passage of the Adoption and Safe Families Act of 1997 (ASFA). ASFA shifted the focus of child welfare systems away from family preservation as the primary goal at all costs toward one that prioritized the health, safety, and well-being of the children.

The law first sought to change the current interpretation of AACWA's "reasonable efforts" requirements. Although ASFA reaffirmed the importance of making reasonable efforts to preserve and reunify families, it held that reunification efforts might not be required or in the best interest of the child when a court determines that certain circumstances would make it unsafe for a child to return to his or her family. Individual states have interpreted such "circumstances" to include "poor prognosis indicators" such as a previous involuntary termination of parental rights to a child's sibling, a history of prior child abuse or neglect, a felony conviction for murder or sexual assault of a child, a history of mental illness or substance use, refusal to seek or a failure to respond to treatment, a human trafficking conviction, or a demonstrated lack of interest in reuniting with the child (CWIG 2018a).

ASFA also introduced significant reforms into the foster care system, including shortening decision-making timelines for assessment and intervention services to children. It also included reforms to speed the placement of foster children into permanent placements. To help prevent children from languishing in foster care, ASFA required that child welfare agencies develop and implement a legal permanency plan within one year of placement and that permanency hearings be held every 12 months to ensure progress toward permanency.

Long-term foster care could no longer be listed as a permanency plan under these new rules, and states were encouraged to develop concurrent plans for cases in which reunification might not be achieved. The act additionally required that states file a petition to terminate parental rights for children who had been in foster care for 15 out of the past 22 months. The only exceptions to this requirement were cases in which a child was residing with a biological relative, when there was a compelling reason why a termination or rights would not be in the best interest of the child, or when the state had failed to provide reunification services.

In cases of severe abuse, including abandonment, torture, and sexual abuse, or in cases where a parent had caused the death of a sibling, states were encouraged to petition immediately to terminate parental rights.

Finally, ASFA encouraged the practice of adoption through a new adoption incentive payment program. In addition, it required HHS to establish new state performance standards and a state accountability system, whereby states could face financial penalties for failure to demonstrate improvements in child outcomes.

In the immediate aftermath of ASFA's passage, yearly foster care adoptions more than doubled, and the average length of time children spent in care and the number of children in care for five years or longer steadily declined (Gelles 2017). The law, however, is not without its critics. Some opponents have argued, for instance, that by shifting the emphasis of child welfare to ensuring that parental rights are terminated and that children are placed in a permanent guardianship or adoptive home in a timely manner, the act served to increase the disproportionate number of permanent family separations among racial minorities (White 2006). Others have pointed out that the law has created situations in which jurisdictions are unable to adequately work with families who face complex issues related to substance abuse, mental health, incarceration, or undocumented immigration status (Golden et al. 2009). Furthermore, the permanency rates for older youth have not been as positive, and the number of youth who emancipated from foster care without achieving permanency actually increased following the passage of ASFA (Golden et al. 2009). This may be due in part to the fact that when parental rights are terminated without a replacement permanency plan, the youth are legally considered to be orphans. Some of these youth never find a permanent family and, consequently, are without any legal family connections upon emancipation (turning 18).

## Increased Focus on Aging Out

In the early to mid-1980s, researchers conducted several surveys revealing that a growing number of older youth were aging out of the foster care system with little support or preparation for adulthood. They also found that a significant number of homeless shelter users had recently been discharged from foster care. In response, Congress created the first federal Independent Living Program. The program authorized an annual entitlement of $45 million for the next two years to provide states with resources to create and implement independent living services for AFDC-eligible children aged 16 and over. In 1988, the program was expanded to permit states to provide services to all youth in foster care aged 16 to 18, not just those who were AFDC eligible. States responded by implementing a variety of assistance options for foster children entering adulthood, including tuition waivers for college, transitional housing, and employment programs, among others.

As foster care caseloads increased in the late 1990s, the plight of older youth who had drifted from foster home to foster home only to be discharged to the streets at 18 without adequate preparation for adulthood became an even more salient issue. One of the major flaws with earlier independent living legislation was the limit on the age of youth who could be served and the fact that youth who aged out of the foster care system were not permitted to use federal funds for room and board. In 1999, Congress enacted the Foster Care Independence Act to better meet the needs of those aging out of foster care by significantly increasing support for those youth. Specifically, the act created the permanently authorized John H. Chafee Foster Care Independence Program (CFCIP). The law doubled the annual funds available to the states and expanded the population of youth eligible to receive independent living services. It did so by extending eligibility for federal funding through the age of 21 and including youth who had recently aged out of foster care. Furthermore, CFCIP gave greater flexibility to the states and tribes to design their own independent living programs and allowed them to support young adults by providing services related to education, employment, financial management, housing, and making connections with mentors. The act additionally gave states the option to enroll former foster youth in state medical assistance programs until the age of 21. In 2001, Congress amended the Chafee Independent Living Program to provide education and training vouchers for foster youth and to create new funding for mentoring the children of incarcerated parents.

Congress once again addressed the issue of youth aging out of care by passing the Fostering Connections to Success and Increasing Adoptions Act in 2008. The act specifically amended various provisions of the Social Security Act to create new funding and programs for supporting relative caregivers, increasing incentives for adoption, improving health and education outcomes for children and youth in foster care, and enhancing services to youth aging out of foster care. The act also gave states the ability to extend eligibility for Title IV-E funding for foster care youth to remain in foster care until age 21, so long as they are either pursuing employment, enrolled in education or employment training, or have a medical condition that prevents them from doing those activities. As of 2019, 27 states and Washington, DC, had implemented a federally approved and funded extended foster care program and 21 states had implemented a state-funded program. More data are necessary, however, to determine whether states and localities are following through on a stipulation that a caseworker must assist foster youth in developing a transition plan during the three-month period before they turn 18 (Gelles 2017). Ultimately, despite the passage of considerable federal and state legislation to help youth who age out of foster care, the struggles faced by many young adults who transition out of foster care remain a persistent social problem.

## Prevention, Family Preservation, and Promoting Family versus Institutional Care

In March 2018, the HHS released a report demonstrating that after over a decade of sustained declines, the number of children in foster care across the United States had increased by more than 10 percent (from 397,600 to 437,500) between 2012 and 2016 (Radel et al. 2018). The HHS study indicated that the rapid increase in caseloads was directly related to the nation's opioid epidemic. Six states where the crisis is particularly acute—Alaska, Georgia, Minnesota, Indiana, Montana, and New Hampshire—saw the number of children in foster care because of parental drug addiction and overdoses more than double between 2012 and 2016, and these numbers have continued to remain elevated. The study additionally highlighted the challenges child welfare agencies face in dealing with the crisis, including a severe shortage of good substance use treatment programs. Family-friendly treatment programs, the report pointed out, were particularly in short supply. In some localities, appropriate treatment options were nonexistent.

Furthermore, the study found that the high volume of cases, the lack of treatment resources, and the sheer magnitude of the problem were overwhelming caseworkers, leading to high stress, burnout, and high turnover. These problems, according to the study, were compounded by an increasing shortage of qualified foster care homes. This shortage was forcing the placement of a growing number of foster children into group settings, apart from their siblings, and often a long distance from their parents.

In an effort to reverse these disturbing trends in the provision of care and to keep at-risk children from having to enter foster care in the first place, Congress enacted the Family First Prevention Services Act (FFPSA) in May 2018. Prior to FFPSA's passage, most funding from the federal and state governments was allocated to assist children and families who were already involved in the system. FFPSA changed this by redirecting funding toward supporting families prior to their children being removed. Specifically, the act sought to prioritize keeping families together, particularly those struggling with the opioid epidemic, by putting federal money toward evidence-based prevention services such as at-home parenting classes, mental health counseling, and substance abuse treatment. Eligible beneficiaries for preventative services under the law include families of children identified as safe staying at home, teen parents in foster care, and those whose children can live with a grandparent or other close relative for a short time. The law also removed the requirement that free preventative services could only be offered to families living below the poverty line.

The act additionally recognized that prevention and family preservation are not always possible. It emphasized that when children are placed in foster care, every effort should be made to place them with a family rather than in an institutional setting. Pursuant to this goal, FFPSA provided $8 million in grants to support the recruitment and retention of high-quality foster families. It also limited placement of children in institutional settings by capping federal funding for group homes or "congregate care" settings. Under the law, states can only be reimbursed for up to two weeks of the time a child spends in a congregate care setting, with exceptions made for children in treatment programs requiring round-the-clock care.

FFPSA contained other investments in child welfare services and amendments to previous programs as well. It extended the eligibility period for education and training vouchers for emancipated youth until the age of 26. It also extended eligibility for the CFCIP's independent living services until the age of 23.

While several prominent child welfare advocates praised FFPSA's passage for bringing about much-needed improvements, others have contended that the law's limitation on funding to group homes is rife with unintended consequences, such as making it hard to house large sibling sets together and threatening funding for important residential drug treatment and mental health programs (Child Welfare Monitor 2018, 2019).

## Strengthening the Child Welfare System for America's Children

In the months leading up to and during the COVID-19 pandemic in 2020, the shortage of eligible foster care families throughout the country became even more pronounced. States and localities reported drastically lower numbers of families willing to provide safe, stable, and loving homes to foster children, even as the number of children in the foster care system continued to rise (Associated Press 2020). Even worse, plans to address these shortages were virtually nonexistent, and no one was looking into why approximately 30–50 percent of licensed foster parents quit within the first year (Riley 2020).

President Donald Trump responded to these trends on June 24, 2020, with an executive order titled Strengthening the Child Welfare System for America's Children. The order requires HHS to build within two years a more "rigorous and systematic approach to collecting State administrative data" to improve data collection on the demographics of children waiting for adoption, the number and demographics of currently available foster families, the average foster parent retention rate, the targeted number of foster homes needed to meet the needs of foster children, and the average length of time required to complete foster and adoptive home certification.

Trump's executive order also promoted collaboration between public, private, faith-based, and other community groups to help keep families together or to place children in permanent families. The order opened new resources to ensure that foster families have flexible educational and therapy options to meet the unique needs of children under their care, and it instructed HHS to develop a plan for addressing the barriers that kin and youth aging out of foster care may face in accessing existing federal assistance and benefits.

Although aimed at addressing persistent problems plaguing the delivery of effective care, it is unclear what impact the executive order will ultimately have. It contains no enforcement measure should state child welfare agencies fail to comply, and because it is a presidential proclamation rather than an official law, it can be revoked at any time. The ACLU has also expressed concern that encouraging partnerships with faith-based agencies may lead to the exclusion of potential foster parents who do not meet the religious requirements of a particular agency, such as LGBTQ parents (ACLU 2020).

## Conclusion

The provision of care for America's abandoned and maltreated children has evolved significantly over the course of U.S. history. The scope and operation of the current system of out-of-home care, commonly referred to as the child welfare or foster care system, is largely the result of state and federal policies adopted over the past century. Today, the foster care system is a complex combination of federal, state, and local governmental organizations working alongside private agencies to oversee the placement of dependent children with relatives, with nonrelative foster families, or in group facilities.

The immediate goal of this out-of-home placement is to provide temporary care for youth of all ages until a parent or guardian can safely resume care. The ultimate goal, however, is to ensure that children live in safe and stable lifelong families. This goal often requires that children be placed in an adoptive home or with a permanent guardian other than their original caretaker. Among children who enter foster care, most will ultimately return to the care of their own families or go to live with relatives or an adoptive family. Many children, however, are moved from placement to placement and never achieve permanency with a loving family. Thus, although the system has come a long way over the course of the nation's history, it still has a long way to go in producing good outcomes for foster children.

The subsequent chapter will explore some of the problems and controversies plaguing foster care and various efforts on behalf of public and private actors to improve the quality of care and the welfare of foster children.

## References

ACLU. 2020. "ACLU Comment on Trump Executive Order on Foster Care." June 24. Accessed September 9, 2021. https://www.aclu.org/press-releases/aclu-comment-trump -executive-order-foster-care

Associated Press. 2020. "Utah Foster Care System Faces Shortages of Parents Statewide." *U.S. News and World Report*. March 7. Accessed April 21, 2021. https://www .usnews.com/news/best-states/utah/articles/2020-03-07 /utah-foster-care-system-faces-shortage-of-parents-statewide

Bremner, Robert H., ed. 1970. *Children and Youth in America: A Documentary History*. Vol. 1. Cambridge, MA: Harvard University Press.

Child Welfare Monitor. 2018. "Sibling Separation: An Unintended Consequence of the Family First Act?" October 9. Accessed April 25, 2021. https:// childwelfaremonitor.org/2018/10/09/sibling-separation -an-unintended-consequence-of-the-family-first-act/

Child Welfare Monitor. 2019. "Family First Act: No Funding for Important Drug Treatment and Mental Health Services." November 18. Accessed April 25, 2021. https:// childwelfaremonitor.org/2019/11/18/family-first-act-no -funding-for-important-drug-treatment-and-mental-health -services/

Children's Bureau. 2020. "The AFCARS Report: Preliminary FY 2019 Estimates as of June 23, 2020—No. 27." U.S. Department of Health and Human Services, Administration for Children and Families. Accessed February 15, 2021. https://www.acf.hhs.gov/sites/default /files/documents/cb/afcarsreport27.pdf

CWIG (Child Welfare Information Gateway). 2016. *Understanding Child Welfare and the Courts*. Washington, DC: U.S. Department of Health and Human Services, Children's Bureau. Accessed March 12, 2021. https://www .childwelfare.gov/pubPDFs/cwandcourts.pdf

CWIG (Child Welfare Information Gateway). 2018a. *Concurrent Planning for Timely Permanence*. Washington, DC: U.S. Department of Health and Human Services, Children's Bureau. Accessed March 12, 2021. https://www .childwelfare.gov/pubPDFs/concurrent_planning.pdf

CWIG (Child Welfare Information Gateway). 2018b. *State vs. County Administration of Child Welfare Services*. Washington, DC: U.S. Department of Health and Human Services, Children's Bureau. Accessed March 12, 2021. https://www.childwelfare.gov/pubPDFs/services.pdf

CWIG (Child Welfare Information Gateway). 2019. *Definitions of Child Abuse and Neglect*. Washington, DC: U.S. Department of Health and Human Services, Children's Bureau. Accessed March 12, 2021. https://www .childwelfare.gov/pubPDFs/define.pdf

CWIG (Child Welfare Information Gateway). 2020. *How the Child Welfare System Works*. Washington, DC: U.S.

Department of Health and Human Services, Children's Bureau. Accessed March 12, 2021. https://www.childwelfare.gov/pubPDFs/cpswork.pdf

Gates, David. 1994. "History of the Orphanage." *Newsweek.* December 11. Accessed March 15, 2021. https://www.newsweek.com/history-orphanage-185444

Gelles, Richard. 2017. *Out of Harm's Way: Creating an Effective Child Welfare System.* New York: Oxford University Press.

Golden, Olivia, Jennifer Macomber, Susan Notkin, and Kristen Weber. 2009. *Intentions and Results: A Look Back at the Adoption and Safe Families Act.* Washington, DC: Urban Institute and Center for the Study of Social Policy. Accessed April 20, 2021. https://www.urban.org/research/publication/intentions-and-results-look-back-adoption-and-safe-families-act

Gordon, Linda, and Felice Batlan. 2011. "The Legal History of the Aid to Dependent Children Program." *Social Welfare History Project.* Accessed April 2, 2021. https://socialwelfare.library.vcu.edu/public-welfare/aid-to-dependent-children-the-legal-history/

Hacsi, Tim. 1995. "From Indenture to Family Foster Care: A Brief History of Child Placing." *Child Welfare* 74 (1): 162–180.

NABSW (National Association of Black Social Workers). 1972. "Position Statement on Trans-Racial Adoptions." September. Accessed April 30, 2021. https://cdn.ymaws.com/www.nabsw.org/resource/collection/E1582D77-E4CD-4104-996A-D42D08F9CA7D/NABSW_Trans-Racial_Adoption_1972_Position_(b).pdf

O'Neill Murray, Kasia, and Sarah Gesiriech. 2004. "A Brief Legislative History of the Child Welfare System." PEW Charitable Trusts. November 1. Accessed April 14, 2021. https://www.pewtrusts.org/en/research-and-analysis

/reports/2004/11/01/a-brief-legislative-history-of-the-child
-welfare-system

Radel, Laura, Melinda Baldwin, Gilbert Crouse, Robin
Ghertner, and Annette Waters. 2018. "Substance Use,
the Opioid Epidemic, and the Child Welfare System: Key
Findings from a Mixed Methods Study." Assistant Secretary
for Planning and Evaluation Research Brief. March 7.
Washington, DC: U.S. Department of Health and Human
Services. Accessed April 20, 2021. https://aspe.hhs.gov
/system/files/pdf/258836/SubstanceUseChildWelfare
Overview.pdf

Renick, Christie. 2018. "The Nation's First Family Separation
Policy." *The Imprint*. October 9. Accessed April 20, 2021.
https://imprintnews.org/child-welfare-2/nations-first
-family-separation-policy-indian-child-welfare-act/32431

Riley, Naomi Schaefer. 2020. "For Foster Kids, a Step
in the Right Direction." *City Journal*. July 9. Accessed
April 30, 2021. https://www.city-journal.org/executive
-order-foster-care

Rymph, Catherine E. 2017. *Raising Government Children:
A History of Foster Care and the American Welfare State.*
Chapel Hill: University of North Carolina Press.

Sabini, Charlene. 2017. "Foster Care: A History." NALS The
Association for Legal Professionals. Accessed January 7,
2021. https://www.nals.org/blogpost/1359892/290477
/Foster-Care-A-History

Warren, Andrea. 1998. "The Orphan Train." *Washington Post*.
November. Accessed March 20, 2021. https://www
.washingtonpost.com/wp-srv/national/horizon/nov98
/orphan.htm

White, Christina. 2006. "Federally Mandated Destruction
of the Black Family: The Adoption and Safe Families
Act." *Northwestern Journal of Law and Social Policy* 1 (1):
303–337.

Yarrow, Andrew L. 2009. "History of U.S. Children's Policy: 1900–Present." First Focus. April 2009. Accessed March 21, 2021. https://firstfocus.org/wp-content/uploads /2014/06/Childrens-Policy-History.pdf

## Introduction

The large number of children in foster care and the struggles that many young adults experience when they exit the foster care system without a permanent family are tremendously concerning issues in America today. Between 2012 and 2019, the number of children in foster care across the United States increased by nearly 10 percent, and the number of children waiting to be adopted grew by more than 20 percent (Children's Bureau 2020b). Foster care is a necessary option for children who face extreme abuse and neglect in their original homes, but there are many indications that the system needs to be improved and is even failing in certain areas.

Each year, thousands of foster youth drift from one placement to the next. At the same time, 20,000 to 30,000 leave the foster care system because they have not reunified with their family of origin or been adopted and are too old to remain in state custody. In addition to the high number of youth aging out of care who are unprepared for adulthood and who lack meaningful, permanent relationships or an effective support system, other features of the system have generated a great

---

A teen runaway. At least 20 percent of youth in foster care have run away at least once. The percentage is higher for teens. Running away is associated with a range of serious negative consequences including higher likelihood of HIV infection, substance use, academic underperformance, and subsequent involvement with the juvenile justice system. (Christy Thompson/ Dreamstime.com)

deal of concern and debate. Some states, for example, have come under scrutiny for being either too zealous or too lax in removing children from potentially threatening situations and for failing to follow state and federal laws, including statutory timelines for searching for kin and pursuing permanency.

One of the most prominent areas of concern in recent years has been the racial disparities within the child welfare system. These disparities have led some reform advocates to call for greater reliance on kinship care and even for defunding foster care altogether, but each of these proposed solutions presents its own set of problems for the children the system is supposed to serve. Finally, many of the troubles plaguing the foster care system are not within the system itself but are caused by societal factors, such as rampant drug abuse, mental health issues, chronic homelessness, unemployment, and the growing prevalence of single-parent homes.

This chapter provides an overview of some of the most persistent problems and controversies plaguing foster care as well as some of the chief controversies related to the delivery of care. It concludes by examining various proposals and actions aimed at improving the experiences and outcomes for children and families who become involved with the child welfare system in the United States.

## Aging Out of Foster Care

Every year, 20,000–30,000 children in foster care age out of the system without a permanent family or social support system. This predisposes them to a range of negative outcomes as young adults (Children's Bureau 2020a).

In 2011, Chapin Hall at the University of Chicago, in collaboration with the University of Wisconsin Survey Center and public child welfare agencies in Illinois, Iowa, and Wisconsin, published the results of the Midwest Evaluation of the Adult Function of Former Foster Youth, also known as the Midwest Study (Dworsky et al. 2011). This longitudinal study followed a sample of young people from Iowa, Wisconsin, and Illinois as they transitioned out of foster care and into adulthood. Foster youth in the three participating states were eligible to participate in the study if they had entered care before their 16th birthday, were still in care at age 17, and had been removed from home for reasons other than delinquency. Baseline survey data were collected from 732 participants when they were 17 or 18 years old. Participants were then reinterviewed at ages 19, 21, 23 or 24, and 26.

The goal of the study was to document how former foster care youth are faring after they age out in areas ranging from employment records, living arrangements, and academic experiences to criminal justice system involvement, physical health, familial relationships, and pregnancy rates. The findings revealed that young people are aging out of foster care without the knowledge, skills, and resources to thrive on their own. The study also found that a large percentage suffer from a range of poor psychological, social, and economic outcomes. Although the data suggested that extending foster care until age 21 may be associated with better outcomes in some domains, the study found that the life outcomes for foster youth who age out remain poor despite a variety of federal and state initiatives to provide them with assistance.

In 2019, the *Kansas City Star* published the results of a comprehensive investigation into the long-term outcomes of youth who have aged out of foster care. The six-part series, titled "Throwaway Kids," demonstrated that a history of childhood trauma combined with a lack of permanency, social connection, and preparedness for adulthood placed youth aging out of foster care at much greater risk than their peers. Of the more than 20,000 youth who age out, 20 percent will immediately become homeless, and more than 50 percent will experience homelessness within four years (Bauer and Thomas 2019). Furthermore, foster youth in general—and particularly those who age out—are far less likely than their peers in the general population to graduate from high school or to find gainful employment. They are also far more likely to be incarcerated (Bauer and Thomas 2019).

### Foster Care Runaways

In addition to the large number of youth who age out of the system, a sizeable percentage also run away from foster care placements. One analysis of administrative data from Florida found that nearly 20 percent of foster youth had run away from foster care at least once (Latzman et al. 2019). Self-report studies suggest, however, that the number is even higher. According to the Midwest Study, 46 percent of the 17-year-olds interviewed reported having run away from a foster care placement at least once (Latzman and Gibbs 2020). Running away is associated with a range of serious negative consequences, including higher likelihood of HIV infection, substance use, academic underperformance, and subsequent involvement with the juvenile justice system (Latzman and Gibbs 2020).

Foster youth who run away from care or who age out of care without a familial or social support system are easy to exploit and manipulate, which makes them particularly susceptible to sex and labor trafficking in the United States. In fact, several recent studies have demonstrated that most of the nation's victims of sex trafficking come from the foster care system (Dolce 2018). For instance, the National Center for Missing and Exploited Children (NCMEC) found that "of the more than 18,500 endangered runaways reported to NCMEC in 2016, one in six were likely victims of child sex trafficking." Of these likely victims, "86 percent were in the care of social services when they went missing" (Dolce 2018).

Other studies have demonstrated similar findings. In 2013, 60 percent of sex trafficking victims rescued in a nationwide 70-city FBI raid came from foster care or group homes. In a 2012 raid in Connecticut, 86 of the 88 children recovered were from the child welfare system. Most alarming, an FBI nationwide bust in 2014 found foster children as young as

11 years old who had never been reported missing by child welfare authorities.

## Placement Instability, Delayed Permanency, and Other System Failures

Although foster care is a necessary alternative for many children living in abusive and neglectful environments, it is not meant to be a long-term solution. Nevertheless, over a quarter of youth placed in care remain in the system for more than two years. Less than 40 percent of states are achieving the goal of an average of two or fewer placement settings for children in foster care (Casey Family Programs 2018).

Some states and localities have particularly poor records when it comes to these measurements. For example, the average length of stay in foster care in Wyoming and Tennessee is a little over a year; however, in Illinois, it is nearly three years, and it is nearly four years in Washington, DC (ASPE 2014). The longer children remain in foster care, the more likely they are to experience multiple placements and to age out without ever being placed with a permanent family. Drifting from placement to placement only compounds the trauma foster youth experience prior to entering care and contributes to their bleak prospects for stability and well-being into adulthood. In fact, research suggests the frequent moves and a lack of permanency and predictability of care not only harms children emotionally by making it difficult for them to form secure and healthy attachments but also harms them physically by interfering with the normal development and function of their brain's prefrontal cortex (Adler 2019). This in turns puts foster youth at greater risk of post-traumatic stress disorder, disruptive behaviors, drug and alcohol abuse, and a range of psychiatric disorders.

A variety of factors are associated with placement instability, including individual child characteristics, placement characteristics, and resource family characteristics (Casey Family Programs 2018). One of the primary factors inhibiting the effective delivery of care and permanency for foster children is a shortage of eligible foster and adoptive parents. This shortage, paradoxically, is not caused by a lack of potential resources. As Thomas C. Atwood, the former president of the National Council for Adoption, has pointed out, there are hundreds of families and at least three places of worship representing a variety of faiths for every child waiting to be adopted in the United States (Atwood 2011). If a greater proportion of these existing places of worship established or expanded efforts to recruit and support eligible foster families, they could potentially alleviate the shortage.

Studies have also found that Americans are highly amenable to the idea of foster care and adoption. According to a survey conducted by the Dave Thomas Foundation for Adoption, at least one in four Americans has considered or is currently considering adopting a child, and nearly 80 percent of potential adopters are interested in adopting out of foster care (Dave Thomas Foundation for Adoption 2017). Furthermore, the number of Americans willing to provide foster care for and to adopt children with special needs has greatly increased over the last few decades (Sheffield 2020).

Despite the openness of many Americans to the idea of foster care and foster adoption, state agencies often fail to respond to inquiries from interested parties and exhibit various weaknesses in recruiting, tracking, training, and matching applicants (Wilson, Katz, and Green 2005). According to one study, only 1 out of 28 initial inquirers into foster adoption eventually ended up adopting a child. Another study showed that only about 8 percent of individuals who inquire into becoming foster parents are eventually licensed (Atwood 2011; North Carolina Division of Social Services 2009). While some level of screening is essential to prevent the licensing of unsuitable applicants, overly cumbersome and unnecessary requirements often deter qualified and well-suited applicants. Countless others, who might be willing and able to foster or adopt, do not even make an initial inquiry because of child welfare agencies' reputation for unresponsiveness and excessive red tape or burdensome requirements. Furthermore, despite foster parents' crucial role in delivering care, states use very little funding to recruit them (Sheffield 2020).

State agencies also have a poor record of retaining foster parents. According to a study commissioned by the Center for State Child Welfare Data at Chapin Hall, a quarter of newly licensed foster care homes close within the first two to four months and nearly 50 percent close within the first year, making the median length of service of foster homes less than a year (Wulczyn et al. 2018). Only a quarter of foster homes remain open to taking children in for more than two years. Most states have spent very little time accounting for this low retention rate, but surveys of current and former foster care providers suggest that a perceived lack of support and respect from child welfare agencies is a leading cause (Atwood 2011; Sheffield 2020; CHAMPS 2019a).

Additional factors contributing to placement instability are delayed permanency decisions and weak enforcement of the Adoption and Safe Families Act's (ASFA) timeline for terminating parental rights. ASFA mandates that child welfare agencies develop and implement a legal permanency plan within one year of placement and that permanency hearings be held every 12 months to ensure progress toward permanency. The act additionally requires that states file a petition to terminate parental rights for children who have been in foster care for 15 out of the past 22 months, except in cases where a child was residing with a biological relative, when there was a compelling reason why a termination of rights would not be in the best interest of the child, or when the state had failed to provide reunification services.

State agencies and courts, however, frequently use the "compelling reasons" exception and other loopholes to ignore timeline rules. According to a Children's Bureau (2018) review, a termination of parental rights was only filed in 52 percent of the applicable cases reviewed. In 26 percent of eligible cases in which a termination of parental rights was not filed, no reason for exemption was included. An earlier Department of Health and Human Services (HHS) report revealed that in 2013, only 14 percent of children who had been in the foster care system for at least 15 of the past 22 months were legally free for adoption because parental rights had been terminated (Children's Bureau 2016).

There are a variety of reasons for lax enforcement of ASFA timelines. One might be the poor incentives created by federal Title IV-E foster care funding (Gelles 2017). Currently, Title IV-E operates as an uncapped entitlement rather than as a block grant program. This means that states receive funding based on the number of children who are in foster care and have little financial incentive to limit their time in care. States lose money when children achieve permanency through reunification, permanent guardianship, or adoption.

Another reason for delayed permanency decisions is that some child welfare practitioners and juvenile and family court judges will purposely prolong such decisions because they are ideologically opposed to terminating parental rights or to placing children with adoptive parents of a different race (Atwood 2011; Sheffield 2020). Others may merely lack a sense of urgency or may have sympathy for birth parents who struggle with substance abuse or have gone off their medication to combat mental illness. Such judges may extend or ignore timelines, telling child welfare agencies to give parents another chance (Riley 2020b).

Despite understandable sympathies for birth parents, time is of the essence for children, especially in the early developmental stages of life. Extending the time allotted for birth parents to comply with reunification requirements leaves children in a state of physical and emotional limbo and greatly diminishes their likelihood of forming secure attachments, developing in a healthy way, being placed in permanent housing, or being loved and cared for by a family through adoption. While it may be appropriate to allow parents more time under special circumstances, if a parent is not progressing toward recovery or is failing to comply with benchmarks set for reunification, children should not be allowed to languish in temporary placements.

Once parental rights are terminated, it is critical that children, particularly those who are very young, be immediately placed in an adoptive home if their guardian or foster parents do not intend to adopt them. The documentary *Unadopted* (2020), directed by 22-year-old former foster youth Noel Anaya, illustrates the importance of this point. Anaya himself entered foster care at age one. He spent his whole childhood and adolescence in foster care but was never adopted, chiefly because he was never placed with a foster family willing to adopt him.

While the number of children placed in foster care who do not receive timely permanency is clearly a problem in need of attention, there are also many children who are never removed from severely abusive situations and placed in foster care. In his book *Out of Harm's Way: Creating an Effective Child Welfare System*, Richard Gelles (2017), a former dean of the University of Pennsylvania School of Social Policy and Practice, recounts the story of Danieal Kelly, a 14-year-old girl with cerebral palsy who died from severe abuse and neglect despite coming to the attention of child welfare authorities on multiple occasions.

Another recent egregious example was highlighted in the Netflix six-part documentary miniseries *The Trials of Gabriel Fernandez* (2020). This miniseries recounts the true story of the abuse and murder of eight-year-old Gabriel Fernandez, from Palmdale, California, by his mother and her boyfriend and the ways that the system had failed to protect him. Through court transcripts and interviews with members of Gabriel's family, journalists, attorneys, and others, the series reveals the magnitude of the systemic failures that left him in such a terrible situation despite tangible evidence of dangerous levels of abuse and torture in the home. Such stories illustrate failures in child welfare agencies caused by a lack of oversight and effective transmission of information, overloaded caseworkers, apathy, and other systemic issues.

## Restrictions on Congregate Care

In May 2015, the Annie E. Casey Foundation published the "Every Kid Needs a Family" study, which highlights the number of foster children placed in group homes or residential treatment facilities, also known as congregate care settings, and the disparate life outcomes for such children. In line with the recommendations made in this report, the Casey Foundation spearheaded a political movement to reduce the use of group homes for foster care. This movement, aided by high-profile stories of corruption and abuse in congregate care facilities, resulted in legislative reform at the state and federal levels. California, for example, passed the Continuum of Care Act in 2015, which effectively ended the placement of foster youth in group settings except for instances of short-term therapeutic care. In 2018, Congress passed and President Trump signed the bipartisan Family First Prevention Services Act (FFPSA). This bill limited the placement of children in institutional settings by essentially cutting off federal funding for placement in group homes or "congregate care" facilities. Under the law, states can only be reimbursed for up to two weeks of the time a child spends in congregate care, with exceptions made for children in treatment programs requiring round-the-clock care. The goal of FFPSA was to incentivize states to reduce their reliance on congregate care. Its supporters believed that children are more likely to thrive in a family as opposed to an institutional setting.

It is widely acknowledged that too many foster children are unnecessarily placed in congregate care rather than with individual foster families. Widespread agreement also exists that, all else being equal, family settings are much better for children than institutional ones. Nevertheless, some child welfare professionals have pointed out several unintended consequences for foster youth from burdensome restrictions on institutional settings as well as the limitations on federal funding for such placements. Every state is currently experiencing a shortage of foster families and beds for the number of children placed in foster care. Closing congregate care facilities has only made this problem worse. With no backup plan, foster children have been forced to sleep in county offices and hotels or to be placed in medical and detention facilities.

Furthermore, while children are more likely to thrive in a family setting, group homes are often more equipped to care for foster youth. This is particularly true of older youth with special needs due to severe behavioral, psychological, or medical issues. Some foster youth are placed in congregate settings because of a lack of other options, but most are there because staying with a foster family did not work out or because they have experienced levels of abuse and neglect that make it nearly impossible for them to function in a family setting.

While the greater cost of congregate care facilities contributes to their unpopularity, the higher costs facilitate a wide range of therapeutic care, round-the-clock supervision, and extracurricular activities for children who need appropriate treatment and a safe environment. Defenders of residential care contend that critics often fail to recognize the wide range of programs available in congregate care and ignore that children in such care are more likely to struggle, at least in part, because the most traumatized and troubled youth are usually the ones placed in residential facilities. Advocates of congregate care acknowledge that some group homes provide poor care and are rife with abuse, but they emphasize that other quality programs have been highly successful at achieving positive outcomes for youth through the effective provision of individualized, trauma-informed care (Cohen 2020a).

Another potential negative consequence of FFPSA and its restrictions on funding for congregate care is a higher number of sibling separations (Cohen 2018). Keeping siblings together whenever possible is critical to the emotional development and well-being of children placed in care. Siblings provide a level of continuity, familiarity, and security for children who have already suffered a traumatic removal from their home. Children who are separated from their siblings in foster care tend to have poorer outcomes than those who remain together (CWIG 2019).

Most cases of separation occur because of the lack of foster homes that can accommodate sibling sets, particularly when there are more than two siblings. In many states, group homes provide a viable means of keeping large sibling sets together. In a few states, including Florida and North Carolina, family-style group homes are specifically designed for this purpose. Unfortunately, FFPSA threatens such options for sibling groups by requiring that group facilities meet criteria as qualified residential treatment programs for children with serious emotional or behavioral disorders to qualify for long-term federal funding.

Sadly, many congregate care facilities that offer highly effective programs are threatened with closure because of state laws and the FFPSA. One example is the San Pasqual Academy (SPA) in San Diego County, California (Cohen 2021). SPA was founded in 2001 by San Diego Juvenile Court judge James R. Milikan in collaboration with the County Board of Supervisors, the director of Child Welfare Services, the Office of Education, and various other members of the community. The goal of SPA is to provide a safe, stable, and caring environment where older foster youth can work toward their high school diplomas, prepare for college or a vocation, and develop independent living skills.

A 10-year research study that followed 478 SPA alumni found that youth who participated in SPA until they were 18 years old or older had GED completion and high school graduation rates far above state and national averages, not only for foster youth but for California's nonfoster youth as well (Lawler et al. 2014). They also demonstrated higher levels of well-being upon aging out than most other foster youth. Despite overwhelming evidence of SPA's life-changing impact on foster youth, the number of youth served by the program has plummeted following a decline in support by child welfare leaders for congregate care and the elimination of federal funds for long-term care in residential facilities.

Supporters of SPA have lobbied the California legislature and the county to adopt a stop-gap solution to keep the academy running while they work to amend state law to make residential schools eligible for reimbursement. Child welfare advocates, recognizing the unintended consequences of the recent crackdown on congregate care, are already working at the federal level to amend FFPSA to add residential campuses with family-style homes as a placement option. FFPSA could also be amended to allow congregate care for sibling groups and to provide new funding to encourage jurisdictions to build foster home communities where siblings can be raised together.

## Ensuring Protection and Permanency for Native American Children

The most controversial and contested law governing child welfare practice over the past several decades has been the Indian Child Welfare Act (ICWA). First passed in 1978, ICWA aimed to redress abusive federal policies that promoted the forced assimilation of American Indians into the broader culture. ICWA prevented state child welfare agencies from removing Indian children from their parents for reasons of poverty or bigotry or placing them outside of their communities. ICWA recognized tribal sovereignty over custodial decisions regarding Indian children living on reservations who were wards of the state. It also gave tribal governments the right to be notified of (and to intervene in) state court proceedings involving the placement of Indian children living off a reservation, imposed stricter evidentiary standards for removal in cases of Indian children, and required that child welfare agencies engage in more extensive efforts to keep Native American children with their families than is required in all other child welfare cases.

Despite its noble intentions, ICWA has been embroiled in controversy and has faced many challenges in court since it became law. Those who favor the maintenance and expansion of ICWA cite the fact that American Indian children are still in foster care at twice the rate of their peers as evidence of continued prejudice and ethnically corrupt practices and as a sign that the law's promises are yet to be fulfilled (Fletcher 2016; Renick 2018). Supporters of the law also contend that because of a lack of federal oversight or data collection related to compliance, state legislatures, public agencies, and courts have been permitted to interpret and apply ICWA's provisions and definitions on their own, resulting in inconsistent implementation of the law (Casey Family Programs 2015). Advocates of the law thus call on federal agencies to support improved monitoring of and compliance with ICWA mandates. Specifically, they contend that federal agencies should allocate funds and resources to promote active efforts to preserve and reunify Indian families. They also want agencies to implement standardized national compliance measures for individual provisions of ICWA accompanied by sanctions for noncompliance.

Critics of the law, however, maintain the disproportionate number of foster care placements from native communities result not from prejudiced removals but from the higher levels of poverty, family disintegration, domestic violence, and drug and alcohol abuse that plague such communities. They emphasize that native children consequently suffer rates of abuse and neglect at nearly twice the national average (Children's Bureau 2019).

Furthermore, while ICWA was supposed to protect Native American children from being arbitrarily and unnecessarily removed from their families and communities, many argue that it has ultimately contributed to a separate and inferior system of child welfare for children with Native American blood that deprives them of their equal rights as citizens (Cohen 2019; Sandefur 2016). A primary reason for this is that ICWA imposes rules on Indian children that are far less protective than the rules that apply to non-Indians.

For example, courts can place children of other races in foster care when there is a "preponderance of evidence" that they are in danger. Under ICWA, however, courts must abide by the more stringent "clear and convincing evidence" standard in cases involving children with Indian heritage. This makes it more difficult for state agencies to remove Indian children from abusive homes when necessary. Moreover, once Indian children are placed in foster care, child welfare agencies must take "active efforts" to reunite them with their families before they can terminate parental rights (as opposed to the "reasonable efforts" required in all other child welfare cases).

The termination of parental rights under aggravated circumstances does not apply under the more demanding active efforts standard, meaning that Indian children must suffer more severe abuse and neglect than other children before they can be cleared for adoption. Furthermore, because there are so few Indian foster and adoptive families, ICWA's requirement that Indian children be adopted by Indian adults, regardless of tribal affiliation, means that many Indian children who are removed from their homes languish in the system without a clear path to permanency.

Critics thus contend that ICWA imposes an unconstitutional form of racial discrimination that violates the individual rights and threatens the well-being of Indian children. Even though federal law prohibits the delay or denial of placement and adoption based on a child's race, ICWA imposes race-matching requirements in foster care and adoption cases, giving tribes the ability to veto the adoption of a Native American child by families who have loved and raised the child since infancy so that the child can be raised by Indian parents, even if the child has never met them or visited their reservation or state. In fact, the adoption of an Indian child by non-Native Americans can be challenged for up to two years after finalization if an Indian family emerges to take the child. In addition, ICWA applies to any child who is genetically eligible for membership in a tribe, regardless of whether the child has a relationship with the tribe and no matter how far removed the child's biological connection. In some cases, tribes have sought to remove children from the custody of their nonnative biological relatives to place them with native relatives they have never met simply because of their partial ethnicity (Sandefur 2016). The law even undermines the ability of Indian parents to offer input or make decisions regarding what they believe is in the best interest of their children. In 1989, the Supreme Court ruled that under ICWA, "the tribe has an interest in the child, which is distinct from, but on parity with, the interest of the parents" (*Mississippi Choctaw Indians v. Holyfield* 1989). In practice, this has meant that the placement preferences of biological parents can be overridden by tribal governments.

ICWA thus overrides the "best interest of the child" standard that applies in child custody lawsuits involving children of other races. According to this standard, custody arrangements should be determined by what best meets the child's needs based on a variety of considerations, including the child's age, attachment level, the need for consistency and safety, evidence of parenting ability, and so on. ICWA instead places the interest and wishes of the tribe above the best interest of the child.

In some cases, this dynamic has led to the placement of children in clearly dangerous environments. One example of this occurred when, because of rules imposed by the ICWA, two-year-old Lauryn Whiteshield and her twin sister were removed from a non-Indian foster family who had cared for them for more than a year. They were placed with their grandfather and his wife, despite the wife's documented history of child abuse and neglect and the fact that there were already five other children living in the home (Cohen 2019). Tragically, Lauryn's stepgrandmother threw her down an embankment and killed her before she reached her third birthday.

ICWA has already been challenged in a series of divided lower court decisions, and the Supreme Court will almost assuredly weigh in on the controversies inherent in the ICWA soon. In the meantime, supporters of ICWA are increasing efforts to recruit and regulate tribal foster care families and to advocate for new federal regulations aimed at a more expansive and consistent application of ICWA provisions (Carpenter 2016).

## Racial Disparities in Child Welfare

Like Native American children, Black children are highly overrepresented in the U.S. foster care system in comparison to their percentage of the general population. According to recent federal data, African American children account for roughly 14 percent of the child population but make up 23 percent of the foster care population (CWIG 2021b). These disparities, which are even more pronounced in large cities such as Chicago and New York, occur at nearly every major decision-making point in the child welfare system, from rates of investigation of suspected maltreatment to confirmed maltreatment leading to out-of-home placement (Dettlaff and Boyd 2020). Black children also spend more time on average in foster care and are less likely to reunify with their families.

While overrepresentation of Black children in child welfare systems is acknowledged by all, great disagreement exists among child welfare practitioners and activists over the reason for the disproportionate numbers. Perhaps the most publicized charge is that overrepresentation is caused by racial bias and discrimination among decision makers and by structural and institutional racism within the child welfare system and society at large. This claim has been advanced by child welfare professionals, politicians, and activists alike. A report published by the Child Welfare Information Gateway (2021b), for example, suggested that structural racism is "embedded in public policies, institutional practices, cultural representation, and other norms within and outside of the child welfare system." New York mayoral candidate Kathryn Garcia pledged in 2021 that, if elected, she would begin her tenure by "rooting out systemic racism" in the New York City foster care system (she later narrowly lost the Democratic primary to Eric Adams). An opinion piece in the *New York Times* went so far as to equate the city's foster care system with state-imposed racial segregation (Shahrigian 2021; Clifford and Greenberg 2017).

The assumption behind these claims is that external (i.e., poverty and neighborhood conditions) and internal factors (i.e., racial bias and racist policies and placement dynamics) within the child welfare system create and perpetuate the risk of the system's involvement among Black families (Dettlaff and Boyd 2020). The argument made by proponents of this theory is that due to historic racism against Black families, the relationship between racism and poverty and poor health and the relationship between racism and blighted neighborhoods, Black families are more likely to experience risk factors associated with maltreatment.

Furthermore, it has been claimed that while external racism promotes conditions of risk leading to increased levels of maltreatment in Black families, racial bias in decision-making within the system worsens and perpetuates racial inequities. Some advocates for racial justice contend that even child welfare policies that were implemented to better protect children have racist undertones and outcomes. They maintain that the Child Abuse Prevention Treatment Act of 1974, which introduced mandatory reporting laws and established mandatory minimum federal definitions of *child maltreatment*, has resulted in expanded state definitions of *abuse and neglect* that have been unduly influenced by racially tinged stories of "welfare queens" and "crack babies." They also argue that legal principles such as "the best interest of the child" standard used in custody cases leave room for substantial subjectivity in application and thereby allow racial biases to permeate decision-making (Dettlaff and Boyd 2020).

Many people who maintain that external and internal racism is responsible for the disproportionate number of Black youth in foster care also contend that placement in foster care has led to worse life outcomes for these youth. Children who spend time in foster care have an increased risk of experiencing a host of poor outcomes throughout their lives, such as economic hardship, ill health, low educational attainment, substance abuse, homelessness, and criminal justice involvement, among others. Some activists argue that these risks are exacerbated for Black children because they already experience racism and inequality (Dettlaff and Boyd 2020).

## Addressing Racial Bias in the Foster Care System

Claims of racial bias and systemic racism within the American foster care system have contributed to a variety of proposals to address racial disproportionality. At one end of the spectrum are those who call for recruiting a more diverse workforce, incorporating workforce retraining in cultural awareness and sensitivity to reduce bias in decision-making, implementing family group decision-making (including biological family and other key figures in the child's life) in planning for services, and expanding reliance on kinship care and subsidized guardianships (CWIG 2021b).

Another widely supported reform is the implementation of a race-blind removal process (Pryce 2020). This process, which is currently being utilized in Nassau County, New York, requires a caseworker to conduct an initial assessment of risk and then present the facts of the case to a committee of child welfare professionals without mentioning demographics, neighborhood, or any evidence of prior unsubstantiated reports of maltreatment. The committee then makes a recommendation on whether a child should be placed in foster care.

Charges of systemic racism in child welfare have also motivated proposals to implement legislation comparable to the ICWA for Black children. In 2019, for example, two Minnesota legislators proposed the Minnesota African American Preservation Act (MAAPA). Like provisions in ICWA, MAAPA would set more stringent standards for removing African American children from their homes than the standards that exist for other children. Among other provisions, it would also require "active efforts," as opposed to "reasonable efforts," to reunify children placed in care with their families.

Moving beyond those who embrace reform strategies aimed at reducing disproportionality, a growing movement of activists and practitioners have called for a more radical re-creation of the system based on the elimination of foster care as an intervention and a fundamental reimagining of child welfare to address elements that have been criticized for oppressing and harming people of color (Dettlaff and Weber 2020).

This movement to abolish foster care dates back to 2004, when a coalition of foundations, nonprofits, and academics organized the Racial Disproportionality Movement and launched a campaign to reduce the representation of Black children in foster care (Cohen 2020b; Bartholet 2009). Reinvigorated by the growth of the Black Lives Matter movement, the Center for the Study of Social Policy joined forces with the Graduate College of Social Work at the University of Houston to launch the UpEnd campaign in June 2020. The explicit goal of UpEnd is to create "a society in which the forcible separation of children from their parents is no longer an acceptable intervention for families in need" (Dettlaff and Weber 2020).

According to its "Pledge to Reimagine Anti-Racist Support for Families," UpEnd seeks to replace the current child welfare system with anti-racist policies and community-based support for the care and well-being of children. Such support includes adequate, safe, and affordable housing; guaranteed minimum income; a child allowance; paid sick leave; affordable and high-quality childcare; quality and accessible public education; affordable and accessible health care, mental health care, and substance use treatment; equitable access to healthy and nutritious food; and meaningful support for children and their families (UpEnd 2020).

Not everyone, however, believes that the foster care system, like other social institutions, is irredeemably racist. Many child welfare advocates and practitioners with experience in the field maintain that those seeking to recreate or abolish the foster care system disregard the suffering of Black children who are abused and neglected. They also highlight evidence demonstrating why Black families have a higher level of involvement than other groups with the child welfare system (Cohen 2020b). Such advocates and practitioners point to data challenging the two assertions behind calls to abolish child welfare: (1) that racism is the chief reason for racial disparities in the foster care system and (2) that involvement in the child welfare system causes pervasive and persistent harm to Black children and that they would be better off if they were left with their parents.

In response to the first charge, scholars and child welfare advocates point out that there is abundant evidence suggesting that race is not the primary factor influencing removal. For instance, the higher representation of Black children in foster care has not been the same for Hispanic and Asian children, who are underrepresented in the system nationally (KIDS COUNT Data Center 2020). Latino and Hispanic children make up 25 percent of children nationwide but only 21 percent of those in foster care. Asian and Native Hawaiian children make up 5 percent of the U.S. child population but only 1 percent of those in foster care. These numbers could be interpreted as proving that the foster care system is anti-Black, but they also counteract the claim that the system is biased against minorities in general or that race is the primary factor in the removal decisions.

Furthermore, experts have argued that the most plausible explanation for disparities is that Black children are for a variety of socioeconomic reasons more likely to be victims of maltreatment and reports (Cohen 2020b). According to recent federal data, in 2019, there were approximately 656,000 cases of substantiated child abuse and neglect, with an average victim rate of 8.9 victims per 1,000 children in the population (Children's Bureau 2019). In comparison, the victimization of American Indian or Alaska Native children was 14.8 per 1,000 children in the population of the same race or ethnicity. For Black children, the rate was 13.7 per 1,000. Moreover, the rate of African American child fatalities from abuse and neglect is 2.3 times greater than the rate of white children and 2.7 times greater than the rate of Hispanic children.

The effects of historic racism, such as family separation policies, may in fact have lingering effects on child welfare. Given that the racial disparities in foster care generally mirror the disparities in rates of child maltreatment, however, many have questioned whether factors other than current racism might be driving discrepancies.

Today, as in the past, the most common shared feature of families with children in the foster care system is poverty. An overwhelming majority of cases in the U.S. Child Protective Services (CPS) system involve some form of neglect, which is generally defined as a failure to meet the basic needs of a child. These typically include the child's need for food, shelter, clothing, medical care, and supervision. Because definitions of *neglect* encompass the deprivation of material goods, some experts contend that children are unnecessarily separated from their families simply because of the effects of poverty and that separation on such grounds disproportionately affects Black families (Azzi-Lessing 2021). According to this contention, simply reducing the number of children in poverty through various income or resource support programs (such as food assistance and housing vouchers) would have the greatest impact on reducing racial disproportionality in foster care as well as the number of children entering foster care in general.

Although it is well established that children placed in foster care almost always come from impoverished backgrounds, poverty alone has little correlation to the abuse and neglect that leads to removal of children and placement in foster care. It is true that a large percentage of children placed in out-of-home care are removed due to neglect rather than physical abuse, but neglect is not synonymous with or merely the result of poverty (Cohen 2020b). The kind of neglect that leads to removal rarely has to do with material deprivation alone. Instead, the neglect in question is usually chronic and serious, such as leaving children in the care of dangerous individuals or known abusers, leaving young children unsupervised or unfed due to parental intoxication, giving children illegal drugs, or exposing children to grossly unsanitary conditions.

Neglect that leads to removal is also frequently accompanied by physical or sexual abuse, even if that abuse is not substantiated. In 2019, 72.9 percent of child maltreatment fatalities were due to neglect or neglect in combination with another maltreatment type (CWIG 2021a). About 45 percent of these maltreatment-related fatalities directly involved physical abuse.

Furthermore, children who experience chronic neglect typically exhibit worse life outcomes, including cognitive, social, and emotional difficulties, than those who experience poverty alone. In an effort to better understand whether there is a correlation between the effects of poverty and neglect, researchers from Pennsylvania State University and the University of Michigan examined 29,154 individuals born between 1993 and 1996 in Milwaukee County, Wisconsin, who either received food assistance or who were reported to CPS before age 16 (Font and Maguire-Jack 2020).

The researchers specifically compared outcomes for children whose living situations were investigated by CPS for possible neglect or abuse in early childhood and adolescence to those who experienced poverty but not CPS involvement. Their findings demonstrated that there is a statistically significant difference in educational, economic, and physical and mental health outcomes for children who grew up in poverty but did not experience CPS involvement and those whose parents were investigated by CPS for abuse and neglect. CPS allegations of neglect are an important risk factor distinct from poverty alone for determining whether children will experience poverty, addiction, criminal justice involvement, or lower educational achievement in adulthood. Consequently, they concluded that targeted efforts to prevent and treat the specific effects of neglect warrant greater priority than those that merely seek to alleviate financial constraints (Font and Maguire-Jack 2020).

As child welfare scholar Naomi Schaefer Riley (2020c) points out, "It is certainly true that poverty can *contribute* to a more neglectful environment for kids." Stress caused by material deprivation may cause even the most loving parents to act aggressively toward their children, and Black families experience poverty at twice the average national rate. However, as Schaefer continues to explain, it is more likely that poverty works in conjunction with the higher rates of illicit drug use and incarceration among Blacks to produce more cases of child maltreatment in those communities.

Moreover, rates of abuse and neglect are highly correlated to family structure. Children are far more likely to be abused or neglected when living with an unrelated cohabiting adult (Faust 2017). In fact, summarizing data from the Fourth National Incidence Study of Child Abuse and Neglect, sociologist Brad Wilcox observed that "children living with their mother and her boyfriend are about 11 times more likely to be sexually, physically, or emotionally abused than children living with their married biological parents" (Wilcox 2011). Citing the same data, Wilcox likewise found that "children living with their mother and her boyfriend are six times more likely to be physically, emotionally, or educationally neglected than children living with their married biological parents." Based on these numbers, it seems that the much higher rates of single motherhood and broken homes among Black families, likely compounded by the social isolation and lack of community support that often plague Black neighborhoods, is a significant contributing factor to the disproportionate need for child welfare services by Black children.

## Do Racial Disparities in Child Welfare Cause Pervasive Harm?

For those children who experience substantiated maltreatment at home, the question remains as to whether out-of-home placement worsens or improves their situation. While chronic child abuse and neglect can cause acute and lasting harm to children's physical and mental health, those who favor recreating or abolishing the child welfare system argue that the cure of out-of-home placement is worse than the disease because it magnifies the negative effects of maltreatment, particularly for Black children. This argument is bolstered by the very real and apparent problems plaguing the U.S. foster care system, including instances of children who experience further maltreatment or multiple placements while in state custody and the large number of youth who age out of foster care every year without achieving permanency. However, attributing the poor outcomes of children with multiple placements or who age out of foster care as representative of the foster care population as a whole is methodologically problematic.

To determine the validity of the contention that placement in foster care is inherently harmful and leads to worse outcomes than if children were never placed in out-of-home care, eight prominent child welfare scholars conducted a review of more than 50 rigorous studies of outcomes following a child welfare intervention. Based on this review, the authors concluded that while measurable benefits are somewhat modest, "current research with adequate comparisons provides no robust evidence to support the idea that children have worse outcomes from CWS involvement" or that Black children are doing worse than their peers because of system involvement (Barth et al. 2020).

In fact, out-of-home placement may have a positive effect in protecting Black youth from certain negative outcomes, such as early death, criminal justice involvement, and early childbearing. Other studies have likewise demonstrated that, although results vary for individuals and the circumstances surrounding their placement, removal from settings in which they were suffering maltreatment improved children's safety and educational outcomes (Gross and Baron 2020; Bald et al. 2019). This is particularly true for children removed from abusive environments prior to age six.

Although substantial concern remains about experiences and outcomes in foster care, the data seem to suggest that children who are removed from situations of significant maltreatment do experience measurable benefits compared to what they would have experienced in the absence of intervention (Barth et al. 2020). Foster care appears to be a less harmful alternative for children whose parents repeatedly injure or severely neglect them. As Font and Gershoff (2020) point out, the differential effects of foster care likely reflect variations in the degree of harm experienced prior to entering foster care, children's individual experiences and encounters in foster care, and children's environments and experiences after exiting foster care. Furthermore, while efforts to eliminate individual-level bias in decision-making for child removal and reunification are laudable, attempts to eliminate racial disparities in child welfare that are not based on sound data may result in worse outcomes for Black children and make them more vulnerable to maltreatment (Cohen 2019).

## The Question of Kinship Care

Another significant subject of debate among child welfare advocates, practitioners, and policy makers is the extent to which the child welfare system should rely on kinship care instead of traditional nonrelative foster homes. Due in part to the high turnover rates of foster parents and inadequate recruitment efforts, more and more children are living with a relative in either informal or formal kinship care. Federal and state laws already require child welfare agencies to identify and provide notice to relatives when a child is being removed from his or her home. These same laws encourage agencies to place children with relatives when such placement is conducive to a child's well-being. Some states have gone beyond the federal mandate to create a clear presumption in favor of kin. The question remains, however, of whether states should continue placing more effort and funding into prioritizing such placements with even minimally qualified relatives over traditional forms of nonrelative foster care.

While there is little research that considers the various qualities of kinship placements, the circumstances surrounding such placements, and the outcomes of such placements, there are many arguments to be made on behalf of kinship care (Epstein 2017). Placement with kin caregivers can minimize the trauma of removal and makes it more likely that a child will retain contact and stay connected with their siblings, friends, neighborhood, school, pets, and the like. Children who are cared for by relatives are also slightly less likely to experience placement instability or to be moved to other care settings for behavioral reasons. Kinship care seems to be particularly beneficial for older children, who are less likely to be adopted out of care and who may be familiar with or have a preexisting attachment to their kin caregiver. This connection to a family member also provides older youth with an ongoing familial relationship and support system once they age out of care.

Despite the many apparent benefits of placing children with relatives, there are also significant drawbacks to preferencing kinship care over nonrelative foster care homes (Riley 2018). One concern is that many states have lower standards in terms of background checks, training, and follow-up assessments for placing children with relatives as opposed to nonrelative foster parents. This may lead to circumstances in which a kinship arrangement is clearly not in the best interest of the child. Often, relative care providers take on suddenly raising a child out of a sense of obligation, even if they are not well suited for such a role. In fact, kinship care providers are less likely to be employed, well educated, or physically and mentally healthy and are more likely to be older, poorer, and single than nonrelative foster care providers (Berrick and Hernandez 2016). Moreover, researchers have found that the same issues of drug abuse, dysfunction, and maltreatment that forced a child to be removed from her or his home are more likely to be present with relative caregivers such as grandparents, aunts, and the like than with a nonrelative caregiver.

Kinship care also potentially creates poor incentives for reunification. Children who are placed with relatives often continue to have regular contact with, and may even at times be supervised by, the parent who abused or neglected them. In fact, birth parents who continue to have access to their children after they have been taken out of the home have less of an incentive to change their behavior or seek help for an addiction or mental illness, which may account for why foster children spend more days on average in kinship care than they do in nonrelative care. Children placed in kinship are also less likely to achieve permanence through adoption. This can be particularly harmful to infants or very young children, who have a strong chance of being adopted if placed with nonrelative foster parents.

The current legal regime preferencing kinship care also creates problems related to permanency and secure attachment when states fail to place statutes of limitation on the legal preference for placement with kin. Stories abound of foster families who have cared for and bonded with children over months and even years only to have them removed when a blood relative (no matter how distant) suddenly expresses an interest in caring for the child and demands custody.

Some states have begun to pass legislation to reduce instances in which foster children are removed from stable, loving homes to be placed with kin who have not been directly involved in their lives and may even be strangers. Arizona, for instance, passed legislation that requires an early and diligent search for relatives who might be willing and able to take in a child. But the state also made a foster family who has cared for a child for at least nine months the legal equivalent of kin (Masterson 2020). Georgia, likewise, has placed some limits on kinship preference by passing legislation stating that "if a relative entitled to notice . . . fails, within six months from the date he or she received the required notice, to demonstrate an interest in and willingness to provide a permanent home for a child, the court may excuse DFCS (the Division of Family and Children Services) from considering such relative as a placement" (Riley 2019a).

## Recruiting and Retaining Foster and Adoptive Families

A necessary step toward improving the delivery of care and placement stability and permanency for children once they are placed in foster care is to increase the supply of good foster and adoptive parents. Most state agencies have inadequate knowledge of the number of foster families they have or the rate at which they are able to retain such families in the provision of foster care services. They also lack an adequate profile of foster families that are most successful at delivering care for the various types of children who enter the system. Thus, one of the best ways to begin improving the delivery and outcomes of foster care is to produce and widely disseminate data on the number of foster families needed; the types of families most likely to succeed at providing safe, stable, and loving homes; and the factors contributing to high or low retention rates among such families. This data can contribute to more effective and targeted recruitment of potential families—particularly those willing to take in youth who are typically harder to place, such as special needs children, older youth, and sibling sets—and a better understanding of how best to retain them.

On June 24, 2020, the Trump administration took a big step toward expanding data-driven foster parent recruitment and retention by issuing an executive order requiring HHS to build within two years a more "rigorous and systematic approach to collecting State administrative data" to improve data collection on the demographics of children waiting for adoption, the number and demographics of currently available foster families, the average foster parent retention rate, the targeted number of foster homes needed to meet the needs of foster children, and the average length of time required to complete foster and adoptive home certification.

The assumption motivating the order is that such data collection will provide a clearer understanding of the various strengths and needs of individual child welfare agencies and localities, including how many children are awaiting adoption in particular locations and how many families they need to recruit. States and agencies can use this data to more effectively allocate limited resources to target, recruit, support, and retain adults who are most likely to succeed at fostering.

Commenting on the new federal demand for data collection and dissemination, child welfare policy expert Naomi Schaefer Riley asserted that acquiring and widely disseminating such data aid both public agencies and private nonprofits in improving their recruitment and retention efforts. She illustrates how FaithBridge, a Georgia-based nonprofit that recruits, trains, and supports foster families through churches, has used that state's data to understand which families they should be targeting with their efforts. The organization discovered, for example, that middle-income people with some college education, parents of mixed ethnicities, older couples, and parents whose biological children were at least 10 years old tend to be the most effective and committed foster parents. Using this information, FaithBridge was able to double the number of foster families they had previously successfully recruited (Riley 2020a).

State agencies should additionally consider adopting measures that would attract a larger number of qualified foster families. While all states offer per diem (per day) compensation to foster parents to help cover the costs of food, clothing, housing, childcare, and other extracurricular expenses, in most states, this funding does not cover all the expenses associated with providing an adequate level of care. Thus, one proposal for increasing the number of families willing to foster children is to supply them with greater financial incentives. While providing adequate compensation is necessary to facilitate the provision of care, however, some observers express concerns about making financial compensation itself a larger motivating factor for foster parenting. Chiefly, those motivated largely by monetary incentives tend not to provide the best level of care. Thus, offering more money might result in worse care for children. In addition, the more foster parents are paid, the more family foster care begins to resemble a form of employment, which counteracts the goal of making children feel like they are part of a normal family, with parents who genuinely care about their well-being (Riley 2019b).

Interestingly, surveys of foster parents rarely mention a lack of money as a primary frustration with the system or their reason for ceasing delivery of care. Instead, research shows that a lack of respect, communication, and support from agencies as well as limited involvement in decision-making about their foster children's future are the leading causes of dissatisfaction and exit among foster parents. Experiences vary from state to state, but foster parents frequently report not being given adequate information about their children's past or medical history and being prohibited from attending placement hearings or sharing information in court that might lead to decisions that are more in line with children's interests (Riley 2019b).

Thus, it seems that one of the most effective ways for states to attract and retain high-quality foster families is to treat them with greater respect; ensure that they are given detailed information about their foster children's medical, educational, behavioral, and placement history; and provide them with a greater voice in the system and the decision-making process. Several states have begun to pursue meaningful reform in this regard. For example, in 2019, Indiana enacted legislation expanding foster parents' rights in a variety of ways, including allowing them to submit written testimony in child protection cases and to file notice with the court if a petition to terminate parental rights has not been submitted according to the timeline laid out by the Adoption and Safe Families Act (CHAMPS 2019b).

The Massachusetts legislature is also reconsidering passage of a foster parent bill of rights, which would give foster parents access to more information about the children under their care (Norton 2021). Together with policies expanding the rights and level of involvement of foster parents, states should consider developing management-level positions to oversee recruitment and retention and to ensure that the system is user-friendly and responsive and that unnecessary requirements and roadblocks that deter prospective foster parents are eliminated. States can also work to make training more accessible and to reform or eliminate unreasonable and unnecessary educational and home licensing requirements that make it prohibitive for some people to serve as foster parents. Most state-imposed standards make sense and are necessary to ensure that children are safe and properly cared for, but others far exceed what is necessary for parents to provide a safe and loving home (Sheffield 2020).

Expanded state partnerships with nonprofit entities is another important step toward more effective recruitment and retention. Private agencies can provide valuable assistance in processing inquiries and assisting in recruiting, training, and supporting foster families. Such entities can help prospective families navigate the oftentimes cumbersome bureaucratic hurdles to becoming licensed foster and adoptive parents and can provide various types and degrees of resources and support services, such as counseling and respite care for foster families, especially those who are caring for children who have special needs or behavioral and emotional issues related to their experience with trauma and neglect.

Faith-based groups, such as churches, are a particularly useful resource because they have relationships with potential foster families in their congregations and a built-in community support network to assist such families. Such support networks result in more successful foster parenting, and foster parents recruited through a church foster longer on average than other foster parents (Sheffield 2020).

Many faith-based groups are already doing important work in recruitment and retention. For example, the Arkansas faith-based group the CALL receives no public funding but has helped recruit nearly half of all foster families in the state. The organization has been particularly effective at recruiting and assisting foster families in rural counties, where the Arkansas Division of Children and Family Services (DCFS) had few placement options and was forced to send children to short-term placements in communities hours away. Another group, One Church One Child, is a national minority adoption recruitment program that was established in Chicago in 1980 by an African American Catholic priest, Father George Clemens, with the goal of recruiting one family in every African American church in Illinois to adopt one child. One Church One Child now has offices throughout the country and has helped placed thousands of children in adoptive homes.

Finally, the business community and employers can play an important role in foster parent recruitment and retention by making it feasible for their employees to serve children in foster care through various forms of support, such as adoption expense reimbursement, family leave for appointments and initial placements, and flexible work hours. States can incentivize such adoption-friendly policies through tax breaks. Nonprofits can also reward businesses through public relations campaigns, such as the 100 Best Adoption-Friendly Workplaces list published by the Dave Thomas Foundation for Adoption, to recognize organizations that are striving to make adoption a supported option for every working parent.

## LGBTQ Rights and Religious Exemptions

The work of nonprofit groups has contributed greatly to foster family recruitment and retention, but this work has not been free from controversy. One of the most debated issues in recent years has been the question of whether nonprofit faith-based adoption and foster care agencies that receive taxpayer funding should be permitted to refuse service to LGBTQ families.

Over the past couple of decades, LGBTQ advocacy groups and civil rights organizations have called on the federal government to restrict the allocation of funding to any agency that engages in discrimination against same-sex couples in their placement decisions and for state social service boards and agencies to revoke the licenses of any such agencies. In the final weeks of his administration, President Obama oversaw the addition of "sexual orientation" as a protected trait under antidiscrimination rules governing federal funds to adoption and foster agencies. In response to a push for further nondiscrimination regulations at the local level, government authorities in several states and localities—including Massachusetts, Illinois, California, and Washington, DC—forbid faith-based agencies from prioritizing married heterosexual couples over same-sex couples in their placement decisions. However, other states—including Alabama, Michigan, Mississippi, North Dakota, South Dakota, Texas, and Virginia—passed legislation adding "conscience clauses" to their foster and adoption laws. These clauses guarantee the right for religious adoption and foster care agencies to refuse any placement that would violate the agency's religious or moral convictions. In 2019, the Trump administration continued this trend by reversing the Obama era restrictions prohibiting the allocation of federal funding to faith-based groups who only place children with married heterosexual mothers and fathers.

LGBTQ and civil rights advocacy groups have contended in response that conscience clauses and religious exemptions amount to state-sanctioned discrimination against otherwise qualified foster and adoptive parents simply because of their identity (Human Rights Campaign 2017). They maintain that faith-based foster and adoption laws question the dignity of LGBTQ individuals and their fitness as parents. These policies, they further argue, place stress on a system that is chronically in need of foster care families by excluding LGBTQ parents who are willing to serve as a family resource for children. Religious exemptions for faith-based agencies thereby deny children the chance to live in a good home simply because the parents are of the same sex.

Those in favor of religious exemptions typically respond to these charges by noting that the continued existence of agencies that prefer to place kids with married heterosexual moms and dads does not prevent LGBTQ individuals from becoming foster or adoptive parents, as every state in the country allows foster or adoption by same-sex couples and there are more than enough private and public agencies willing to work with and place children with them (Kao 2018). They additionally contend that shuttering faith-based agencies that wish to continue operating according to the tenets of their faith will lead to fewer quality options and placements, especially since these agencies have a high level of success in placing older and disabled children.

In June 2021, the Supreme Court weighed in on the issue of LGBTQ rights and religious exemptions in *Sharonell Fulton, et al. v. City of Philadelphia*. The controversy leading to this case arose when individuals associated with Catholic Social Services (CSS) sued the City of Philadelphia for violating their religious free exercise rights after city officials barred CSS from continuing its work with foster children and families because it refused to place children with same-sex parents. On June 17, 2021, the Supreme Court issued a narrow ruling declaring that the City of Philadelphia's decision to cancel CSS's foster care contract on account of the group's religious beliefs violated the First Amendment right to free exercise of religion. Nevertheless, the majority opinion made clear that the court had only sided with CSS in this case because the city contract contained language allowing discretionary exemptions on a case-by-case basis, but Philadelphia would not consider CSS's claim to an exemption. Thus, the decision left intact the principle that governments can require contracting agencies that receive taxpayer funding, including faith-based ones, to comply with nondiscrimination laws. Consequently, the controversy is unlikely to wane anytime soon, as local governments can get around the decision by simply eliminating language allowing for case-by-case exemptions in their legal code.

## Increased Focus on Older Youth

Any effort to improve outcomes in foster care needs to include a specific focus on increasing permanency and support for older youth. The longer children remain in foster care and the older they are upon entrance into state care, the less likely they are to achieve meaningful permanency and the more likely they are to exhibit poor life outcomes. Most children awaiting adoption are 8 years old or older, and the older they get the less likely they are to achieve permanency through adoption. Once a waiting child reaches the age of 9 in foster care, he or she is more likely to remain in foster care than be adopted. Youth who enter or remain in foster care after the age of 12 have a 75 percent chance of aging out of the system without ever finding a permanent family (Atwood 2011; Gelles 2017).

Older foster youth, however, are just as much in need of loving homes and the emotional and financial stability offered by a family as their younger counterparts. Placing older children into permanent homes dramatically improves their overall well-being and their odds of success in adulthood (Punnett 2014). Furthermore, while state and federal policies have largely focused on ensuring that youth aging out of care have adequate economic and educational assets for independent living, the benefits of supportive, interdependent relationships with caring adults have also been well documented (Munson et al. 2010). Thus, one of the most important areas of work in this regard has been the promotion of adoption and adult mentorship of older foster youth.

One organization at the forefront of such efforts is the Dave Thomas Foundation for Adoption (DTFA), the only agency dedicated solely to foster care adoption. Through its Wendy's Wonderful Kids program, the foundation provides funding to adoption agencies to hire recruiters to use a child-focused recruitment model to find permanent homes for children in foster care. Recruiters specifically focus on children for whom it has traditionally been difficult to find adoptive families, primarily older children and children with mental health disorders but also children who are part of sibling groups, those with previously failed adoption efforts, children with special needs, and children who have lingered in foster care. A comprehensive and rigorous evaluation demonstrated that foster care youth served by the Wendy's Wonderful Kids program are 1.7 times more likely to be adopted than those not served. The study also found that older children and those with mental health challenges are three times more likely to be adopted when served by Wendy's Wonderful Kids recruiters (Malm et al. 2011).

Another organization doing substantive work for older foster youth is the DC Family and Youth Initiative (DCFYI). DCFYI is a nonprofit dedicated to helping teenagers in foster care find adoptive families and make lifelong connections with caring adult mentors who can provide advice, guidance, affection, and a sense of belonging that they otherwise might not have. DCFYI works annually with 35 to 40 foster youth, ages 12 to 21. Youth participants are connected with adult volunteers in DCFYI-sponsored environments, such as shared meals, outings to bowling alleys, and softball games, among others. Through these environments, participating youth develop relationships that lead to one-on-one mentorships, connections with "host families" who welcome them for regular visits, and official adoptions. Since DCFYI's inception in 2010, no participant has left foster care without a loving adult in his or her life, and more than 25 youth were adopted within the first few years of operation alone.

## COVID-19 and Child Welfare Challenges and Opportunities

The onset of the COVID-19 pandemic in early 2020 and the corresponding government shutdowns over the course of 2020 and 2021 served to magnify the problem of child maltreatment in American society. At the same time, it revealed many inherent flaws and shortcomings in the delivery of foster care and other child welfare services that warrant immediate and long-term attention.

Following the imposition of disease mitigation measures, such as stay-at-home orders, which began in late March 2020, states across the country witnessed an up to 50 percent drop in calls to child abuse and neglect reporting hotlines compared to the previous year (LeBlanc 2020). In Massachusetts alone, reports of alleged abuse dropped nearly 55 percent between the first week of March and the last week of April. According to experts, this drastic decline in reporting did not stem from a sudden, simultaneous decline in maltreatment. Rather, the more likely cause for the dramatic downturn in reports of potential abuse or maltreatment is that with schools and childcare facilities closed, doctor visits postponed, and increased social isolation in general, children experiencing maltreatment were less likely to be noticed by mandatory reporters, such as teachers, day care providers, school counselors, and pediatricians, who have regular contact with children. Stay-at-home orders and social distancing also isolated many high-risk children from their extended family and members of their community, and thousands of students in high-poverty districts never even logged on to their synchronous virtual classes (Font 2021; Richards 2020).

Compounding the steep drop in reports of suspected cases of maltreatment, easily verifiable cases also went unnoticed as caseworkers began to scale back investigations of abuse and neglect because of fear of spreading or catching the virus, a shortage of personal protective equipment, workforce furloughs, and difficulty accessing case files while working remotely (Font 2021). California governor Gavin Newsom, under pressure from the union that represents child welfare workers, even temporarily dropped a requirement mandating in-person visits by caseworkers to approximately 60,000 children in the California foster care system and another 14,000 children still living with parents but under state supervision because of histories of abuse and neglect (Therolf, Lempres, and Alzhan 2020). In Los Angeles County, many previously abused children deemed to be living under "high" or "very high" risk of future abuse were not checked in on for months.

Even as pandemic precautions led to declines in child maltreatment reports and investigations, experts noticed that as the pandemic became more severe, hospitals reported spikes in severe and even fatal child abuse cases (Zheng 2020). Stress factors associated with the social isolation, job losses, and the increased caregiving burden for children that accompanied the COVID pandemic undoubtedly contributed to the well-documented rise in substance abuse and intimate partner violence across the country, both of which are risk factors highly correlated with child maltreatment (Font 2021).

Meanwhile, the pandemic and the nationwide response to it resulted in prolonged stays in foster care and further barriers to permanency for thousands of children (Ho and Fassett 2021). For instance, the pandemic made it more difficult for a large percentage of parents whose children had been removed from their care to meet the requirements of reunification. The pandemic hammered families in many ways, including increased joblessness, reduced access to public transportation, limited access to drug testing and psychiatric evaluations, and a delay or pause in in-person visitations, leaving parents with weakened bonds with their children.

Additionally, many required services and treatment programs were shut down, closed to new clients, or moved to online platforms requiring reliable internet access and electronic devices. The number of adoptions also decreased as courts canceled hearings, delayed cases, went virtual, or temporarily shut down. Some court proceedings to terminate parental rights because of abuse or maltreatment were delayed indefinitely. According to one Associated Press analysis, at least 22,600 fewer children left foster care in 2020 compared with 2019 (Ho and Fassett

2021). All of this occurred during a period in which increased social isolation and the deprivation of normalcy undoubtedly exacerbated the existing challenges of life for children in foster care, a sizeable percentage of whom were housed in overcrowded hotels or shelters because of a shortage of foster families or proper care facilities.

Despite the struggles of America's child welfare system to meet and adapt effectively to the challenges brought on by COVID-19, the pandemic has also presented a valuable opportunity to transform and improve the operation of foster care in the United States. In a report on the lessons to be learned from the pandemic, sociology professor Sarah A. Font (2021) lays out several recommendations for better protecting children through the pandemic and beyond. These recommendations include developing new strategies and making better use of existing technologies for detecting child maltreatment outside of traditional settings such as school, designating caseworkers as essential workers and requiring timely in-person investigations of alleged abuse and consistent monitoring of open cases, permitting virtual participation in court hearings and mandating that other requirements for moving children toward permanency continue without delay, encouraging innovative foster family recruitment and support services, and partnering with community-based agencies and nonprofits to sustain or increase services to foster, kin, and biological families.

## Conclusion

Family relationships are essential to children's healthy growth, development, and overall well-being. Every child has a fundamental right to be cared for and protected by loving parents. Ideally, every child would be raised, loved, and adequately cared for by their parents of birth. Unfortunately, a sizeable percentage of American children are endangered by abuse and neglect at the hands of their parents. When a child's parents are unwilling or incapable of providing a safe environment for a child—or even worse, pose a direct threat to her or him—the state has an obligation to step in to protect the vulnerable child from further harm. At times, this may only require the provision of services to enable parents to resume their appropriate role as caretakers, but there are also times that children endangered by abuse and neglect must be removed and cared for outside of their homes.

When circumstances mandate removal and placement in foster care, the government has a social responsibility to either safely reunify children with their biological family or to provide them with a new family in a safe and timely manner. Many children do experience safety and well-being and ultimately achieve permanency through the foster care system. Unfortunately, however, a sizeable percentage of foster youth—due to past trauma, failures in foster care practices and policies, or some combination of both—never achieve permanency or stability in their living situations. When such children age into adulthood, they are more likely to experience poor life outcomes, including higher levels of drug abuse, criminal behavior, mental illness, joblessness, and homelessness, than youth in the general population. Such poor outcomes, combined with continued heated debates over racial disparities in the foster care system and competing visions about whether the system should prioritize family preservation or child protection, have led some activists to call for recreating and even abolishing the system altogether.

The problems and controversies that have been inherent in the delivery of foster care were further heightened during the COVID-19 pandemic. However, the return to normal life following the pandemic provides an important opportunity to continue to evaluate the system's effectiveness and to identify opportunities for improvement. Ultimately, despite the many problems and controversies related to the delivery of foster care in the United States, individuals, faith-based groups, and other public and private organizations across the country are expanding their efforts in new and creative ways to reduce the need for foster care, to improve experiences and outcomes for foster youth, and to increase the likelihood that children placed in foster care will be raised in healthy environments with a permanent and loving family.

## References

Adler, Eric. 2019. "Frequent Moves Don't Just Harm Foster Kids' Emotions—They Hurt Their Brains." *Kansas City Star.* December 15.

Annie E. Casey Foundation. 2015. "Every Kid Needs a Family: Giving Children in the Child Welfare System the Best Chance for Success." KIDS COUNT Policy Report. May 19. Accessed May 15, 2021. https://assets.aecf.org/m/resourcedoc/aecf-EveryKidNeedsAFamily-2015.pdf

ASPE (Assistant Secretary for Planning and Evaluation). 2014. "A Temporary Haven: Children and Youth Are Spending Less Time in Foster Care." U.S. Department of Health and Human Services. September 1. Accessed June 15, 2021. https://aspe.hhs.gov/sites/default/files/private/pdf/77056/rb_FosterCare.pdf

Atwood, Thomas C. 2011. "Foster Care: Safety Net or Trap Door?" Backgrounder No. 2535. March 25. Washington, DC: Heritage Foundation. Accessed June 1, 2021. https://www.heritage.org/marriage-and-family/report/foster-care-safety-net-or-trap-door

Azzi-Lessing, Lenette. 2021. "Reform the Child Welfare System to Protect Vulnerable Children." *The Hill.* February 3. Accessed April 1, 2021. https://thehill.com/opinion/judiciary/537188-reform-the-child-welfare-system-to-protect-vulnerable-children

Bald, Anthony, Erich Chyn, Justine S. Hastings, and Margarita Machelett. 2019. "The Causal Impact of Removing Children from Abusive and Neglectful Homes." National Bureau of Economic Research. Working Paper

25419. Accessed June 16, 2021. https://www.nber.org /papers/w25419

Barth, Richard P., Melissa Johnson-Reid, Johanna K. P. Greeson, Brett Drake, Jill Duerr Berrick, Antonio R. Garcia, Terry V. Shaw, and John R. Gyourko. 2020. "Outcomes Following Child Welfare Services: What Are They and Do They Differ for Black Children." *Journal of Public Child Welfare* 14 (5): 477–499.

Bartholet, Elizabeth. 2009. "The Racial Disproportionality Movement in Child Welfare: False Facts and Dangerous Directions." *Arizona Law Review* 51:871–932.

Bauer, Laura, and Judy L. Thomas. 2019. "We Are Sending More Foster Kids to Prison Than College." *Kansas City Star*. December 15. Accessed May 25, 2021. https://www .kansascity.com/news/special-reports/article23820 6754.html

Berrick, Jill Duerr, and Julia Hernandez. 2016. "Developing Consistent and Transparent Kinship Care Policy and Practice: State Mandated, Mediated, and Independent Care." *Children and Youth Services Review* 68:24–33.

Carpenter, Kristen. 2016. "Indian Status Is Not Racial: Understanding ICWA as a Matter of Law and Practice." *CATO Unbound* (August). Accessed April 20, 2021. https://www.cato-unbound.org/print-issue/2102

Casey Family Programs. 2015. "Indian Child Welfare Act: Measuring Compliance." March. Accessed April 20, 2021. https://www.casey.org/media/measuring-compliance -icwa.pdf

Casey Family Programs. 2018. "What Impacts Placement Stability." October 3. Accessed June 10, 2021. https://www .casey.org/placement-stability-impacts/

CHAMPS. 2019a. "A CHAMPS Guide on Foster Parent Recruitment and Retention: Strategies for Developing a Comprehensive Program." April. Accessed June 10, 2021.

https://fosteringchamps.org/wp-content/uploads/2019/04
/CHAMPS-Guide-on-Foster-Parent-Recruitment-and
-Retention.pdf

CHAMPS. 2019b. "Summary of Indiana P.L. 210-2019, SB
1." Accessed June 15, 2021. https://fosteringchamps.org
/fact-sheet/summary-of-indiana-p-l-210-2019-sb-1/

Children's Bureau. 2016. "Child Welfare Outcomes
2010–2013: Report to Congress." Department of Health
and Human Services, Administration for Children and
Families. Accessed June 10, 2021. https://www.acf.hhs.gov
/cb/report/child-welfare-outcomes-2010-2013-report
-congress

Children's Bureau. 2018. "Child and Family Services Reviews
Aggregate Report Round 3: FYs2015–2017." Department
of Health and Human Services, Administration for
Children and Families. Accessed June 10, 2021. https://
www.acf.hhs.gov/sites/default/files/documents/cb/cfsr
_aggregate_report_2015_2017.pdf

Children's Bureau. 2019. *Child Maltreatment 2019.*
Department of Health and Human Services,
Administration for Children and Families. Accessed
September 9, 2021. https://www.acf.hhs.gov/sites/default
/files/documents/cb/cm2019.pdf

Children's Bureau. 2020a. "The AFCARS Report:
Preliminary FY 2019 Estimates as of June 23, 2020—No.
27." U.S. Department of Health and Human Services,
Administration for Children and Families. Accessed
February 15, 2021. https://www.acf.hhs.gov/sites/default
/files/documents/cb/afcarsreport27.pdf

Children's Bureau. 2020b. "Trends in Foster Care and
Adoption: FY 2010–FY 2019." U.S. Department of Health
and Human Services, Administration for Children and
Families. Accessed March 11, 2021. https://www.acf.hhs
.gov/sites/default/files/documents/cb/trends_fostercare
_adoption_10thru19.pdf

Clifford, Stephanie, and Jessica Silver-Greenberg. 2017. "Foster Care as Punishment: The New Reality of 'Jane Crow.'" *New York Times.* July 24. Accessed June 16, 2011. https://www.nytimes.com/2017/07/21/nyregion/foster -care-nyc-jane-crow.html

Cohen, Marie K. 2018. "Sibling Separation: An Unintended Consequence of the Family First Act?" Child Welfare Monitor. October 9. Accessed June 5, 2021. https:// childwelfaremonitor.org/2018/10/09/sibling-separation -an-unintended-consequence-of-the-family-first-act/

Cohen, Marie K. 2019. "Race, Tribe, and Child Welfare: How Identity Policy Trumps Children's Needs." Child Welfare Monitor. January 7. Accessed May 20, 2021. https://childwelfaremonitor.org/2019/01/07/race-tribe -and-child-welfare-how-identity-policy-trumps-childrens -needs/

Cohen, Marie K. 2020a. "Therapeutic Residential Care: A Necessary Option for Foster Youth with Greater Needs." Child Welfare Monitor. November 11. Accessed June 15, 2021. https://childwelfaremonitor.org/2020/11/11 /therapeutic-residential-care-a-necessary-option-for-foster -youth-with-greater-needs/

Cohen, Marie K. 2020b. "'Upending Child Welfare' Means Devaluing Black Children's Lives." Child Welfare Monitor. November 2. Accessed June 15, 2021. https:// childwelfaremonitor.org/2020/11/02/upending-child -welfare-means-devaluing-black-childrens-lives/

Cohen, Marie K. 2021. "When Ideology Outweighs What's Best for Kids: The Case of San Pasqual Academy." Child Welfare Monitor. March 10. Accessed March 11, 2021. https://childwelfaremonitor.org/2021/03/10/when -ideology-outweighs-whats-best-for-kids-the-case-of-san -pasqual-academy/

CWIG (Child Welfare Information Gateway). 2019. "Sibling Issues in Foster Care and Adoption." Department of

Health and Human Services, Administration for Children and Families, Children's Bureau. Accessed June 10, 2021. https://www.childwelfare.gov/pubPDFs/siblingissues.pdf

CWIG (Child Welfare Information Gateway). 2021a. "Child Abuse and Neglect Fatalities 2019: Statistics and Interventions." Department of Health and Human Services, Administration for Children and Families, Children's Bureau. March. Accessed June 16, 2021. https://www.childwelfare.gov/pubpdfs/fatality.pdf

CWIG (Child Welfare Information Gateway). 2021b. "Child Welfare Practice to Address Racial Disproportionality and Disparity." Department of Health and Human Services, Administration for Children and Families, Children's Bureau. April. Accessed June 10, 2021. https://www.childwelfare.gov/pubpdfs/racial_disproportionality.pdf

Dave Thomas Foundation for Adoption. 2017. "U.S. Adoptions Attitude Survey." Harris Poll. Accessed June 5, 2021. https://www.davethomasfoundation.org/library/2017-adoption-attitudes-survey-us/

Dettlaff, Alan, and Kristen Weber. 2020. "Now Is the Time for Abolition." *The Imprint.* June 22. Accessed June 16, 2021. https://imprintnews.org/child-welfare-2/now-is-the-time-for-abolition/44706

Dettlaff, Alan J., and Reiko Boyd. 2020. "Racial Disproportionality and Disparities in the Child Welfare System: Why Do They Exist, and What Can Be Done to Address Them?" *Annals of the American Academy of Political and Social Science* 692 (1): 253–274.

Dolce, Michael. 2018. "We Have Set Up a System to Sex Traffic American Children." *Newsweek.* January 12. Accessed May 20, 2021. https://www.newsweek.com/we-have-set-system-sex-traffic-american-children-779541

Dworsky, Amy, Mark E. Courtney, Jennifer Hook, Adam Brown, Colleen Cary, Kara Love, Vanessa Vorhies, et al. 2011. *Midwest Evaluation of the Adult Functioning of Former Foster Youth.* Chicago: Chapin Hall at the University of Chicago. Accessed October 12, 2020. https://www.chapinhall.org/research/midwest-evaluation-of-the-adult-functioning-of-former-foster-youth/#

Epstein, Heidi Redlich. 2017. "Kinship Care Is Better for Children and Families." American Bar Association. July 1. Accessed June 17, 2021. https://www.americanbar.org/groups/public_interest/child_law/resources/child_law_practiceonline/child_law_practice/vol-36/july-aug-2017/kinship-care-is-better-for-children-and-families/

Faust, Katy. 2017. "Biology Matters." Them Before Us. May 6. Accessed June 17, 2021. https://thembeforeus.com/biology-matters/

Fletcher, Matthew L. M. 2016. "Family, Tribes, and the Indian Child Welfare Act: Limit Government Intrusion in Indian Families' Lives." *CATO Unbound* (August). Accessed April 20, 2021. https://www.cato-unbound.org/print-issue/2102

Font, Sara A. 2021. "What Lessons Can the Child Welfare System Take from the COVID-19 Pandemic?" American Enterprise Institute. January. Accessed June 20, 2021. https://www.aei.org/wp-content/uploads/2021/01/What-Lessons-Can-the-Child-Welfare-System-Take-from-the-COVID-19-Pandemic.pdf

Font, Sara A., and Elizabeth T. Gershoff. 2020. "Foster Care: How We Can, and Should, Do More for Maltreated Children." *Social Policy Report* 33 (3). Accessed June 17, 2021. https://srcd.onlinelibrary.wiley.com/doi/epdf/10.1002/sop2.10

Font, Sara A., and Kathryn Maguire-Jack. 2020. "It's Not 'Just Poverty': Educational, Social, and Economic Functioning among Young Adults Exposed to Childhood Neglect, Abuse, and Poverty." *Child Abuse and Neglect* 101:104356. https://doi.org/10.1016/j.chiabu.2020.104356

Gelles, Richard. 2017. *Out of Harm's Way: Creating an Effective Child Welfare System*. New York: Oxford University Press.

Gross, Max, and E. Jason Baron. 2020. "Temporary Stays and Persistent Gains: The Causal Effects of Foster Care." Social Science Research Network. Accessed June 16, 2021. https://papers.ssrn.com/sol3/papers.cfm?abstract_id =3576640

Ho, Sally, and Camille Fassett. 2021. "AP Analysis: COVID Prolonged Foster Care Stays for Thousands." *U.S. News and World Report*. June 9. Accessed June 21, 2021. https://www .usnews.com/news/politics/articles/2021-06-08/ap-analysis -covid-prolonged-foster-care-stays-for-thousands

Human Rights Campaign. 2017. "Disregarding the Best Interest of the Child: Licenses to Discriminate in Child Welfare Services." December. Accessed September 22, 2021. https://assets2.hrc.org/files/assets/resources/licenses -to-discriminate-child-welfare-2017.pdf

Kao, Emily. 2018. "Faith-Based Adoption Agencies, under Assault by the Left." *National Review*. March 13. Accessed September 22, 2021. https://www.nationalreview.com /2018/03/faith-based-adoption-agencies-under-assault -from-left/

KIDS COUNT Data Center. 2020. "Black Children Continue to Be Disproportionately Represented in Foster Care." Annie E. Casey Foundation. April 13. Accessed June 16, 2021. https://datacenter.kidscount.org/updates /show/264-us-foster-care-population-by-race-and-ethnicity

Latzman, Natasha E., and Deborah A. Gibbs. 2020. "Examining the Link: Foster Care Runaway Episodes and Human Trafficking: OPRE Report No. 2020-143." Washington, DC: Office of Planning, Research, and Evaluation, Administration for Children and Families, U.S. Department of Health and Human Services. Accessed May 21, 2021. https://www.acf.hhs.gov/sites/default/files

/documents/opre/foster_care_runaway_human_trafficking
_october_2020_508.pdf

Latzman, Natasha E., Deborah A. Gibbs, Rose Feinberg,
Marianne N. Kluckman, and Sue Aboul-Hosn. 2019.
"Human Trafficking Victimization among Youth Who Run
Away from Foster Care." *Children and Youth Services Review*
98 (March): 113–124.

Lawler, Michael J., Liat Sayfan, Gail S. Goodman, Rachel Narr,
and Ingrid M. Cordon. 2014. "Comprehensive Residential
Education: A Promising Model for Emerging Adults in
Foster Care." *Children and Youth Services Review* 38:10–19.

LeBlanc, Paul. 2020. "Child Abuse Reports Are Down during
the Pandemic. Experts Say That's a Bad Sign." CNN. May
17. Accessed June 20, 2021. https://www.cnn.com/2020
/05/17/politics/child-abuse-pandemic/index.html

Malm, Karin, Sharon Vandivere, Tiffany Allen, Kerry
DeVooght, Raquel Ellis, Amy McKlindon, Erick Williams,
Jacqueline Smollar, and Andrew Zinn. 2011. *Evaluation
Report Summary: The Wendy's Wonderful Kinds Initiative.*
Washington, DC: Child Trends. Accessed June 19, 2021.
https://www.davethomasfoundation.org/wp-content
/uploads/2018/02/wwk-research-evaluation-summary.pdf

Masterson, Rebecca Smith. 2020, "There's a Better Way to Do
Foster Care." *Tampa Bay Times*. July 3. Accessed June 11,
2021. https://www.tampabay.com/opinion/2020/07/03
/theres-a-better-way-to-do-foster-care-column/

*Mississippi Choctaw Indians v. Holyfield*, 490 U.S. 30 (1989)

Munson, Michelle R., Susan E. Smalling, Renée Spencer,
Lionel D. Scott Jr., and Elizabeth M. Tracy. 2010. "A
Steady Presence in the Midst of Change: Non-Kin Natural
Mentors in the Lives of Older Youth Existing Foster Care."
*Children and Youth Services Review* 32:527–535.

North Carolina Division of Social Services. 2009. *Treat
Them Like Gold: A Best Practice Guide to Partnering*

*with Resource Families.* January. Raleigh, NC: Child Welfare Services Section. Accessed June 11, 2021. http://centerforchildwelfare.fmhi.usf.edu/kb/Implementation/Partnering_with_Resource_Families.pdf

Norton, Michael. 2021. "Massachusetts House Approves Bill Updating Child Protection Law." MassLive. March 8. Accessed June 15, 2021. https://www.masslive.com/politics/2021/03/massachusetts-house-approves-bill-updating-child-protection-laws.html

Pryce, Jessica. 2020. "The Case for Race-Blind Foster Care Removal Decisions." *The Imprint.* January 13. Accessed June 15, 2021. https://imprintnews.org/opinion/the-case-for-race-blind-foster-care-removal-decisions/39898

Punnett, Susan. 2014. "For Teens in Foster Care, Adoption Is a Lifeline." *Washington Post.* January 3. Accessed June 19, 2011. https://www.washingtonpost.com/opinions/for-teens-in-foster-care-adoption-is-a-lifeline/2014/01/03/cf36e5b8-7330-11e3-9389-09ef9944065e_story.html

Renick, Christie. 2018. "The Nation's First Family Separation Policy." *The Imprint.* October 9. Accessed April 20, 2021. https://imprintnews.org/child-welfare-2/nations-first-family-separation-policy-indian-child-welfare-act/32431

Richards, Erin. 2020. "America's Missing Kids: Amid COVID-19 and Online School, Thousands of Students Haven't Shown Up." *USA Today.* September 28. Accessed September 13, 2021. https://www.usatoday.com/story/news/education/2020/09/28/covid-online-schools-back-to-school-missing-kids/3519203001/

Riley, Naomi Schaefer. 2018. "Reconsidering Kinship Care." *National Affairs* (Summer). Accessed June 15, 2021. https://nationalaffairs.com/publications/detail/reconsidering-kinship-care

Riley, Naomi Schaefer. 2019a. "Georgia's Foster Care Reform Bill: Blood Relatives Shouldn't Always Have Legal Preference." *USA Today.* May 20. Accessed June 10, 2021.

https://www.usatoday.com/story/opinion/2019/05/20
/georgia-foster-reform-kinship-preference-blood-relative
-limits-children-column/3733367002/

Riley, Naomi Schaefer. 2019b. "Honor Your (Foster) Mothers and Fathers." American Enterprise Institute. September. Accessed November 9, 2020. https://www.aei.org/research -products/report/honor-your-foster-mothers-and-fathers/

Riley, Naomi Schaefer. 2020a. "For Foster Kids, a Step in the Right Direction." *City Journal*. July 9. Accessed June 5, 2021. https://www.city-journal.org/executive-order -foster-care

Riley, Naomi Schaefer. 2020b. "Foster Care Still Needs Time Limits." *City Journal*. September 24. Accessed June 5, 2021. https://www.city-journal.org/covid-foster-care -time-limits

Riley, Naomi Schaefer. 2020c. "Is Foster Care Racist?" *Quillette*. June 26. Accessed June 16, 2021. https://quillette .com/2020/06/26/is-foster-care-racist/

Sandefur, Timothy. 2016. "Family, Tribes, and the Indian Child Welfare Act: Treat Children as Individuals, Not as Resources." *CATO Unbound* (August). Accessed April 20, 2021. https://www.cato-unbound.org/print-issue/2102

Shahrigian, Shant. 2021. "NYC Mayoral Candidate Kathryn Garcia Gets Personal, Vows to Fight 'Systemic Racism' in Foster Care System." MSN. April 12. Accessed June 12, 2021. https://www.msn.com/en-us/news/politics/nyc -mayoral-candidate-kathryn-garcia-gets-personal -vows-to-fight-systemic-racism-in-foster-care-system /ar-BB1fzXZl

Sheffield, Rachel. 2020. "A Place to Call Home: Improving Foster Care and Adoption Policy to Give More Children a Stable Family." United States Congress, Joint Economic Committee, *Social Capital Project* Report No. 4-20 (August). Accessed December 10, 2020. https://www.jec .senate.gov/public/index.cfm/

republicans/2020/9/a-place-to-call-home-improving-foster
-care-and-adoption-policy-to-give-more-children-a-stable
-family

Therolf, Garrett, Daniel Lempres, and Aksaule Alzhan. 2020. "They're Children at Risk of Abuse, and Their Caseworkers Are Stuck Home." *New York Times*. August 7. Accessed June 21, 2021. https://www.nytimes.com/2020/08/07/us /virus-child-abuse.html

*Unadopted*. 2020. Directed by Noel Anaya. Oakland, CA: YR Media. Accessed October 4, 2020. https://unadopted film.com/

UpEnd. 2020. "Initial Pledge to Reimagine Anti-Racist Support for Families." Accessed June 16, 2021. https:// upendmovement.org/upend-movement-pledge/

Wilcox, W. Bradford. 2011. "Suffer the Little Children: Cohabitation and the Abuse of America's Children." *Public Discourse*. April 22. Accessed June 16, 2021. https://www .thepublicdiscourse.com/2011/04/3181/

Wilson, Julie Boatright, Jeff Katz, and Robert Green. 2005. "Listening to Parents: Overcoming Barriers to the Adoption of Children from Foster Care." Harvard University, John F. Kennedy School of Government, Faculty Research Working Paper Series No. RWP05-005. February. Accessed June 9, 2021. https://www.hks.harvard .edu/publications/listening-parents-overcoming-barriers -adoption-children-foster-care

Wulczyn, Fred, Britany Orlebeke, Kristen Hislop, Florie Schmits, Jamie McClanahan, and Lilian Huang. 2018. *The Dynamics of Foster Home Recruitment and Retention*. Chicago: Center for State Child Welfare Data. September. Accessed February 16, 2021. https://fcda.chapinhall.org /wp-content/uploads/2018/10/Foster-Home-Report-Final _FCDA_October2018.pdf

Zheng, Lili. 2020. "Fort Worth Hospital Sees Spike in Severe Child Abuse Cases over Last Week." NBCDFW. March 21. https://www.nbcdfw.com/news/local/fort-worth-hospital -sees-spike-in-severe-child-abuse-cases-over-last-week /2336014/

## Introduction

This chapter includes seven essays written by authors from a variety of perspectives and personal and professional backgrounds on a range of topics related to the issue of foster care in America. The chapter opens with an essay by Darcy Olsen, the founder and CEO of Gen Justice, an advocacy group focused on promoting and protecting the legal and constitutional rights of foster children. Olsen addresses the lesser status of abused children's rights under the law and the need to extend to children the same constitutional and statutory rights that are afforded to their predators.

The second and third essays are written by former foster youth. Tori Petersen highlights the detrimental effects that negative stereotypes can have on life outcomes of foster youth and recounts the opportunities and encouragement that helped her overcome such stereotypes in her own life. Jaymie Gonzales gives voice to the trauma, fear, loneliness, and frustration experienced by many foster youth by telling the story of his own adolescence in foster care.

In the fourth essay, Terri Galindo, the vice president of clinical services at 4Kids, Inc., focuses on the treatment that abused and neglected children receive for mental and behavioral health

---

Two fathers cook dinner with their foster kids. One of the primary factors inhibiting effective delivery of care and permanency for foster children is a shortage of eligible foster and adoptive parents. (Scott Griessel/Dreamstime.com)

issues. She contends that the assessment of such children is inconsistent across medical and mental health services and that mental health professionals typically diagnose such children exactly as they would children in the general population rather than more effectively prescribing treatment through the lens of trauma. She makes the case for trauma-informed treatment that includes the whole child—mind, body, and spirit.

The fifth essay was provided by Natalie Goodnow, a child and family policy expert. Goodnow profiles the important work of faith-based agencies (FBAs) in recruiting foster and adoptive families, supporting families through the licensing and placement process, and finding homes for children who are typically harder to place, such as older children, children with special needs, and sibling sets. She contends that the valuable work of FBAs in these areas merits their preservation and protection.

The final two essays are written from the perspective of foster family members. Vienna Scott recounts her family's experience with fostering amid the opioid crisis and how her family learned firsthand how parental opioid abuse affects child victims. She also discusses the challenges that foster families face in providing them with appropriate care. Finally, Diana Hayes draws attention to the losses and beautiful gains involved in foster adoption as she tells the story of how she became a forever mother to five precious, unique children.

## Changing Laws, Changing Lives
*Darcy Olsen*

In January 2020, Phoenix police responded to a report of child abuse. This was not the first call for this address, and when the officers arrived, they found five children, ages six, four, one, and two newborns. They were infested with lice and wearing diapers wet with urine and soiled with feces. They had insects crawling out of their ears.

Police immediately removed four of the children for medical treatment. One of the infants could not breathe due to a brain bleed, and the toddler had multiple skull fractures. The fifth child, a baby born just weeks before, was not taken for help. This baby was taken to the morgue.

Like the Arizona infant, thousands of children die every year in America despite being known to authorities. In Ohio, we read about Dylan, a two-month-old, tortured, chained, and thrown down a well after the child protection agency returned him to his meth-addicted father. In California, we read about Anthony, age 10, who despite a long history of being abused was returned to his California parents to be tortured, beaten, starved, and ultimately murdered.

Every one of these kids—just like the five Phoenix children—were known to their local child safety agency. Authorities knew these children and had multiple opportunities to keep them safe—and failed. In fact, this is the rule in child welfare, not the exception. More than half of the children killed each year in their homes have former or open cases with child protection. That is a damning indictment of a system whose very purpose is to keep children alive.

Journalists often jump to the conclusion that a caseworker must have erred or the agency must have failed to follow protocol. While human error and failure to follow rules contribute to fatalities, they are a small piece of the puzzle.

Repetitious violence against children and high death rates are endemic to child protection due to systemic inequities in the justice system. Even the best caseworkers, agencies, and judges have a limited capacity to remediate this situation.

The bottom line is that predators have more rights under the law than the children they abuse. Consider the right to an attorney, one of America's most basic constitutional privileges. The criminally accused have a constitutionally protected right to counsel, but child victims do not. This means abused children are not guaranteed attorneys in their own court cases. Only half of U.S. states currently provide traditional legal representation for children involved in dependency court and foster care proceedings (First Star and Children's Advocacy Network 2015).

Not surprisingly, the Chapin Hall Center for Children at the University of Chicago found that children with attorneys have better life outcomes than children without. Children represented by lawyers exit the foster care system one to three-and-a-half times faster than other children. Likewise, for the subset of children who need adoptive families, researchers found that those with attorneys have "much higher rates of adoption" (Zinn and Slowriver 2008). It is important to note that higher rates of adoption do not come at the expense of reunification. Family reunification rates were unchanged. The higher rates of adoption reflect children on the path to adoption or aging out.

Guiding Supreme Court precedent has by and large ignored the constitutional rights of abused children. A judge recently summed up the legal regime this way: "Birth mother's rights are constitutional; baby's rights are *only statutory*."

The court has indeed upheld as fundamental the mother's right to direct the upbringing of her children and to familial association. These rulings protect the sanctity of family against the overreach of the state. However, the abused child's natural right to his or her own life interests, which is also a fundamental right, has not been adjudicated.

Violence against children was further institutionalized by the Supreme Court in the guiding *DeShaney* case. In this case, the court held that the government bore no responsibility for a child in its care who was so brutally beaten at age four that he now lives in a vegetative state.

Taken together, these common legal practices and high court decisions have created a system where violence against children is endemic. The lesser status of abused children under the law must be remedied.

It is too late for the baby taken to the Phoenix morgue. It is too late for the tens of thousands of children in our nation's child protection system who have already died under the state's watch. But it is not too late to protect children's lives going forward by making it a priority to extend to children the equivalent rights and protections afforded their predators.

## References

First Star and Children's Advocacy Institute. 2015. *A Child's Right to Counsel: A National Report Card on Legal Representation for Abused and Neglected Children.* 3rd ed. Accessed December 22, 2020. http://www.firststar.org/wp -content/uploads/2015/02/First-Star-Third-Edition-A -Childs-Right-To-Counsel.pdf

Zinn, Andrew, and Jack Slowriver. 2008. *Expediting Permanency: Legal Representation for Foster Children in Palm Beach County.* Chicago: Chapin Hall Center for Children at the University of Chicago. Accessed December 22, 2020. https://legalaidresearchnlada.files.wordpress.com/2020/01 /palm-county-legal-representation.pdf

*Darcy Olsen has two decades of success in shaping policy related to patients with life-threatening illnesses' right to try medication before it receives market approval, but she considers the 10 infants she has fostered her most important work. After seeing the injustices facing abused kids, Olsen decided she needed to act. She founded Gen Justice, an advocacy group focused on promoting and protecting the legal and constitutional rights of foster children, in honor of these children, including "Baby A," who lived just 56 days.*

## Combating "Stereotype Threat" among Foster Youth
*Tori Petersen*

No one knows how I did well in school or how I keep a job. The statistics say, as a former foster youth, that I am unlikely to thrive, that my son and daughter are destined to end up abused, and that every relationship I enter into is doomed to crumble (IFoster 2019).

A variety of factors contribute to poor statistical outcomes among foster youth, including a lack of familial and community support systems, limited opportunities, social constraints, poverty, and the trauma of abuse and neglect. Additionally, an invisible phenomenon known as *stereotype threat* further hinders the likelihood of positive life outcomes for foster youth.

Studies on the psychological phenomenon referred to as *stereotype threat* demonstrate how detrimental negative stereotypes can be for society's most vulnerable members (APA 2006). *Stereotype threat* refers to the phenomenon in which stereotypes themselves contribute to individuals' risk of conforming to the negative stereotypes of their social group (APA 2020). The effects of stereotypes increase when people expect discrimination due to their identification with a negatively stereotyped group. Repeated experiences of stereotype threat lead to a vicious cycle of diminished confidence, poor performance, and loss of interest in long-term achievement or success.

There are a variety of negative stereotypes that plague various populations. While in the foster care system, I personally dealt with a variety of negative stereotypes associated with being a "foster youth." One of the most detrimental of these stereotypes was the assumption that foster youth are troubled and therefore prone to lying. I reported abuse in two of my foster homes. The first time, I was separated from my biological sister, a heartbreaking experience that I still carry with me today. Both times I reported abuse I was treated as being manipulative and untrustworthy. No serious investigation was conducted, and corruption was brushed under the rug.

Unfortunately, the dismissal of accusations of abuse in foster homes, without a serious investigation, is more common than many people realize. Caseworkers have a conflict of interest in that they are supposed to advocate on behalf of foster children but are often seeking to meet government-imposed mandates that often contradict what is best for the child (Wexler 2017). Reports made by foster youth are easily dismissed because of stereotypes that they are incapable of forming healthy relationships and that they are prone to manipulation and sabotage. Consequently, abuse and neglect continue to run rampant in places where children are supposed to be safe.

As a foster youth, I was also plagued by stereotypes about what type of future I would be capable of achieving.

Caseworkers, teachers, foster parents, and other community members tended to assume that I would "just become another statistic." I began to believe those assumptions and to fear the future. Fortunately, I was able to break free from those poor expectations, thanks in large part to my high school track coach. He told me that I did not have to be another statistic and that I could accomplish great things. He also laid out concrete goals for me to pursue. The year after my coach first began to speak words of encouragement into my life, I became a five-time state champion in track and field in Ohio. This accomplishment enabled me to receive a full-ride scholarship to a prestigious college. In 2018, I became part of the 3 percent of foster youth who graduate with a bachelor's degree or higher. My college education additionally opened doors to invaluable employment opportunities, enabling me to support my family and to live a healthy lifestyle. A loving church community and my faith in God further contributed to my eventual ability to defy the odds and break free from the stereotypes and statistics that plague foster youth.

While I have been fortunate to overcome stereotypes, many foster youth never receive the same opportunities or encouragement. Those of us who care about empowering foster youth should continually strive to raise awareness. We should promote the stories of foster youth, so they have the chance to prove that they do not have to be defined by the stereotypes that society places on them. By God's grace and the contribution of mentors who believed in my capabilities, I have overcome many of the negative stereotypes associated with foster youth and have achieved great things. Foster youth need adult allies willing to see past stereotypes and to encourage them to become the young men and women whom God created them to be.

## References

APA (American Psychological Association). 2006. "Stereotype Threat Widens Achievement Gap." July 15. Accessed August 1, 2020. www.apa.org/research/action/stereotype

APA (American Psychological Association). 2020. "Stereotype Threat." *APA Dictionary of Psychology*. Accessed August 1, 2020. https://dictionary.apa.org/stereotype-threat

IFoster. 2019. "Foster Care Statistics 2019: 6 Quick Statistics on the Current State of Foster Care." Accessed August 1, 2020. www.ifoster.org/6-quick-statistics-on-the-current -state-of-foster-care/

Wexler, Richard. 2017. "Confessions of a Caseworker: We Remove Kids to Protect Ourselves." *Youth Today*. March 1. Accessed August 1, 2020. https://youthtoday.org/2017/02 /confessions-of-a-caseworker-we-remove-kids-to-protect -ourselves/

*Tori Petersen is a former foster youth, current foster mom, biological mom, foster care advocate, and wife. In 2018, Tori became a part of the 3 percent of former foster youth who earn a college diploma. She graduated from Hillsdale College after studying Christian Studies and Psychology. Tori is a national speaker and writer who advocates for and raises awareness about vulnerable populations, especially those in foster care and suffering families.*

## My Life in Foster Care
*Jaymie Gonzales*

I was placed into foster care at age 11, when my grandmother Frances fell ill. From the time I was a baby, I was tossed around from relative to relative, beginning with my grandmother Frances, to my cousin, then to my other grandmother, until finally returning to Frances. Change had been the only constant in my life, so I thought I would adapt to the change of being in foster care as well.

My first placement was with a woman named Helen. I had no idea how to relate to her. She provided me with basic care but not much else. Helen did not show any love toward me and did not provide me with the opportunity to build trust. I soon learned that I did not have anyone to whom I could confide, and I was not prepared for this reality. I was 11 years old, alone, scared, and silenced.

Helen was a strange woman. She showed little empathy, and whenever she tried to, it came off awkward. It just did not fit her. I immediately learned that I could not open up to her. My social worker did exhibit empathy, and at first, I felt that I could confide in him and come to him with my problems. However, I soon learned that I could not trust him to listen to me either. When I would express the problems I was having with Helen, my social worker would note it and move on. He never offered any solutions. I soon became disillusioned with both persons.

Helen was a religious woman. I happily went to church with her, as I saw church as a nice escape. For my first 11 years, I had grown up with accepting and loving people of faith, so I was not expecting the rejection that I felt. At this point of my life, I began to discover things about myself, and I changed my mannerisms and clothing style to reflect that change. Instead of extending compassion, Helen would look at me strangely and would publicly degrade my appearance. She would frequently remind me that I was a boy, and I should look like one.

Helen's humiliating degradation of my appearance, and her failure to realize that I was longing for my family, caused me to lash out, and our relationship became strained. I would frequently complain to my social worker, would inform him of our latest spats, and would voice my wish to be removed from her house, but all he would do was note it and move on. I ran away several times to get his attention, but he would just note it and move on. After seven months of this endless cycle, I developed a not so clever preteen plan of going to my school principal and threatening to kill Helen. Of course, I had no intention of doing any such thing, but I was desperate. I knew this act would be serious enough to warrant my removal, and it was. My social worker finally recommended I be placed into another foster home.

My next placement was with Loretta and Gerald. I felt an immediate sense of love and care. They welcomed me with open arms, even though they were fully aware of the dumb stunt I had pulled. In the beginning, life with Loretta and Gerald was much different than what I had been accustomed to. Loretta showed empathy for my situation and attempted to extend kindness to me the best she could. However, I soon felt that even Loretta did not fully understand me or take me seriously. This feeling, coupled with my still lingering desire to be with my family, led me to act out.

I soon began lashing out at home, yelling at my foster parents or my social workers and running away in an effort to be heard. I assumed that cussing, yelling, and being standoffish would lead others to treat me like an adult. Although I was only in my early teens, I was dealing with grown-up experiences and the aftermath of trauma. Being ripped from my family through no fault of my own and having already gone through several placement changes in my adolescence, all while going through puberty, was a lot to handle. I should have been allowed an avenue to express my feelings openly, so they could be prudently resolved. But this did not occur.

My anger and the stunts I pulled led others to believe I was mentally troubled, so I was placed on medication against my will. I was forced to take pills that I knew deep in my heart I did not need, and I emphatically emphasized to all persons in authority over me that I did not want them. In my naive early-teen mind, I assumed that being more standoffish and more defiant would cause these people to listen to me and heed my wishes. I was wrong, and my defiance led to many years of pain and psychiatric trauma. Looking back, I understand now why I dug myself in such a big hole and said and did things that I regret today.

Regardless of the turbulence in our relationship, I loved my foster parents deeply. I felt a connection to them at a level that I had only experienced with my grandmother Frances, who is very dear in my life. But I still felt rejection. When I was in ninth grade, I got in trouble at school (which was a regular occurrence), and the school informed my foster parents that I was gay. I reluctantly confirmed this. Gerald did not seem to care, but Loretta dismissed me as foolish. This crushed me, and I was scared to share my identity for many years to come.

When Loretta developed a terminal illness, I cranked up my defiance to a level 10 and really made life hard for them both. I was even expelled from school; I did not know how else to respond. I was stuck in a vicious cycle: I rebelled, so my medications were upped, and I rebelled at that. To make matters worse, my parents were not open and honest about what was going on with Loretta's illness. I did not know Loretta was terminally ill until it became incredibly obvious. I knew something was wrong, and it made me even more angry that my foster parents had not confided in me. All my life, I was whisked away—first from Frances, then from my cousin, then my other grandmother, and then from Frances again—without being asked my opinion or feelings. Now it was happening again. Loretta was being whisked away from me, much like everyone else in my life, and I was angry.

I was angry that Loretta was dying. I was angry I could not find a stable home and could not be with my family. And I was angry that I was forced to take pills against my will and that I could not be open about my identity. I was mean and nasty, got into fights with others, and bullied everyone, which only made my life worse. Loretta's death in 2015 shook me to my core. It was the first major death I had experienced. I began to settle down, but the deepness of my guilt for my behavior and anger began to hang over me like a dark cloud—and it still does.

I wish my story had a happy ending, but it does not. I wish I could build a time machine and go back to change how I had behaved, but I cannot. As I look back on my life now, at the age of 21, I am not excusing how I acted as a preteen and teenager, but I can understand why I acted the way I did based on the instability, sense of rejection, and loneliness I had experienced since birth. The only thing I can do now is tell my story, so others can have a glimpse of what youth in the foster care system, like myself, have gone through and are going through. Foster youth often experience feelings, pain, and trauma that are too much to handle at such a young age. They deserve to be heard.

*Jaymie Gonzales recently graduated with a bachelor's degree in political science from California State University, San Bernardino. He plans to pursue a career in public administration or law.*

## Improving Trauma-Informed Treatment of Foster Children
*Terri Galindo*

It is a common belief that children who are removed from their homes are "rescued" from abusive or neglectful parents. To some, this implies that they live "happily ever after" following foster care placement. But removal from familial abuse and neglect is not the end of the story; it is just the beginning. Merely being placed in a home that is not their own can be traumatic for children. They are removed from a home they know, albeit a home that might be filled with fear and anxiety, and placed in a home with strangers who live differently than they are accustomed—different sounds and smells, different cultural traditions and spiritual beliefs, different routines, and often different races or ethnicities. Abused and neglected children face more than their histories when coming into care, which places them at serious risk of mental and behavioral health issues. Unfortunately, the treatment of these issues is not always based on responding to the unique trauma experienced by children in foster care.

### Defining Trauma
*Trauma* is the response to a serious or life-threatening event that leads to severe psychological distress that can be demonstrated in anxiety, depression, guilt, anger, and post-traumatic

stress (Psychology Today 2020). According to the National Child Traumatic Stress Network (2020), children in our society suffer from numerous types of trauma: bullying, community violence, complex trauma, disasters, early childhood trauma, traumatic grief, and others. It is evident that children are at risk of exposure to and can be victims of trauma throughout their life cycles.

As many as 70 percent of children who are placed in foster care meet the criteria for complex trauma (Greeson et al. 2014). *Complex trauma* refers to children's exposure to multiple and severe traumatic events, such as abuse or profound neglect. Foster children have often been chronically and cumulatively exposed to traumatic incidences that lead to placement in foster care, and these incidences sometimes continue while they are in foster care.

Infants and children up to age five can be especially vulnerable, as these are years of great growth and development. These children frequently experience multiple delays in the areas of physical growth, emotional regulation, and development. Brain development can be stunted as well as speech, motor skills, and capacity for learning. Children in foster care are furthermore less likely to develop secure attachments due to the trauma they have experienced (Jankowska et al. 2015). In later years, former youth are often not prepared to enter adulthood. In their first few years of adulthood, they often experience homelessness, substance abuse, unplanned pregnancies, and poverty (Berzin, Rhodes, and Curtis 2011).

## Risk

Children who enter foster care are at serious risk of mental health and other health problems. These children also deal with being separated from siblings, placement changes, illness or death of family members (Scheid 2020), and court-mandated visits with the accused biological parents. Studies show that more than 80 percent of youth in foster care display significant problems, including behavioral, emotional, or developmental problems (Kang-Yi and Adams 2017; Schmidt et al. 2013; Ellermann 2007). The Urban Institute's national study of the child welfare system indicated that children placed in foster care or with relatives exhibited increased behavioral problems and increased suspensions and expulsions from school, and they were more likely to have received mental health services (Kortenkamp and Ehrle 2002).

**Assessment and Diagnosis**

The assessment of children in foster care is not consistent across medical and mental health services, and diagnosis and treatment is not always prescribed within the lens of trauma. As Tullberg et al. (2017) observe, "Few child welfare agencies fully integrate trauma knowledge into their practice." Often, instead of diagnosing and treating foster youth for trauma (with more common diagnoses of post-traumatic stress disorder or trauma- and stressor-related disorders unspecified), mental health professionals are diagnosing them exactly as they would children in the general population. The most common diagnoses of foster children are attention deficit hyperactivity disorder, anxiety, conduct disorders, and depression (Rubin et al. 2012). These possible misdiagnoses may also lead to psychopharmacological treatment. Often this type of treatment is found to be ineffective because the diagnosis is incorrect, or the child might experience possible unexpected results, such as increased suicidal ideation, as a reaction to antidepressants. Because of this, psychotropics should never be the first type of treatment recommended for foster children (Scheid 2020).

Instead of traditional diagnoses and treatment, mental health practitioners must look at the root of the behaviors. The dysregulation that may be evident should be seen through the lens of trauma and treatment prescribed accordingly. When tempted to diagnose a child with a traditional diagnosis, for example, bipolar disorder, the practitioner must look deeper to see whether those symptoms might be better explained by trauma (Scheid 2020). It is through correct diagnosis that correct treatment can be defined.

## Spiritual Beliefs

Another overlooked area in the lives of children in foster care is their beliefs. The findings of a Casey Field Study revealed that 95 percent of children and youth believe in God, that He is the creator (70 percent), and that He is love (70 percent), and 79 percent believe that prayer is a good spiritual practice (Jackson et al. 2010). Over half said that their response to "bad or tragic things happening" was prayer (59 percent).

If children are separated from their parents and extended family, they may be left with a spiritual void in an area that could contribute to their resilience in the face of adversity (DiLorenzo and Nix-Early 2004). Failure to address all three parts of the child—mind, body, and spirit—ignores the essential role that all three contribute to how children identify themselves, feel about themselves, cope with difficulties, and relate to the world.

Most studies identify religious beliefs as a positive aspect of mental health (Malinakova et al. 2020). Those who consider God to be distant have more anxiety and poorer mental health. Those who are closer to God experience better mental health and an overall feeling of well-being. They demonstrate less substance abuse, depression, and suicidal tendencies and better cognitive functioning (Malinakova et al. 2020). Regnerus and Elder (2003) (as quoted in Jackson et al. 2010) confirm this in their study of 9,000 youth who experienced reduced vulnerability to becoming alcoholics or substance users and were less likely to have school problems or delinquency issues if they were "religious."

## The Role of the Foster Parent(s)

The final overlooked area in the assessment of the foster child is the impact of the foster parents. They are often looked upon as temporary babysitters. Judges often do not include them in decisions made, and mental health providers will often not include them as part of the treatment team. Children are seen in individual therapy sessions and are expected to process their trauma in the safety of the therapy session and then return home to the unsuspecting and uninformed foster parents.

Foster parents can have a profound effect on the progress made by the children placed in their homes. Proper training and information can significantly contribute to the outcomes of these children. Significant healing can take place when foster parents, like the rest of the treatment team, view their foster children through the lens of trauma rather than through their own pasts and beliefs and the children's behaviors.

### Trauma Treatment

Once a thorough assessment is made that has looked at all aspects of the foster child and a correct diagnosis is assigned, treatment can proceed. Trauma treatment must include the whole child—mind, body, and spirit. For foster children especially, this treatment should include a multifaceted, trauma-informed team of a therapist, family support staff, foster parents, child welfare staff, and volunteers who meet the special needs of the child and foster family.

Foster children, surrounded by loving and caring people, can develop the resilience to overcome the problems of their pasts and look forward to a better future.

### References

Berzin, S. C., A. M. Rhodes, and M. A. Curtis. 2011. "Housing Experiences of Former Foster Youth: How Do They Fare in Comparison to Other Youth?" *Children and Youth Services Review* 11:2119–2126.

Dilorenzo, P., and V. Nix-Early. 2004. *Untapped Anchor: A Monograph Exploring the Role of Spirituality in the Lives of Foster Youth.* Philadelphia: Philadelphia Department of Human Services.

Ellermann, C. R. 2007. "Influences on the Mental Health of Children Placed in Foster Care." *Family & Community Health* 30:S23–S32.

Greeson, J. K. P., E. C. Briggs, C. M. Layne, H. M. E. Belcher, S. A. Ostrowski, S. Kim, R. C. Lee, R. L. Vivrette, R. S. Pynoos, and J. A. Fairbank. 2014. "Traumatic Childhood Experiences in the 21st Century: Broadening and Building on the Ace Studies with Data from the National Child Traumatic Stress Network." *Journal of Interpersonal Violence* 3:536–556.

Jackson, L. J., C. R. White, K. O'Brien, P. DiLorenzo, E. Cathcart, M. Wolf, D. Bruskas, P. J. Pecora, E. V. Nix, and J. Cabrera. 2010. "Exploring Spirituality among Youth in Foster Care: Findings from the Casey Field Office Mental Health Study." *Child & Family Social Work* 15 (1): 107–117.

Jankowska, A. M., A. Lewandowska-Walter, A. A. Chalupa, J. Jonak, R. Duszynski, and N. Mazurkiewicz. 2015. "Understanding the Relationships between Attachment Styles, Locus of Control, School Maladaptation, and Depression Symptoms among Students in Foster Care." *School Psychology Forum: Research in Practice* 9:44–58.

Kang-Yi, C. D., and D. R. Adams. 2017. "Youth with Behavioral Health Disorders Aging Out of Foster Care: A Systematic Review and Implications for Policy, Research, and Practice." *Journal of Behavioral Health Services & Research* 44 (1): 25–51.

Kortenkamp, K., and J. Ehrle. 2002. "The Well-Being of Children Involved with the Child Welfare System: A National Overview." *New Federalism: National Survey of America's Families*, Series B, No. B-43. Urban Institute. Accessed December 23, 2020. https://www.urban.org/sites/default/files/publication/59916/310413-The-Well-Being-of-Children-Involved-with-the-Child-Welfare-System.PDF

Malinakova, K., P. Tavel, Z. Meier, J. P. van Dijk, and S. A. Reijneveld. 2020. "Religiosity and Mental Health:

A Contribution to Understanding the Heterogeneity of Research Findings." *International Journal of Environmental Research and Public Health* 17 (2): 494.

National Child Traumatic Stress Network. 2020. "Types of Trauma." Accessed December 23, 2020. https://www.nctsn .org/what-is-child-trauma/trauma-types

Psychology Today. 2020. "What Is Trauma?" Accessed December 23, 2020. https://www.psychologytoday.com/us /basics/trauma

Rubin, D., M. Matone, Y.-S. Huang, S. DosReis, C. Feudtner, and R. Localio. 2012. "Interstate Variation in Trends of Psychotropic Medication Use among Medicaid-Enrolled Children in Foster Care." *Children and Youth Services Review* 8:1492–1499.

Scheid, J. M. 2020. "Challenges and Strategies in Foster Care." *Psychiatric Times* 37 (5). Accessed December 23, 2020. https://www.psychiatrictimes.com/view/challenges -and-strategies-foster-care

Schmidt, J., M. Cunningham, L. Dalton, L. Powers, S. Geenen, and C. Orozco. 2013. "Assessing Restrictiveness: A Closer Look at the Foster Care Placements and Perceptions of Youth with and without Disabilities Aging Out of Care." *Journal of Public Child Welfare* 7 (5): 586–609.

Tullberg, E., B. Kerker, N. Muradwij, and G. Saxe. 2017. "The Atlas Project: Integrating Trauma-Informed Practice into Child Welfare and Mental Health Settings." *Child Welfare* 95 (6): 107–125.

*Terri Galindo is a licensed clinical social worker (LCSW) and licensed marriage and family therapist (LMFT) with almost 40 years of experience in the mental health field, primarily with trauma and at-risk children and their families. She is the vice president of clinical services at 4KIDS, Inc., where she leads the EPIC team of therapists who provide clinical therapy services and parent support and training to foster, adopted, and other community children and families.*

## Faith-Based Agencies and Communities Are Essential in Child Welfare Work
*Natalie Goodnow*

Faith-based agencies (FBAs) and religious communities have long played an essential role in the care of vulnerable children. FBAs and private organizations were the foundation of child welfare work in the United States going back to at least the early 1800s, predating the federal child welfare structure by roughly a century (U.S. Department of Health and Human Services 2008).

While the important work of faith communities continues through hundreds of FBAs, over the last two decades, several state and local governments have been terminating child welfare contracts with FBAs over the agencies' religious beliefs. This prevents FBAs from continuing to provide services such as foster care placements and adoptions. The valuable contribution of FBAs to child welfare work merits their preservation and protection.

### The Benefits of FBAs

There are three key areas FBAs particularly excel in that make them useful partners for state and local child welfare agencies: recruiting foster and adoptive families, providing support during the licensing and placement processes, and placing more traditionally challenging populations.

### *Recruitment of Foster and Adoptive Families*

The recruitment skills of FBAs are critical right now, as at least 20 states saw their number of licensed foster homes decrease between 2018 and 2019, with 11 of those states experiencing a decline greater than 10 percent (Kelly 2019). FBAs are uniquely positioned to tap into faith populations—which are more willing to step forward—to recruit foster and adoptive parents. Practicing Christians are more than twice as likely as the general population to adopt and about 50 percent more likely to foster (Medefind 2014).

The talents of organizations such as the CALL in Arkansas, which has helped recruit almost half of the state's foster families through its work with hundreds of churches, are indispensable (Hardy 2017). The CALL "recruits potential foster parents, trains them, guides them through the state's certification process and provides ongoing assistance once the kids begin arriving" (Hardy 2017). Thirty-six percent of CALL families said they would not have become foster or adoptive parents were it not for the organization, and 40 percent were unsure (Howell-Moroney 2013b).

### Support during the Licensing and Placement Processes

With a natural community structure, faith groups like churches provide a built-in network of support. Almost half of foster families exit foster parenting within a year of their first placement (Clements 2018), often because they do not feel supported or respected (CHAMPS 2019). Research has found that foster parents recruited through faith-based organizations, however, foster 2.6 years longer than other foster parents (Cox, Buehler, and Orme 2002). This makes sense, as many foster parents say strong faith or church support facilitated successful fostering, providing them both motivation and a means of coping with the challenges of fostering (Buehler, Cox, and Cuddleback 2003).

FBAs can offer more personalized support than other child welfare agencies to foster and adoptive parents as they go through the licensing process, serve as foster parents, and even after adoption. This is crucial because many prospective foster and adoptive parents drop out before they finish the licensing process, with some training programs experiencing dropout rates of up to 90 percent (Wiltz 2019). Families engaged through the CALL and Project 1:27, a faith-based foster care recruitment and support organization in Colorado, found the licensing process easier to navigate and personnel more helpful and generally felt more supported compared to respondents from a national sample (Howell-Moroney 2013a).

### *Placing More Traditionally Challenging Populations*

FBAs do a particularly good job of finding homes for children that often have a harder time being adopted, such as sibling groups, teens, and children with special needs (Medefind 2018). In 2016, 45 percent of adoptions that took place through Catholic Charities—one of the most well-known networks of FBAs—were children with special needs (Goodnow 2018). Organizations such as Encourage Foster Care in Ohio even focus their foster care ministry specifically on finding families for siblings, teens, and children with medical needs.

### The Consequences of Pushing Out FBAs

Many states embrace partnerships with FBAs, with at least 10 states passing legislation protecting the religious freedom of these organizations so they can continue to contribute to their communities in accordance with their religious beliefs, such as the belief that children should be placed in homes with a married mother and father. However, since the early 2000s, some states and cities have begun terminating their partnerships with FBAs, including San Francisco, Boston, and the State of Illinois (Goodnow 2018).

Ultimately, pushing FBAs out of child welfare work does three things:

- It eliminates partners that excel in recruiting and supporting foster and adoptive parents and placing more challenging children. This is especially important with well over 400,000 children in foster care, over a quarter of whom are waiting for adoption. Foster families licensed through FBAs may be unwilling to switch agencies, which might require relicensing. Some of these families have developed a strong relationship with their FBA and benefited from personalized and even spiritual support (Free to Foster 2020). Without that, they may choose to stop fostering.

- This in turn reduces recruitment diversity of foster and adoptive parents. States are encouraged to recruit populations that reflect the diversity of their communities and the backgrounds of the children in foster care (Child Welfare Information Gateway n.d.). Eliminating FBAs reduces the outreach opportunities to these potential foster and adoptive parents.

- It sends a message to people of faith, who are currently the most likely to step forward, that they are not welcome unless they leave their faith at the door. Even if other agencies tried to replicate the recruitment efforts of FBAs among the faith community (which is dubious given how overburdened many child welfare agencies already are), people may be less willing to become foster parents if they feel the state's policies and the available licensing agencies are hostile to their values.

### Fulton v. City of Philadelphia

In June 2021, the U.S. Supreme Court decided *Sharonell Fulton, et al. v. City of Philadelphia*. The court was faced with the leading arguments for and against faith-based providers in child welfare work and unanimously ruled in favor of FBAs. Fulton, the lead plaintiff, had fostered more than 40 children over 25 years through Catholic Social Services (CSS). The case addressed Philadelphia's decision to shut down CSS unless it violated its religious beliefs and licensed people in same-sex relationships as foster parents. At the time Philadelphia suspended its relationship with CSS, the city also announced a need for hundreds of foster families (Terruso 2018).

CSS has served the City of Philadelphia for over 100 years, during which no same-sex couple sought foster care certification from the organization (Becket Fund for Religious Liberty 2020). The Becket Fund, which represented Fulton, noted that while CSS cannot endorse same-sex or unmarried couples due to its religious beliefs, it would work with them "to find a match from among the 29 other nearby foster agencies" so they could still foster (Becket Fund for Religious Liberty 2018).

This counters the argument that allowing FBAs to operate according to their religious beliefs would reduce the number of foster and adoptive parents (ACLU 2019). Qualified candidates could simply choose to work with a different agency instead of an FBA with whom their beliefs may not align. Same-sex couples would not, as the ACLU claimed, "be denied the opportunity to provide a loving home to children in need" (ACLU 2019). Chief Justice Roberts, who authored the opinion for the court, wrote: "Maximizing the number of foster families and minimizing liability are important goals, but the City fails to show that granting CSS an exception will put those goals at risk. If anything, including CSS in the program seems likely to increase, not reduce, the number of available foster parents" (*Fulton v. City of Philadelphia* 2021, 14).

The court's ruling in favor of *Fulton* is a significant victory for FBAs, providing greater protection for their services. However, this does not mean the issue is closed. The Supreme Court ruled for *Fulton* because the City of Philadelphia had a policy permitting exemptions from the same-sex certification requirement and did not offer a good enough explanation for denying an exemption to CSS. Other cities and states may eliminate all exemptions in the future and refuse to work with FBAs unless they are willing to compromise their religious beliefs.

### Conclusion

Faith-based agencies and communities are pillars in the child welfare world, and their role remains critically important. Recognizing their value and allowing them to continue to serve vulnerable children and families is a pressing issue right now in the United States. Without them, there would certainly be a void that would be difficult to fill, leaving communities struggling to meet the needs of foster children. States should embrace their FBAs and faith communities as key partners in child welfare work and take advantage of all the benefits they have to offer in finding loving homes for children in foster care.

## References

ACLU. 2019. "Coalition Letter on Discrimination in Child Welfare System." February. Accessed October 1, 2020. https://www.aclu.org/letter/coalition-letter-discrimination-child-welfare-system

Becket Fund for Religious Liberty. 2018. "*Sharonell Fulton, et al. v. City of Philadelphia*." May 16. Accessed September 14, 2020. https://www.becketlaw.org/case/sharonell-fulton-et-al-v-city-philadelphia/

Becket Fund for Religious Liberty. 2020. "Supreme Court Will Decide Fate of Faith-Based Foster Care." February 24. Accessed on September 14, 2020. https://www.becketlaw.org/media/supreme-court-will-decide-fate-faith-based-foster-care/

Buehler, Cheryl, Mary Ellen Cox, and Gary Cuddeback. 2003. "Foster Parents' Perceptions of Factors That Promote or Inhibit Successful Foster Parenting." *Qualitative Social Work* 2 (1): 61–83. Accessed October 10, 2020. https://perma.cc/F3KE-BU3F

CHAMPS. 2019. "CHAMPS Policy Goals: Research Highlights." Accessed September 14, 2020. http://fosteringchamps.org/wp-content/uploads/2019/01/CHAMPS-Research-Highlights-for-Policy-Goals.pdf

Child Welfare Information Gateway. n.d. "Working with Faith-Based Communities." Accessed September 14, 2020. https://www.childwelfare.gov/topics/systemwide/diverse-populations/faith-based/

Clements, Irene. 2018. "We Have to Stop Losing Half Our Foster Parents in the First Year." *The Imprint*. March 18. Accessed September 14, 2020. https://imprintnews.org /opinion/stop-losing-half-foster-parents-first-year/30904

Cox, Mary Ellen, Cheryl Buehler, and John G. Orme. 2002. "Recruitment and Foster Family Service." *Journal of Sociology & Social Welfare* 29 (3): 151–177. Accessed October 12, 2020. https://perma.cc/P4SV-MTP4

Free to Foster. 2020. "Stories of Foster Care Heroes." Accessed on October 10, 2020. https://freetofoster.com/family-stories

*Fulton v. City of Philadelphia*. No. 19-123 (U.S. Supreme Court, June 17, 2021).

Goodnow, Natalie. 2018. "The Role of Faith-Based Agencies in Child Welfare." Heritage Foundation. May 22. Accessed September 14, 2020. https://www.heritage.org/civil-society /report/the-role-faith-based-agencies-child-welfare

Hardy, Benjamin. 2017. "In Arkansas, One Faith-Based Group Recruits Almost Half of Foster Homes." *The Imprint*. November 28. Accessed September 14, 2020. https://imprintnews.org/featured/arkansas-one-faith-based -group-recruits-almost-half-foster-homes/28821

Howell-Moroney, Michael. 2013a. "Faith-Based Partnerships and Foster Parent Satisfaction." *Journal of Health and Human Services Administration* 36 (2): 228–251. Accessed October 1, 2020. http://www.jstor.org/stable/23621779

Howell-Moroney, Michael. 2013b. "On the Effectiveness of Faith-Based Partnerships in Recruitment of Foster and Adoptive Parents." *Journal of Public Management & Social Policy* 19 (2): 168–179.

Kelly, John. 2019. "Fewer Foster Youth, More Foster Homes: Findings from the 2019 Who Cares Project." *The Imprint*. October 10. Accessed September 14, 2020. https:// imprintnews.org/featured/less-foster-youth-more-foster -homes-findings-from-the-2019-who-cares-project/38197

Medefind, Jedd. 2014. "New Barna Research Highlights Christian Adoption and Foster Care among Three Most Notable Vocational Trends." Christian Alliance for Orphans. February 12. Accessed September 14, 2020. https://cafo.org/2014/02/12/new-barna-research -highlights-christian-adoption-foster-care-among-3-most -notable-vocational-trends/

Medefind, Jedd. 2018. "Heritage Foundation Forum: Where Faith, Foster Care, and Adoption Go Together." Christian Alliance for Orphans. June 23. Accessed October 1, 2020. https://cafo.org/2018/06/23/heritage-foundation-forum -how-faith-foster-care-and-adoption-go-together/

Terruso, Julia. 2018. "Philly Puts Out 'Urgent' Call: 300 Families Needed for Fostering." *Philadelphia Inquirer.* March 8. Accessed June 22, 2021. https://www.inquirer .com/philly/news/foster-parents-dhs-philly-child-welfare -adoptions-20180308.html

U.S. Department of Health and Human Services, Office of the Assistant Secretary for Planning and Evaluation. 2008. "Evolving Roles of Public and Private Agencies in Privatized Child Welfare Systems." March. Accessed September 14, 2020. https://aspe.hhs.gov/basic-report /evolving-roles-public-and-private-agencies-privatized-child -welfare-systems

Wiltz, Teresa. 2019. "As Need Grows, States Try to Entice New Foster Parents." Pew Charitable Trusts. March 1. Accessed October 10, 2020. https://www.pewtrusts.org /en/research-and-analysis/blogs/stateline/2019/03/01 /as-need-grows-states-try-to-entice-new-foster-parents.

*Natalie Goodnow works in child and family policy and is a visiting fellow at the Independent Women's Forum. She holds a master's in public policy from the Harvard Kennedy School of Government and lives with her husband and their children in Virginia.*

## Fostering amid the Opioid Crisis: My Family's Story
*Vienna Scott*

Every year in New Hampshire, the number of opioid cases and deaths rise. The state is at the center of the national epidemic with one of the highest rates of death due to drug overdose in the country. With so many teens and adults suffering from addiction, children statewide are suffering as well. A rise in substances abuse cases is correlated with higher levels of child abuse and neglect and a larger number of infants going through withdrawal in hospitals (neonatal abstinence syndrome). There has been a fivefold increase in infant opioid addiction over the past 10 years. This enduring crisis has resulted in a massive influx of children into the foster care system. My family experienced firsthand the effect of this crisis on its child victims and the challenges that foster families face in providing them with appropriate care.

I was in elementary school when we got our first call about a foster placement. My father was out of town and unreachable, and my mother was given less than an hour to make a decision with no information about the child's or mother's health. She said yes, and we had a child at our kitchen table less than two hours later.

When social services showed up at our door, we met a child, about a year and a half old, with a smoker's cough and the facial dysmorphology that goes along with fetal alcohol syndrome. We will call her Emily (her name has been changed to protect the identity of the child). It was clear that Emily was incredibly hungry, so my mom cut up some fruit for her. She ate so much so fast that we were afraid she would throw up. The case agent said she had probably never tried fresh fruit before. As she inhaled the blueberries and grapes, the case agent filled in some of the missing details.

Emily had a teenage mom who was about 17 years old and pregnant for the second time. Her mom had already failed her drug screenings twice for the new pregnancy, and doctors were certain the child would be born with special needs. He would probably enter the foster care system right after being born (he did). Emily had previously lived with her grandparents. She reeked of smoke and had rashes on her body from lack of care. Her skin was so raw with blisters that her flesh smelled.

We learned quickly what it is like to care for a child struggling with the aftermath of an addicted parent. Within three days, Emily's rashes had cleared up, and her appetite had stabilized. Her personality started to come through. Emily was sweet and a little shy. She loved music and dancing. Slowly but surely, she melded into our family. I really wanted to bring her into my class for show and tell, but my mom gently shut that idea down.

While the physical effects of neglect, like the rash and smokers cough, subsided, Emily's trauma manifested in a new way. She began to throw incredible tantrums. With no discernible trigger, she would suddenly throw herself on the floor, crying and thrashing and screaming.

On follow-up visits, Emily's pediatrician informed us that the spontaneous emotional turmoil was related to brain damage caused by her mother's substance abuse. Emily could not predict when the spells were going to take over her, and she felt totally out of control. As she got older, the pediatrician explained, she could learn strategies to control them, but puberty would be especially hard because hormones might make the tantrums even more volatile.

We adjusted our family life to accommodate her explosions. We stayed in more, and mom and dad drove separate cars to church and other events so that one of them could leave immediately if Emily had a hard time. We made sure to put rugs down on our hardwood floors and covered sharp furniture edges so that she would not hurt herself falling into an outburst. When she fell into one of her mini-rages, I remember trying every solution my eight-year-old mind could think of. I would grab one of her books and cuddle up next to her on the floor to read or sing until the fits subsided. I am not sure it really helped, but at least I felt like I was being a good big sister.

But I wasn't her big sister—not really. The goal of the foster care system is reunification with the birth parents. Foster care is designed to be temporary. Until their rights have been terminated, birth parents retain some legal control over their child, even while they live with a foster family. Emily's birth mother used this control to prevent my family from taking her out of state. We could not even travel to visit our family for Christmas while she was in our care.

Although the primary aim of the foster care system is eventual familial reunification, the opioid epidemic makes such reunification markedly more difficult. Serious addictions to heroin, fentanyl, and other illicit opioids are often deadly, making reunification impossible. For children born to parents who are addicts, reunification is difficult for all parties involved because the children's medical and emotional needs require additional care from parents who are rehabilitating and still learning to care for themselves. Many parents are never fit to regain custody of their children, so the kids become adoptable. For a system that is overwhelmed by too many cases from the crisis, sibling groups are often split up because adoptive families are not always willing or able to take on multiple children with specialized needs.

Emily's story is bittersweet. Her biological mother was not able to overcome her addiction, and her father's identity is unknown. Although she was never reunified with her birth family, New Hampshire's Child and Family Services was able to ensure that she and her baby brother were adopted into the same home. Emily's story, however, is not the norm. Most children are permanently separated not only from their birth parents but also from their siblings.

Foster care is complicated for families, medically, legally, and personally. Despite the challenges, I hope to someday become a foster parent myself and to work with child welfare systems to give stability and permanency for children like Emily: the youngest victims of the opioid crisis.

*Vienna Scott is a senior at Yale studying political science and religious studies. Her family has fostered for several years, and she has several adopted siblings.*

## They Call Me Mom
### Diana Hayes

Today, I am the proud mother of five children, but becoming a mother did not happen for me the way it does for most people. My journey to motherhood began when I was 21 years old. My husband and I were newly married and recovering from a miscarriage when we found out that our 2-year-old niece, Amber, had been abandoned by her parents. We did not hesitate to bring her into our home, and she became our first foster child. After two years, Amber's birth mother returned and went through the process to reunify with her.

When Amber was four-and-a-half years old, we went to juvenile court and were asked what we thought should happen next. At the time, we were confident that Amber should return to her mother. We sincerely believed that children should be with their biological parents. As much as we would miss her, we wanted to support what we thought would be best for Amber. The court agreed, and Amber returned to live with her then pregnant mother and her mother's boyfriend. Years later, Amber informed us that when we left her at her mother's house that day, she sat on the front porch waiting for hours in hopes that we would return to pick her up.

After she returned to her mother, we would invite Amber to visit and have her stay a few nights. She would share stories of being left alone for long periods of time, sometimes days. She would tell us about drug addicts who stayed in the home and about her lack of food or clean clothes. We would call Child Protective Services (CPS), but when they interviewed her, she would not repeat what she had told us out of fear. By this time, Amber's mother had had two additional children, Adam and Elaine, and Amber had taken on a mother-like role toward them. She was afraid that if she did not return home, they would be neglected and hurt.

In the meantime, my husband and I, knowing that we were meant to be parents, tried unsuccessfully to have our own biological children. We also pursued adoption through the county by filling out paperwork, attending classes, and completing a home study. The day finally arrived for us to sign the final papers to be officially placed on a waiting list. Our appointment with our adoption worker was set at 9:00 a.m. That same morning, at 7:00 a.m., we received a call from a CPS worker asking if we could pick up Amber (age 10), Adam (age 5), and Elaine (age 3). They had been removed from their home the night before. We immediately abandoned our pursuit of adoption and instead became foster parents to our nephew and two nieces.

The first night that all three children were with us, they insisted on sleeping together in a twin-size bed. We could not separate them. They had only brought with them a black trash bag filled with broken, dirty toys and stained, soiled, and torn clothing of disproportionate sizes. All three kids also had a severe case of lice that would take about four weeks to eradicate. We made an outdoor game of it, in which we would take turns removing the nits and swimming in the pool. It became a summer full of fun memories.

All three children had different fathers, which complicated the entire process. Their mother had simply left each of the fathers and had not maintained contact. Amber's father's whereabouts were unknown. Adam's father was actively pursuing reunification, and Elaine's father was being dragged to court and through the process of reunification against his will by her grandfather.

After one year, Adam's father regained custody of him. Elaine's father failed to reunify, and the court rescinded her grandfather's visitation rights. Amber's father was located back east. He was remarried with children and felt it best that she stayed with us. He voluntarily relinquished his rights.

Now that we were legally able to do so, we chose to adopt Amber, who was 12, and Elaine, who was 6. Elaine immediately began calling us mommy and daddy, but not Amber. This was a difficult transition for her. She always saw us as her parents, but the terms of endearment that she preferred to use were "uncle" and "aunt." She had only bad memories of her biological parents, and it took a long time before she understood the importance of those terms and started to refer to us as "Mom" and "Dad." When we went to finalize the adoption, she also asked to keep her last name. It was not because she loved her name or hated ours; it was simply because her last name was part of her identity, something she had that completely belonged to her.

Two years passed. We had settled into our forever family, but our foster license was still active. One day, our licensing worker called and asked whether we still wanted to maintain our eligibility. My husband and I had discussed fostering again, since we had learned so much from our experience. We told the worker that we were considering infant foster care.

Two days later, I received a call from CPS for placement of a one-day-old baby boy, straight from the hospital. He had been given up at birth and would be placed with an adoptive family when one was found for him. We agreed to take him in, and CPS workers brought him over within hours. He arrived before my husband even got home from work! We were all excited to welcome this new baby into our family. I kept a daily log of everything we did as well as videos and pictures. I marked all his firsts on the calendar. At one point, he needed to be admitted to the hospital for observation when he was just a couple of months old. I intended on staying with him. The nurses where dumbfounded because they said foster parents never stayed overnight. We treated him as our own, and though we did not know what his future held, we hoped he would become a permanent member of our family.

When he was two days short of four months old, I handed him into the arms of his new mother and watched him join his adoptive family that the county had arranged for him. Handing him over to a new family was hard for us. I was a mess the entire week leading up to his departure. I would cry by his crib each night. My husband would sit in the parking lot at work and cry. Elaine was happy to be the baby again, but Amber was heartbroken. She loved him so much.

Within days of our first baby leaving, we switched our license from foster care to adoption. We requested either a boy or girl from newborn to six months old. We wanted a baby to call our own forever. It was March, and our adoption worker told us that we would have a long wait ahead of us. We were confident that a baby would be placed with us soon, and we were right.

In June, we received the call for a relinquishment baby, which is a child voluntarily given up for adoption by the birth mother. Our son, Josiah, was born two months premature at three pounds and had been in the hospital for six weeks. He was in a foster home. We were told we could meet him on June 30 and take him home on July 1. We were ecstatic. He was so little, just eight pounds at three months old. He had several health complications the first year due to being born premature. We battled pneumonia and years of asthma, but he recovered well. We were able to adopt him quickly.

In the years that followed, we found that Elaine, who had endured a great deal of abuse while living with her birth mother, had some learning difficulties and behavioral issues. We pursued therapy for her and hired tutors to help her through school. She was easily angered and very aggressive. She lacked proper social skills and would get into trouble with other children. Because of the need to give proper attention and care to these issues, we decided not to take in any more children.

Many years later, when Josiah was 11, Amber was on her own, and Elaine was attending college and had a good job, we decided that we were still called to help children in crisis and pursued becoming foster parents again. The following year, we received our license, and in March, we welcomed a five-day-old baby boy, Joshua, from the hospital. We had no information for him other than that he had tested positive for methamphetamines. He arrived with the clothes the worker provided and a bag of bottles and formula from the hospital. Nothing else. We had no idea how long he would stay with us or what the plan was for him.

Joshua's story took months to unfold. We were told he had a one-year-old sister, Olivia, who was still with their birth father. We were asked whether we would take her as well if she were ever removed. In time, we learned that his birth mother was an addict and had not expressed a desire to reunify. When CPS intervened, she changed her mind and started a case for reunification. Joshua's birth father was also pursuing reunification. Two months later, however, Olivia was removed from his care and came to live with us as well.

After 10 months with us, Olivia and Joshua were reunited with their birth parents. It was very difficult to hand over the baby whom I had cared for from five days old. I had watched him crawl for the first time and had witnessed his first tooth come in and his first steps. I placed him in the car seat, and I will never forget the look on his face; it was as if to say, why am I leaving you? Even though Olivia had been with us for a shorter amount of time, I was heartbroken saying goodbye to her as well. She had grown so much with us and had made wonderful improvements.

Saying goodbye to these children was the hardest thing I ever did. Nevertheless, we supported reunification, as we had been taught that it was best for the children. We wanted the best possible outcome for these children whom we treated and loved as our own. We encouraged and supported the birth parents every step of the way and stayed in touch after the children were returned to them.

Ten months after reunification, however, Joshua and Olivia were once again removed. We had to wait two weeks to get our license in order for them to come back to live with us. It was the longest two weeks of my life, wondering how they were doing in a stranger's house and what they must be going through. Finally, we were all together and began a whole new adventure. It was a roller-coaster ride through court hearings, delays, continuances, therapy, counseling, visitation that would increase and decrease and increase again, and so on. At one point, we were told they were going home at the next hearing. I packed all their things. I made notes, wrote letters, labeled their toys, and even taught them some practical things, like the importance of handwashing and eating breakfast.

We arrived at court ready to say goodbye, but their stay with us was extended another six months. There would be other close encounters of thinking they would return to their birth parents only to have reunification delayed. It was a very complicated case. At one point, after they had been in foster care for two years, everything was set in motion for them to return to their birth parents, until CPS called for an emergency court hearing. Based on the birth parents' failure to comply with reunification requirements, CPS requested termination of services and asked us whether we would like to adopt the children. A few months later, the birth parents' rights were terminated, but they chose to appeal that decision. It took another year for us to finalize Joshua and Olivia's adoption. They were five and six years old, respectively. They had spent four and a half years in foster care. It had been a chaotic and emotional time for them, and they spent years in therapy for PTSD as a result.

Despite all the ups and downs, I am grateful for the family my husband and I have because of foster adoption. Our oldest daughter, Amber, is 37 years old and is happily married with three children. Our second oldest daughter, Elaine, is 31 years old and is in the process of earning a bachelor's degree in special education. She also works with autistic children. Our oldest son, Josiah, is 23 years old. He recently got married and is a wildland firefighter. Our youngest daughter, Olivia, is 12 years old. She is an excellent piano player and loves to read and cook. Our youngest son, Joshua, is extremely energetic and possibly has sensory processing disorder, but he is intelligent, inquisitive, and likes to work with wood.

Through my journey to motherhood through foster adoption, I learned the importance of sacrifice and putting the needs of each child first as you strive to love them as your own. My family was created through both significant losses and wonderful gains. We loved each child who came to us as our own, even when we did not know whether they would stay. Today, my children have a mom and dad, sisters and brothers, and extended family. We are not the ones they were born from, but who they were born into. I am proud and grateful that I earned the privilege of them all calling me "Mom."

*Diana Hayes is the mother of five children whom she and her husband adopted out of the San Bernardino County foster care system. She has taught training courses to prospective foster families and has mentored several families as they navigated the challenges of foster adopting.*

## Introduction

There are currently hundreds of governmental and nonprofit organizations and individuals working in various capacities to serve children and families involved with the child welfare system in the United States. Although not exhaustive, this chapter highlights the work of some key national and local organizations. Among these organizations are government-sponsored entities, policy and research institutions, faith-based groups, and other private nonprofits dedicated to providing direct services to foster youth, promoting better policy, and recruiting, equipping, and assisting strong, loving foster families.

## AdoptUSKids

AdoptUSKids is a national project that is managed through a cooperative agreement with the Children's Bureau of the Administration for Children and Families of the U.S. Department of Health and Human Services. The project works to ensure that children and teens in foster care get safe, loving, permanent families. The AdoptUSKids.org website first launched in 2002 as an internet adoption service to recruit and connect foster and adoptive families with waiting children throughout the United States. The secure website features a

A foster parent fills out adoption paperwork for her foster children. Several nonprofits are successfully working to recruit and support adoptive parents to lower the number of eligible foster children waiting to be adopted. (Lucian Milasan/Dreamstime.com)

national database of photographs and biographies of children in the foster care system who are available for adoption. The project also provides information and referral services to prospective adopters and approved families as well as training and technical assistance to states and tribes to increase their capacity to provide adoption services to children in foster care and to increase retention and recruitment of foster and adoptive parents. AdoptUSKids further helps prospective families through the entire adoption process.

Since its inception, AdoptUSKids has helped connect more than 10,000 children with adoptive families. Recently, AdoptUSKids has partnered with the Ad Council to launch a series of public service advertisements raising awareness of teens in foster care and encouraging prospective parents to consider adopting them. The campaign highlights stories from real families to demonstrate why teen adoption is so important and rewarding for both the adoptive parents and the adopted youth.

## Aging Out Institute

The Aging Out Institute (AOI) is a social enterprise founded in 2010 by former foster youth Lynn Tonini with the goal of connecting foster youth across the country with resources and strategies that can help prepare them for aging out of foster care and building successful adult lives. Today, AOI offers a variety of services and resources, including a database of organizations, programs, online tools, and other resources focused on helping older and former foster youth; a podcast series, *Preparing Foster Youth for Adulting*, which highlights the experiences, tools, and strategies being used across the nation to help foster youth get ready for adulthood; a list of books and movies about aging out of foster care; and a collection of YouTube videos about how to find an apartment. AOI also runs an annual national awards program that recognizes organizations and individuals for doing innovative and effective work in helping youth age out of foster care successfully.

## Annie E. Casey Foundation

The Annie E. Casey Foundation is a private philanthropy, now based in Baltimore, that was founded in 1948 in Seattle by UPS founder James E. Casey and his siblings and named in honor of their mother. Today, the foundation aims to promote a brighter future for the millions of children at risk of poor educational, economic, social, and health outcomes by focusing on three core goals: strengthening families, building stronger communities, and ensuring access to opportunity. The organization supports research to promote evidence-based strategies for improving child well-being and opportunities for success. It also provides grants to federal agencies, states, counties, cities, and neighborhoods to help them pursue more innovative, cost-effective responses to the issues that negatively affect children, such as poverty and disconnection from family.

Among the foundation's many successful initiatives are the Child Welfare Strategy Group (CWSG) and the Jim Casey Youth Opportunity Initiative. CWSG provides intensive consulting, coaching, and technical assistance to child welfare agencies, so agencies are more effective at strengthening the connections between children and their families and in helping children heal and recover from maltreatment. CWSG additionally develops tools that agencies can use to collect quality data and to evaluate and update services and policies.

The Jim Casey Youth Opportunities Initiative is an effort at the local, state, and national levels to advance policies and practices that help young people transitioning from foster care to adulthood. The Jim Casey Initiative focuses on four pillars of success: ensuring that transitioning youth are connected to caring, supportive adults; ensuring that transitioning youth have a safe and stable place to live; ensuring that transitioning youth earn a high school diploma and postsecondary credentials and have access to work opportunities and training in financial management; and ensuring that transitioning youth have the tools and skills needed to make informed decisions about parenthood and that those who are expecting or parenting have resources and support.

Every year, thousands of young people transitioning from foster care participate in the Jim Casey Initiative's Opportunity Passport program, a matched savings program that helps participants pay for education, housing, and automobiles.

## Better Together

Better Together is a privately funded nonprofit founded in 2015 by Megan Rose, who after 10 years working in the Florida child welfare system became frustrated with the lack of programs aimed at providing services to help prevent the need for placement of children in foster care. The organization aims to preserve families at no cost to the state by promoting employment and assisting them during periods of hardship.

Better Together's Better Families program provides an alternative to foster care for families that are in distress or experiencing crises such as job loss, illness, substance abuse, homelessness, or jail time. When a family calls or is referred for help, Better Together's professional staff meets the parent or parents to better understand their story, needs, and objectives. If parents voluntarily place their children with a host family, they will be assigned a family advocate and matched with a couple best suited to help. Together with their family advocate, the birth parents and host family agree on temporary living arrangements. After parents reunify with their children, Better Together volunteers maintain regular visits with families and continue to support and mentor them. Since its inception, the Better Families program has served more than 2,500 children in Southwest Florida and reports that it has kept 98 percent of them out of the foster care system.

Better Together also sponsors a Better Jobs program, which helps churches run virtual and in-person job fairs for families suffering economic hardship due to unemployment. Before meeting with prospective employers, participants receive interviewing tips, resume help, and coaching on how to best articulate their skills. Church-based organizers recruit volunteer hairstylists and collect business attire to help attendees look and feel their best. The Better Jobs program has helped nearly 28,000 individuals find work through church-based job fairs across 20 states.

## The CALL

A Christian nonprofit founded in 2007 by a group of church leaders and child advocates in Pulaski County, Arkansas, the CALL now operates in more than 50 counties throughout the state. The organization recruits potential foster parents, trains them, guides them through the state's certification process, and provides ongoing assistance to families that have taken children in. Even though the CALL receives no public funding, it has become the source of nearly half of all foster homes in Arkansas. The organization has been particularly effective at recruiting and assisting foster families in rural counties, where the Arkansas Division of Children and Family Services (DCFS) had so few placement options that it was forced to send children to short-term placements in communities hours away. When face-to-face training sessions were canceled in response to the COVID-19 pandemic, the CALL quickly organized a virtual online training program and has more than doubled the number of families trained per month to open their homes to abused and neglected children. Since the organization's inception, CALL families have served thousands and have adopted hundreds of children in the DCFS system.

## Casey Family Programs

Casey Family Programs was established in Seattle, Washington, in 1966 by United Parcel Service founder James E. Casey with the mission "to provide and improve—and ultimately prevent the need for—foster care" in the United States. Today, the organization operates in 50 states, several tribal communities, and the District of Columbia and Puerto Rico and is the nation's largest foundation focused entirely on foster care and improving the child welfare system. The organization provides nonpartisan research and technical expertise to child welfare system leaders, members of Congress, and state legislators in an effort to promote improvements in practice and policy. Since its inception, Casey Family Programs has donated more than $1.6 billion in programs and services to benefit children and families in the child welfare system and has developed several tools used by child welfare agencies, including the Casey Life Skills Assessment. This free tool assesses the behaviors and competencies youth need to achieve their long-term goals. The self-evaluation assessment is meant to help mentors, educators, and caseworkers assist youth in maintaining healthy relationships, developing good work and study habits, planning and goal setting, budgeting, using community resources, and improving computer literacy, among other efforts.

## Center for State Child Welfare Data

A growing body of research suggests that child welfare agencies that use research evidence to inform their policies and practices achieve improved outcomes for both children and families. In an effort to provide high-quality research on family welfare issues, Dr. Fred Wulczyn founded the Center for State Child Welfare Data in 2004 as a partnership between state child welfare agencies, Chapin Hall at the University of Chicago, the American Public Human Services Association, and the Center for Social Services Research at the University of California, Berkeley. Funding for the Data Center comes from the Annie E. Casey Foundation and Casey Family Programs.

The Data Center collects and uses data to develop knowledge about children, families, communities, and agencies. It then works to put that knowledge in the hands of public and private child welfare agencies and system leaders, so they can make evidence-based policy and practice decisions to improve outcomes for children and families. The Data Center further offers training in data analysis, reporting, and application to help child welfare staff build evidence-use skills.

In addition to its direct work with agencies, the Data Center pursues a rich research program devoted to measuring the effects of child welfare policy and research evidence use among child welfare agencies. Foundation- and government-supported research conducted by the center has addressed topics such as using technology for assessing young people's mental health, adolescents leaving care to permanency, the dynamics of foster home recruitment and retention, racial disparities within the foster care system, and the role of family support centers in reducing maltreatment investigations.

## CHAMPS

CHAMPS, which stands for Children Need Amazing Parents, is a national policy campaign that aims to communicate the vital role of foster parents in children's lives and to advance research-based policy improvements nationally and in the states to ensure better outcomes for children and youth in foster care by promoting the highest-quality parenting. The campaign—which is led by a coalition of partners, including researchers, advocates, pediatricians, faith-based leaders, foster parents, youth, service providers, and others—offers policy makers a policy playbook and related tools to help agencies recruit, retain, and support stable foster parents. All aspects of the campaign are grounded in research that shows that loving, supportive families—whether birth, kin, foster, or adoptive—are critical to children's healthy development.

### Child Welfare League of America

The Child Welfare League of America (CWLA), established in 1920, is the nation's oldest and largest membership-based child welfare organization. CWLA provides training, consultation, and technical assistance to child welfare professionals and agencies while educating the public on emerging issues that affect abused, neglected, and at-risk children. Through publications and conferences, CWLA shares information on emerging trends, federal and state policy, and specific topics in child welfare practice (family foster care, kinship care, adoption, etc.).

CWLA develops new standards and regularly revises existing standards through a rigorous, inclusive process that challenges child welfare agency representatives and a diverse group of national experts to address persistent and emerging issues, debate current controversies and concerns, review research findings, and develop a shared vision that reflects the best current theory and practice. In 2012 and 2013, CWLA worked with members and experts across the country to develop the National Blueprint for Excellence in Child Welfare. This National Blueprint serves as the foundation for updating and creating CWLA program-specific Standards of Excellence for child welfare practices.

## Children's Bureau

The Children's Bureau is a federal agency within the U.S. Department of Health and Human Services' Administration for Children and Families. Created by President William H. Taft in 1912, it was the first federal agency in the United States (and in the world) to focus exclusively on improving the lives of children and families.

Today, the Children's Bureau partners with federal, state, tribal, and local agencies to improve the overall well-being of our nation's children and families. Many of its efforts focus on improving child abuse prevention, foster care, and adoption. The Children's Bureau, which operates an on annual budget of nearly $10 billion, is composed of eight divisions and teams and participates in a variety of projects that provide guidance on federal law, policy, and program regulations; fund essential services, helping states and tribes operate every aspect of their child welfare systems; support innovation through competitive, peer-reviewed grants for research and program development; offer training and technical assistance to improve child welfare service delivery; monitor child welfare services to help states and tribes achieve positive outcomes for children and families; and share research to help child welfare professionals improve their services.

## Children's Rights

Children's Rights started as a project of the New York and American Civil Liberties Unions and then became its own entity in 1995. Since its inception, Children's Rights has worked to reform and improve failing child welfare, juvenile justice, education, and health care systems through legal advocacy and action. Representatives from Children's Rights team up with local child advocates to investigate and expose pervasive problems in child welfare systems and to develop long-term solutions and negotiate court-enforceable plans to transform local public agencies so that they better serve kids in need. Children's Rights has won landmark legal victories on behalf of children throughout the country. These victories include, among many others, decreasing the number of institutionalized children aged 12 and younger in Connecticut by nearly 90 percent, increasing the frequency of caseworker visits to children in foster care in Atlanta, and ensuring that more sibling groups are placed together in Tennessee.

In addition to its legal efforts, Children's Rights engages in research and state and national policy advocacy to improve the laws governing child welfare practice. The organization is particularly focused on exposing and responding to the exclusion of LGBTQ foster parents, the mistreatment of LGBTQ foster youth, racial discrimination in child welfare systems, and over-medication of foster youth.

## Congressional Coalition on Adoption Institute

The Congressional Coalition on Adoption Institute (CCAI) is a nonprofit, nonpartisan organization that seeks to raise awareness about the millions of children around the world in need of permanent, safe, and loving families and to eliminate barriers that hinder these children from realizing their basic right to a family. Its origins can be traced to 1985, when several members of Congress, including U.S. senators Lloyd Bentsen (D-TX) and Gordon Humphrey (R-NH) and U.S. representatives Tom Bliley (R-VA) and Jim Oberstar (D-MN), joined together in an effort to eliminate barriers to adoption. In pursuit of this goal, they formed the Congressional Coalition on Adoption caucus, which has contributed to the passage of historic legislation, such as the Adoption and Safe Families Act of 1997 and the John Chafee Foster Care Independence Act. In 2001, they created the CCAI to provide information and resources for members of Congress and their staffs.

Today the CCAI has five core programs: the Foster Youth Internship (FYI) Program, the Angels in Adoption Program, the Congressional Resource Program, the 20/20 Vision Program, and National Adoption Day.

The FYI Program is a highly esteemed congressional internship for young adults who spent time in the foster care system. The program began in 2003 as an effort to raise awareness to federal policy makers about the needs and unique perspectives of children and youth in foster care. During the internship program, CCAI organizes retreats, advocacy training, and various networking opportunities with experts in the child welfare field. FYI Program interns additionally spend time researching policy issues that affect children and youth in the foster care system and create a policy report that is presented to members of Congress and their staffs and released to child welfare advocates across the country.

The Angels in Adoption Program honors a wide spectrum of individuals and organizations making extraordinary contributions in the areas of adoption, permanency, and child welfare.

The Congressional Resource Program shares objective, relevant, and timely information to help educate policy makers on information critical to federal adoption and child welfare policy and connects policy makers with individuals with personal experience with adoption and foster care.

The 20/20 Vision Program is a public-private partnership delegation model designed to build relationships and increase positive dialogue among members of Congress, foreign and domestic government officials, and private sector leaders to share information and improve adoption and child welfare policy and practices around the globe.

Finally, CCAI emphasizes the importance of a loving family by promoting National Adoption Day efforts and celebrations throughout country.

## Court Appointed Special Advocates

Court Appointed Special Advocates (CASA), named after the title given to its volunteers, is a national association that recruits, trains, and supports court-appointed advocates for abused and neglected children. CASA was founded in 1977 by Seattle juvenile court judge David W. Soukup after he realized that the state's Child Protective Services agency was not providing him with sufficient information to make life-changing decisions for children suffering from child abuse and neglect.

The organization is made up of volunteers, also referred to as CASA, who complete extensive and ongoing training and instruction in court observation. These CASA are generally appointed by a judge at a child's first child welfare hearing, and they stay with each case until it is closed and the child is in a safe, permanent home. They get to know the child and everyone involved in the child's life, including parents, family, foster parents, educators, and service providers and legal and child welfare professionals. These interactions better equip them to make well-informed recommendations to the court in the best interest of the child.

CASA's network of programs and volunteers closely follow issues affecting children who have experienced abuse and neglect, including those targeted for sex trafficking, those affected by the opioid crisis, those living with incarcerated parents, and those preparing to age out of the foster care system.

Since its founding, CASA has extended its services to the District of Columbia and every state (except for North Dakota), has recruited nearly 100,000 volunteers, and has served millions of children nationwide. Children assigned to a CASA volunteer are more likely to receive services, are less likely to run away while in foster care, are more likely to succeed in school, and are more likely to find a safe, permanent home.

## Dave Thomas Foundation for Adoption

The Dave Thomas Foundation for Adoption (DTFA) is the only public nonprofit charity in the United States that is exclusively focused on foster adoption. The foundation was established in 1992 by Wendy's founder Dave Thomas, who was himself adopted. It is currently led by president and CEO Rita Soronen.

The DTFA's signature program is Wendy's Wonderful Kids program. Through this program, the foundation provides funding to adoption agencies to hire recruiters to use a child-focused recruitment model to find permanent homes for children in foster care. Recruiters specifically focus on children for whom it has traditionally been difficult to find adoptive families—primarily older children and children with mental health disorders as well as children who are part of sibling groups, those with previously failed adoption efforts, children with special needs, and children who have lingered in foster care.

In an effort to learn what works in adoption recruitment, the DTFA commissioned an unprecedented five-year study of the foundation's child-focused recruitment model. The study presents the most comprehensive, rigorous empirical evaluation to date of adoption recruitment practices and the policies aimed at improving the likelihood of permanent adoption for children in foster care. The control group research showed that children in foster care served by the Wendy's Wonderful Kids program were 1.7 times more likely to be adopted than those not served. It also found that older children and those with mental health challenges were three times more likely to be adopted when served by Wendy's Wonderful Kids recruiters.

The foundation additionally sponsors the Adoption-Friendly Workplace program and publishes the 100 Best Adoption-Friendly Workplaces list to recognize organizations that provide employees with financial reimbursement for adoption costs and offer paid leave after they bring an adopted child into their home.

## DC Family and Youth Initiative

The DC Family and Youth Initiative (DCFYI) is a nonprofit organization, staffed largely by volunteers, that helps teens in foster care make lifelong connections with caring adults. These mentors become their support system and provide advice, guidance, affection, and a sense of belonging that they otherwise might not have.

DCFYI works annually with 35 to 40 foster youth, ages 12 to 21. Youth participants are connected with adult volunteers in DCFYI-sponsored environments, such as shared meals, outings to bowling alleys, softball games, and the like. Eventually, relationships develop that lead to one-on-one mentorships, connections with host families who welcome youth for regular visits, and official adoptions. Many youth participants have been adopted through DCFYI programs, and all participants leave foster care connected to at least one adult mentor.

## FaithBridge

Founded in 2007 with a grant from the Mt. Bethel United Methodist Church, FaithBridge Foster Care is Georgia's largest Christian Child Placement Agency. The organization recruits, trains, and supports foster care families in local churches and licenses them to provide community-based, short- and long-term traditional and therapeutic care for foster children. FaithBridge pioneered the Community of Care model, which is designed to surround every foster family with a community of support from trained volunteers and professionals who offer assistance in providing safe and stable homes for foster children.

In many foster care placements developed by FaithBridge, the foster parents are encouraged to interact with the birth parents by sharing meals, attending family outings and church services together, and sharing parenting skills. Nearly a quarter of FaithBridge foster families maintain relationships with their foster children even after they have been reunited with their parents. They continue to provide encouragement and support to help birth parents keep their lives on track. In 2020, The U.S. Department of Health and Human Services (HHS) cited FaithBridge as a model foster care agency because of its focus on reuniting foster children with healthy birth families.

## Family and Youth Law Center

Established in 1998 as the National Center for Adoption Law and Policy, the Family and Youth Law Center (FYLaw) is a nonprofit legal organization at Capital University Law School that partners with local, state, and national agencies and organizations to improve laws, policies, and practices associated with child protection, adoption, and juvenile justice systems.

In all services, FYLaw partners with Capital University and Capital University Law School to provide experiential and service-learning opportunities to law and social work students interested in working in child welfare and other related fields.

FYLaw's student-oriented programming includes a national moot court competition, a fellowship program, externships, and pro bono opportunities.

In conjunction with the Nationwide Children's Hospital, FYLaw also sponsors an Adoption Academy, an eight-week training series designed to provide prospective adoptive parents with neutral information about adoption options and the various components of the adoption process.

Over the past few years, FYLaw has expanded its services beyond advocacy, training, and education to include direct representation of systems-involved youth. FYLaw launched the Foster Youth Advocacy Center (FYAC) to provide civil legal services to youth ages 16 to 25 who are transitioning out of the child welfare system or who have already aged out. FYAC staff are able to assist such youth in the following areas: obtaining personal records and documents, credit checks and repair, housing, juvenile and adult criminal record sealing and expungement, small claims, public benefits, education, power of attorney, self-advocacy, and other civil legal issues. In 2020, FYAC expanded its operations to add these services to families at risk of systems involvement.

## Family Equality

Family Equality, originally titled the Gay Fathers Coalition, was founded in 1979 by a group of gay fathers seeking to promote legal protections and equality for gay fathers through community building, education, and policy change. Eventually, the national nonprofit expanded its mission to include lesbian, bisexual, transgender, and queer families and changed its name to Family Equality in 2007.

Among its many focus areas, Family Equality seeks to ensure that child welfare and support systems are free from discrimination that might inhibit permanency for LGBTQ foster youth or deter LGBTQ foster parents from seeking family formation through adoption, foster care, assisted reproductive technology, or other means. The Family Equality Policy Team tracks legislation at the federal and state levels that affects existing LGBTQ families or individuals seeking to form families. Family Equality specifically opposes laws that grant religious exemptions that legally protect the right of faith-based agencies to deny services to LGBTQ foster parents.

In 2020, Family Equality launched Every Child Deserves a Family Campaign to develop recommendations for LGBTQ-affirming and progressive policies in the child welfare system. These recommendations led to the introduction into Congress of the John Lewis Every Child Deserves a Family Act of 2021. The act prohibits any foster care or adoption agency that receives public funding from refusing to provide services to qualified prospective LGBTQ parents.

## Foster America

Foster America was launched in 2016 by attorney and policy maker Sherry Lachman and community builder Marie Zemler Wu. Foster America's core and immediate focus is a fellowship program that recruits, trains, and deploys talented professionals with diverse skills from backgrounds in data and technology, design and marketing, finance, and strategy and planning into the child welfare system. The program draws inspiration from other successful fellowship models such as Teach for America and the Broad Residency. The goal is to effect change within a bureaucratic system from the inside out by placing successful postgraduate and midcareer professionals to work under change-minded government and nonprofit agency leaders in pursuit of short-term improvements and long-term transformations.

Fellows are encouraged to focus on a previously identified problem that affects children in foster care and to work on an innovative project in one of the following areas: preventing abuse and neglect outside of foster care; seeing that children who do enter foster care can live with loving, stable foster families rather than in group settings; ensuring that every child in foster care has consistent quality support from a highly capable caseworker; and securing children's health, mental health, safety, and educational success as the multiple systems in their life work together for their well-being.

## Foster Care Alumni of America

The idea for Foster Care Alumni of America (FCAA) was generated in 1999 when Casey Family Programs began extensive interviews with more than 1,800 alumni of foster care for its National Alumni Study. As it became clear that alumni wanted to be more involved in shaping policy and improving the system, alumni leaders proposed the establishment of an independent, nonprofit, alumni-led organization. Thanks to significant investment by Casey Family Programs, FCAA was established in 2004. Today, the organization has chapters across the country that operate with the avowed mission of connecting the voices of the foster care alumni community to transform policy and practice.

The FCAA policy agenda seeks to capture the expertise of its members' collective experience to advocate for foster care reform at the local, state, and federal levels and to educate key stakeholders about important policy issues pertaining to foster care. FCAA's priority areas include housing stability, higher education, physical and mental health, sex trafficking prevention, aging out, LGBTQ services and support, employment, financial stability, sibling connections, and child welfare finance reform.

FCAA further seeks to ensure that individuals from foster care can experience the same traditions, opportunities, and love that most people get from their families by planning alumni reunions, which include "family" barbeques and holiday events. In recognition that a majority of college scholarships for foster care alumni are limited to students younger than 25 and do not fund graduate programs, the organization also sponsors a scholarship program for foster care alumni aged 25 and over.

## Foster Care to Success

Foster Care to Success (FC2S) is the oldest and largest non-profit organization working to help foster youth transition from foster care to adulthood through education. FC2S was founded as a small Washington, DC, community outreach program in 1981 by Joseph Rivers, who had spent his entire childhood in a New York orphanage and knew firsthand how difficult it was to enter adulthood without a caring support system. Initially, program volunteers helped participating youth meet their immediate needs for housing, jobs, and transportation and also with long-term goal development. With four small $500 grants, Rivers created what is now the FC2S scholarship program. After Rivers's death in 1990, his foster sister and FC2S board member Eileen McCaffrey became executive director and helped the organization grow into the largest provider of college funding and support services for foster youth in the nation.

Today, FC2S provides over $15 million in funding to over 5,000 youth for college, training, and student support programs annually. In addition to financial backing for college in the form of scholarships and grants, FC2S provides participating youth and young adults academic and personal mentoring, help with internships and employment readiness skills, and family-like encouragement and care packages with school supplies, health and personal care items, motivational items, treats, and gift cards.

## FosterClub

FosterClub is a national peer support network that provides encouragement, motivation, education, and benefits for foster youth. The idea for FosterClub dates back to 1996, when Celeste and Jeff Bodner agreed to provide foster care to two young boys who had been sneaking into a shed on their property for shelter. The Bodners received foster parent training and binders of informational material, but they were struck by the fact that the boys received no information. They had not received a list of their rights, an explanation of what foster care is or how to navigate it, or any information concerning resources or peers with experience in foster care whom they could contact.

Celeste Bodner founded FosterClub in 2000 and started a website to provide foster youth access to peer support groups and information that would help them navigate the foster care system. The Jim Casey Youth Opportunities Initiative became the first official funder of FosterClub, and the site soon became popular among youth in foster care. Children and youth who became members were able to connect with peers, confidentially share their experiences with others, read inspiring stories about famous former foster kids, and find answers to their questions using the first 24/7 resource built specifically for them.

Within two years of its inception, FosterClub was contracted to host three-day Teen Conferences in several states. These conferences were initially staffed in part by a small group of foster youth interns. Over time, the internship program grew into the current All-Star Program, a group of more than 20 competitively selected youth who are sponsored by their states to serve in a yearlong internship. The All-Star interns are now recognized as leaders on the national foster care scene.

Today, FosterClub, which is headquartered in Seaside, Oregon, has over 60,000 members. Each year, the FosterClub All-Stars teach and inspire thousands of foster youth across the country. They also travel to Washington, DC, and state capitals to raise awareness about the need for changes in policy and practices and to advocate for policies that will better serve foster youth. FosterClub's All-Stars were instrumental in lobbying for the passage of the Fostering Connections to Success and Increasing Adoptions Act of 2008.

## Fostering Court Improvement

The passage of the Adoption and Safe Families Act of 1997 brought increased attention to the need for state dependency courts and child welfare agencies to collaborate on measuring and working to improve outcomes for children and families in the foster care system. Fostering Court Improvement (FCI) is a nonprofit organization that provides a platform of shared data that dependency courts and child welfare agencies in every state can use to make informed decisions, manage operations, monitor performance, and make systemic changes. FCI combines the expertise developed at the University of North Carolina School of Social Work, the Barton Child Law and Policy Center of the Emory University School of Law, the American Bar Association Center on Children, and Fostering Results—a public education and outreach campaign supported by PEW Charitable Trusts and the Children and Family Research Center at the University of Illinois at Urbana-Champaign's School of Social Work—to convert existing data from the Adoption and Foster Care Analysis and Reporting System (AFCARS) and the National Child Abuse and Neglect Data System (NCANDS) into reports that can be used to inform the core work of dependency courts and child welfare agencies.

## 4KIDS, Inc.

4KIDS, Inc., is a faith-based nonprofit in South Florida motivated by the vision of securing hope, homes, and healing for foster children who have been removed from their homes for the first time, foster siblings who need to stay together, young moms facing an unplanned pregnancy with no place to go, and young adults who need a place to belong.

4KIDS initially began as two separate ministries. The first was Calvary Chapel Fort Lauderdale's Child SHARE Ministry, which was established in 1997 as a ministry to recruit and train foster parents and was later expanded with a family-style home called Kids Place. Kids Place was designed to serve kids who would otherwise be difficult to place in traditional foster homes, including teens and large sibling groups. The second ministry was Project TeamWork 4Kids. Launched in 1999 by Rick and Joan Englert with support from the Stacy Foundation, Project TeamWork was the first Christian foster care agency with the vision of bringing the South Florida church community together. In 2000, Project TeamWork piloted an innovative program called SafePlace, an emergency intake center for children awaiting a more permanent home.

In 2003, Child SHARE and Project TeamWork 4Kids merged to create 4KIDS of South Florida. A couple years later, 4Kids launched an additional ministry, the 4KIDS Spirit of Success Institute. The Spirit of Success Institute is an independent living program designed to give young adults aging out of foster care the opportunity to finish high school, get jobs, start college, and otherwise transition out of foster care successfully. Around the same time, 4KIDS merged with His Caring Place, a crisis maternity home. His Caring Place allows 4KIDS to care for moms and babies who could be separated in the foster care system. The goal is to break the cycle of separation by equipping young moms to live with and care for their children on their own. Over the years, 4KIDs has expanded its homes and ministries throughout South Florida and the Treasure Coast.

In 2014, 4KIDS adopted the EPIC Therapeutic Approach, which aims to help every child experience healing with a family equipped to love and support them by addressing the emotional, physical, intellectual, and character-based (EPIC) needs of children. The EPIC approach consists of three major components: training, therapy, and EPIC Camp. The 4KIDS EPIC training is a 12-hour program designed to equip parents, teachers, or other caregivers to connect with kids using an evidence-based, trauma-informed approach. The EPIC therapy component involves licensed, master-level therapists creating a unique plan for each individual child and family that will best help each child experience healing and wholeness. Finally, the EPIC Camp consists of a camp experience where therapists help kids understand their individualized sensory needs, learn the tools they need to help them calm their bodies, and learn new ways to cope with their strong emotions. After the camp, therapists help parents and caretakers implement and solidify the techniques the kids learned.

## Gen Justice

Arizona-based Gen Justice was founded by child welfare policy expert Darcy Olsen. Through her own experience as a foster mother of 10 children over 10 years, Olsen witnessed firsthand the many failures of the child welfare system. Olsen, along with Gen Justice cofounder and vice president Rebecca Masterson, concluded that one of the primary underlying problems with foster care is that while those accused of child abuse and neglect are provided with constitutional rights, such as the rights to an attorney and to a speedy and public trial, alleged child victims are not afforded the same legal rights and protection. Moreover, many children within the system suffer because of weak laws or poor compliance with good laws. Gen Justice works to address these failures through nonpartisan policy reform, a pro bono Children's Law Clinic, and lawsuits designed to bring about social change.

Since its inception in 2017, Gen Justice Children's Law Clinic has helped hundreds of Arizona foster children through direct representation, advocacy, and training. Within its first two years in operation, Gen Justice successfully engineered bipartisan support for six new child safety laws in Arizona and assisted legislators in Georgia with the passage of another. Reforms included improved legal representation for abandoned, abused, and trafficked children; reduced wait times for adoption; placement of foster newborns with permanent families within one year (versus four years previously); and a requirement that child services expedite the search for relatives in the first 30 days, thus satisfying the presumption that kids in foster care are best off with family. In 2019, at a White House policy summit and ceremony, Gen Justice was awarded the inaugural Peterson Prize in Venture Philanthropy.

## Healthy Foster Care America

Healthy Foster Care America (HFCA) is an initiative of the American Academy of Pediatrics and its partners to improve the health and well-being outcomes of children and teens in foster care. Partners have included representatives from child welfare, family practice, social work, nursing, government, the legislative and judicial fields, child psychiatry and psychology, advocacy organizations, alumni, and families.

HFCA partners first met in Washington, DC, in April 2005 to develop a collaborative plan among the various disciplines working with children and teens in foster care. Since its inception, HFCA has worked to achieve multiple goals. The first is the development of a National Foster Care Alliance made up of key national organizations and agencies to pursue common short- and long-term strategies to improve the health and well-being of children and teens in foster care. The second is to research, identify, and implement best practices by examining programs and practices already in place and to create a think tank to set a national research agenda for foster care. The third is to create a political/policy agenda aimed at improving the health and well-being of children and teens in foster care and strategies for pursuing that agenda. The fourth is to involve health professionals at the national, state, and local levels in advocating for and treating children and teens in foster care. The fifth is to empower children and teens in foster care and their families by increasing their involvement in all aspects of their own health care and providing respite and therapeutic services for foster parents and kin. The sixth is to develop comprehensive tools to share information and data among key stakeholders while protecting patient confidentiality. The seventh is to design and launch a media campaign to build the public will to improve foster care, to decrease negative stigma associated with foster care, and to recruit new families for children and teens in care.

## Heart Gallery

The Heart Gallery is a traveling photographic and audio art exhibit consisting of professional photographs of local and nationwide children who are currently in foster care and waiting to be adopted. There are over 80 Heart Galleries across the United States, all of which work in collaboration to increase the number of adoptive families for children in need of a forever family. The galleries display the personalities of children and their siblings awaiting adoption by capturing them in settings outside of a caseworker's office. The goal is to demonstrate that their smiles are those of the children you see playing in your neighborhood, the children that your child goes to school with, and the children that you could see as an addition to your family.

The work of Heart Gallery became even more important as recruiting adoptive families during the COVID-19 crisis became more complicated. In response to the crisis, the Heart Gallery of Sarasota, Florida, launched the Family Finder program, which uses ads targeted to prospective adoptive families to match them with children in the child welfare system. People who respond to ads receive information, videos, and photos of children awaiting adoption.

## iFoster

iFoster is a national nonprofit that bridges the gap between youth in the child welfare system and the external corporations, programs, foundations, and government agencies that have the products, services, and resources they need to become successful, independent adults. iFoster was founded in 2010 by

Serita and Reid Cox, both of whom had overcome adversity in their own lives to build successful careers in the business world. It has since grown into the largest national online network of resources for foster youth.

iFoster currently operates a resource portal, a jobs program, and TAY (transition-age youth) AmeriCorps. The iFoster Resource Portal has over 500 resources for foster youth, such as free tutoring, free vision exams and eyeglasses, discounted laptops, free career and employment preparation courses, and other valuable products and services.

The iFoster Jobs Program is a trauma- and evidence-informed training program that provides foster youth with the job skills they need to succeed in the workforce. iFoster has over 25 major corporate employer partners who offer interviews to each of the youth who graduate from training. Over 450 foster youth earned living wage jobs in the program's first three years of existence. In response to the COVID-19 pandemic, iFoster launched a virtual version of the Jobs Program in October 2020, which uses self-directed online job readiness training and interactions with iFoster trainers via Zoom.

Launched in March 2019, TAY AmeriCorps is iFoster's newest program. Thanks to a grant from the Corporation for National and Community Service (CNCS), iFoster is deploying 100 current and former foster youth to serve as AmeriCorps members at 45 host sites, including high schools, colleges, and youth workforce centers throughout Los Angeles County and the San Francisco Bay Area. These participants connect other transition-age foster youth to resources such as tutoring and financial aid services. The program is designed to be a stepping-stone for transition-age youth to gain the skill sets they need to find permanent employment in the public sector.

As of mid-2021, iFoster has over 60,000 members across all 50 states, Guam, and Puerto Rico, with an estimated 300 new members joining every month.

## Isaiah 117 House

When children are removed from their homes out of concern for their welfare, they are usually brought to the Department of Children's Services (DCS) office or a state equivalent to await placement with a foster family. This wait can be several hours to nearly a full day or more. The children are often dirty, hungry, lonely, and scared and often have no other option than to sit or lie on office floors while caseworkers call and beg foster families to take them in.

Headquartered in Elizabethton, Tennessee, Isaiah 117 House is a nonprofit organization that was started in 2017 by former foster parents Ronda and Corey Paulson. Isaiah 117 House, which is named for a Bible verse in Isaiah calling for "defend[ing] the cause of the fatherless," provides a safe, comforting home where children can be brought to wait while child welfare officers complete necessary paperwork and identify a foster placement. Volunteers work to make the transition to state care less stressful and traumatic by providing these children with clean clothes, toys, food, comfortable beds, and blankets. Once a placement is found, children are able to meet and get to know their foster family in a comfortable environment. The house also supports foster families by providing backpacks, car seats, and other supplies for children's immediate needs.

As of 2021, Isaiah 117 House operates in 19 counties in Tennessee and 7 counties in Indiana. In addition, it has expanded into Florida and Virginia with its first homes in those states.

## Love Fosters Hope

Love Fosters Hope is a Texas-based nonprofit that strives to bring hope and healing to children and teens in foster care through summer camps, mentoring, and visits to residential treatment centers.

The centerpiece of the organization is its summer camps for foster youth. At Love Fosters Hope's Royal Family Kids Camp, children ages 7 to 11 participate in outdoor recreation, arts and crafts, a talent show, and a shared birthday party. Camp counselors, called "cousins," become each participant's cheer-leader, encourager, confidant, and friend. Love Fosters Hope also sponsors Teen Reach Adventure Camps (T.R.A.C.). These all-boys and all-girls camps, for youth ages 12 to 15, are conducted according to guidelines established by the national T.R.A.C. organization and provide a positive atmosphere for recreation and self-expression in which participants are taught self-respect, teamwork, and trust.

Lover Fosters Hope operates a year-round mentoring program, in which mentors offer support, counsel, and friendship to foster youth ages 12 to 19, with the goal of helping them reach their potential. Mentors serve as role models by demonstrating the exemplary behavior and positive values that will increase participants' chances for success and happiness. The mentors also support, advocate for, and challenge participants. They work to discover what each young person is passionate about and what they are good at. They help participating youth research career options, discover what training they will need or what college programs to take, and connect them with resources as they work to help them overcome hurdles. Love Fosters Hope mentors additionally visit residential treatment centers, encouraging young residents and inviting them to participate in fun activities and skill-building workshops.

Love Fosters Hope also sponsors a Rescue Home, a safe and nurturing home for teens who have previously participated in their program but who have aged out of foster care and would otherwise be homeless.

## Mayfly Project

The Mayfly Project is a nonprofit organization that seeks to support and build relationships with children in foster care through fly-fishing and an introduction to local water ecosystems. The project was founded in Arkansas in 2015 by Jess and

Laura Westbrook. Jess Westbrook came up with the idea to use fly-fishing as a tool to support children in foster care because he had used fly-fishing as a therapeutic tool to manage his own anxiety. After he was introduced to mentoring children in foster care through an organization at his church, he realized that he could use fly-fishing to give these children the opportunity to get out on an adventure while they engaged in a therapeutic practice.

Jess and Laura Westbrook developed the Mayfly Project as a mentoring program based on the mayfly life cycle. Participating kids go through several different stages or sessions. In the Egg Stage, children are introduced to fly-fishing, the fly rod, and the Mayfly Project mentors. In the Nymph Stage, they are introduced to casting, knot tying, and catch and release. The Emerger Stage consists of setting the hook, conservation education, and casting. And the Dun Stage consists of reading water, mending line, and roll casting. During the final session "The Big Catch Stage," the kids and a mentor go out for a daylong fishing trip. During each outing, the children participate in a conservation initiative in which they are taught the three C's: catch and release, clean rivers, and contamination. Each outing includes a "conservation mentor" who educates the children on how to care for the environment and for the fish they get to experience.

In 2016, the Westbrooks partnered with Kaitlin Barnhart to expand the program to Idaho and to establish the National Mayfly Project so the program might be implemented in other states as well.

## Monument Academy

Monument Academy is a weekday boarding charter school for fifth through eighth graders in Washington, DC, whose mission is to provide students, particularly those who have had or might have contact with the foster care system, with the requisite academic, social, emotional, and life skills to be successful in college, career, and community.

Founded in 2014 and supported by both public and private funds, Monument Academy uses a houseparent model in which 10 students live with two adults in a wing of the school building during the week, eating their meals together and learning discipline, mutual support, and life skills such as doing laundry and setting the table. Participating students are dropped off early Sunday evening and picked up on Friday afternoon by their primary caregivers, who are given a chance to speak with the staff. The purpose of the structured drop-off and pickup is to establish and develop relationships between caregivers and staff to ensure a seamless transition between home and school life.

Students begin each day with a family-style breakfast with their houseparent and student life family. After sharing a personal daily goal, students engage in community building and skills practice and then move through their daily class schedule. After the academic day, students engage in enrichment activities, which may include sports, cooking club, choir, theater, or service clubs before they attend a family-style dinner and then have time to relax, read, and complete homework. Before students prepare for bed, they reflect on the daily goal they set in the morning and then read or journal in their rooms until lights out. The boarding aspect of the program addresses one of the biggest challenges for foster students—the frequency with which they move and are forced to change schools.

## Multi-System Trauma-Informed Collaborative

Every year millions of children experience trauma related to violence in their homes, schools, and communities and are consequently at increased risk for mental health issues, substance abuse, suspension from school, long-term medical problems, and involvement in the criminal justice system.

In 2010, the U.S. Department of Justice's Office of Juvenile Justice and Delinquency Prevention (OJJDP) embarked on an effort to foster enhanced collaboration between child-serving public agencies to identify and support children who have experienced violence-induced trauma. This effort led to the creation of the Multi-System Trauma-Informed Collaborative (MSTIC).

MSTIC has four key objectives: (1) to increase the capacity of state child-serving systems to collaborate effectively to identify, screen, assess, and treat youth exposed to violence; (2) to increase knowledge of evidence-based policies, practices, and programs; (3) to enhance the ability of state systems to identify, implement, and monitor impacts of effective trauma-informed practices; and (4) to improve the capacity of systems to blend funding sources to sustain implementation of evidence-based practices that are trauma informed.

In an effort to achieve these objectives, OJJDP chose Chapin Hall at the University of Chicago and the American Institutes for Research (AIR) to provide training and technical assistance to state-level leaders of child-serving agencies from Illinois, Connecticut, and Washington. Working closely with senior administrators representing juvenile justice, child welfare, education, early childhood, public health, and mental health public agencies, Chapin Hall and AIR experts are supporting the three states through a comprehensive planning process to develop actionable strategic plans that are evidence based in the hope of better serving children who have witnessed or experienced violence and maximizing opportunities to leverage state and federal funds.

## National Foster Parent Association

The National Foster Parent Association (NFPA) is a nonprofit that was established in 1972 to better meet the needs of foster families in the United States by providing them with advocacy, networking opportunities, and education. Today, its primary activities include the delivering services and supports to state and local foster parent associations and foster families; promoting networking; advocating for policy change at the local, state, and national levels; and developing and disseminating training and other educational materials to the public. In conjunction with the multinational health services company Centene Corporation, NFPA launched the NFPA Training Institute. The Training Institute creates new curriculums and online training to give caregivers and others associated with the child welfare system quick and easy access to education that addresses targeted issues that they commonly encounter.

Since its inception, the NFPA has grown from an original group of 926 foster parents, 210 social workers, and 59 other professionals to an organization that represents thousands of foster families nationwide through foster parent affiliate associations organized by a Council of State Affiliates.

## Native American Youth and Family Center

The Native American Youth and Family Center (NAYA) was founded by tribal volunteers in Portland, Oregon, in 1974 to build cultural connections between tribal youth and families and to help native people develop strengths and resiliency. NAYA officially became a nonprofit organization in 1994 and has since expanded to meet the various needs of the Native American community in Portland through a variety of services, including in-home support, elder services, housing, and education.

In partnership with the City of Portland, the Oregon Children's Fund, the Children's Trust Fund of Oregon, and the Kellogg Foundation, NAYA operates a Foster Care Support Program to assist youth and families involved with the state or tribal foster care systems. The Oregon Department of Human Services and child welfare agencies refer children and families to the program and comanage the cases of children and youth who engage in NAYA services. The program's services include monthly sibling and family visits, coaching, training, educational support, and the Generations Project. NAYA's monthly Sibling and Family Visit Night provides a positive natural environment for youth in foster care to visit with siblings, family members, and other people they have connections with. These evenings include a time for learning about culturally specific ideas, activities, and traditions.

NAYA provides various forms of coaching to help foster and birth parents navigate the system and develop a parenting plan. NAYA additionally offers Positive Indian Parenting curriculum four to five times a year to all community members. The Generations Project is an intergenerational housing program in which tribal elders live in a housing complex with foster youth and their caretakers to support the youth through tutoring and mentoring in cultural ways.

## One Church One Child

One Church One Child is a national minority adoption recruitment program that was established in Chicago in 1980 by Father George Clemens, an African American Catholic priest. Clemens came up with the idea for the organization during Illinois's adoption crisis in the 1970s when it became evident that a disproportionate number of African American children available for adoption were lingering in the foster care system. The primary goal of the One Church One Child program is to recruit families for adoption and foster care. The name comes from the mission of the first One Church One Child program in Chicago, which was "to find one family in every African American church in Illinois to adopt one child."

Today, One Church One Child programs operate throughout the country and recruit families through presentations to targeted faith-based audiences. In addition to recruiting families, One Church One Child programs provide resource materials and monthly parenting classes for adoptive parents utilizing the expertise of child welfare professionals. The organization has helped place thousands of children in adoptive homes throughout the country.

## One Simple Wish

One Simple Wish—based in Trenton, New Jersey—is an innovative wish-granting platform for kids impacted by foster care, abuse, and neglect. The idea for One Simple Wish began in 2006, after its founder, Danielle Gletow, and her husband became foster parents and realized how many children in the foster care system do not have access to the simple things, experiences, and joyful parts of childhood that other children might take for granted, such as new shoes, bicycles, eyeglasses, braces, music lessons, participation in school sports, and fun excursions. Gletow left her job in the corporate world to start One Simple Wish, and the online wish registry platform became fully operational in 2008.

Through its platform, agencies that work with children in foster care join One Simple Wish's Community Partner Network and submit wishes on behalf of the children they are helping. One Simple Wish then shares the wishes throughout its network, and individual donors help make those wishes come true. Wishes are categorized on the website as arts and music, education and employment, health and wellness, experiences, just for fun, and essentials. Wish grantors can select price and age ranges as well as the state where the child lives. The age range goes up to 30 to enable wish fulfillment for those who have aged out of the foster care system but do not have permanent or stable connections.

Several corporations, such as Volkswagen, Disney, and TJX, have partnered with One Simple Wish, and a network of nearly 800 foster agencies in 48 states help deliver gift items. In 2018–2019 alone, One Simple Wish granted more than 20,000 wishes. Individuals can make a general donation toward the mission of One Simple Wish, or they can click on and pay for a specific request and learn more about the child behind it.

Donors can also follow a specific child and support subsequent wishes from that child and can send notes of encouragement to a child through the system.

In addition to its online platform, One Simple Wish sponsors wish parties. These parties provide a place for foster families to unite, a place for siblings who are placed in separate foster homes to visit each other, and a place for underserved families to bond and form a network of support. Families who attend these parties enjoy a meal, make crafts, and play games while they make new connections and learn about One Simple Wish's services and other local resources.

## Project 1.27

Project 1.27 is a ministry founded by Pastor Robert Gelinas of Colorado Community Church with the mission to inspire, recruit, and resource churches and families to foster and adopt the kids in their own backyard.

In December 2004, Pastor Gelinas began to speak with the Colorado state government to explore how Colorado churches could work to provide families for the hundreds of children in the Colorado foster care system who were legally available for adoption with no identified adoptive family. Based on these meetings, Gelinas founded Project 1.27 to act as a bridge between the church community and the kids in foster care that need families. Project 1.27 partners with local churches and agencies to recruit more families and to provide training, encouragement, and support to foster and adoptive parents through the state certification process.

## Safe Families for Children

Safe Families for Children is a volunteer-driven nonprofit founded in 2003 to reduce the need for foster care by providing extended family-like support to vulnerable families in times of crisis. In many crisis situations—such as those resulting from homelessness, hospitalization, domestic violence, and so on—parents or guardians may be incapable of providing a safe and caring environment for their children, putting them at risk of abuse and neglect. To make matters worse, a sizeable percentage of families today are socially isolated and do not have extended family or neighbors who are available to step in to help in times of crisis by caring for their children for short periods of time.

Safe Families for Children operates based on three objectives: to prevent child abuse or neglect during periods of family crisis; to support and stabilize families in crisis by surrounding them with a caring, compassionate community; and to reunite families and reduce the number of children entering the child welfare system.

Parents in need can approach Safe Families for Children through a self-referral or other referral sources. Volunteers provide much-needed preventative support to these families on several different levels. Screened and approved host families take in children for short periods of time. Parents can opt to reunify with their children at any time and never lose custody of their children. Volunteers may also serve as Family Friends, supporting parents in need by befriending, coaching, and offering support in such areas as transportation, babysitting, meals, and the like.

A Safe Families Church is a spiritual community that supports Safe Families for Children as a ministry of its church. As of 2021, Safe Families for Children engages more than 25,000 volunteers and nearly 4,600 churches in over 100 cities across the United States, the United Kingdom, and Canada.

## Safe Haven Services

Safe Haven Services, LLC, is a family-owned social service agency contracted through the Arizona Division of Developmental Disabilities (DDD) to provide safe, loving, and compassionate homes to individuals, including foster children, with developmental disabilities. After serving as a director of a Developmental Home Program and seeing the need for support and advocacy for in-home care providers and individuals with developmental disabilities, Rebecca Nichols, along with her husband, Brandon, established Safe Haven Services, LLC, in February 2019.

Safe Haven Services offers both child developmental home services and adult developmental home services. Child development home providers care for children with developmental disabilities who cannot live with their natural families and help them achieve permanency, either through reunification with their parents, adoption, or another court-ordered plan. Adult developmental home providers provide care to adults with developmental disabilities to teach them important skills and to help them live satisfying and successful lives. Safe Haven Services also offers respite care for children and adults living with developmental home providers to provide short-term relief for the primary caregivers.

## Utah Youth Village

Founded as Utah Girls' Village in 1969 before changing its name in 1988, Utah Youth Village is one of Utah's largest and most respected charities. The organization currently serves thousands of individuals a year in a network of group homes and treatment foster homes with supervision and support centralized in Salt Lake City. Children and youth are placed in these homes through the State Division of Child and Family Services (DCFS), Youth Corrections, and, in some cases, by their families.

All Youth Village affiliates subscribe to the Teaching-Family Model (TFM) of treatment. TFM is a philosophy and practice of care and treatment that prioritizes therapeutic relationships with caregivers in supportive family-style settings as the primary conduit of effective treatment. An independent study of residential treatment facilities conducted in Utah revealed that the Youth Village had an 86 percent success rate at releasing children to less restrictive levels of care and treatment as compared to the combined average of 37 percent for other agencies. The study also revealed that Youth Village homes had far fewer runaways than other agencies.

The state's DCFS, juvenile courts, and Division of Juvenile Justice and many pediatricians, therapists, and church leaders also use the Youth Village's Families First Program to teach parents how to interact with children with behavioral issues whom they might not otherwise be able to care for. The organization additionally runs a Smarter Parenting website to give all parents the tools they need to raise happy, responsible, and ethical children.

## Introduction

This chapter contains figures and primary resources for further research on the topic of foster care in the United States. The first section presents data on the nature and scope of foster care with a focus on the sex, race, and ethnicity of children in care, the circumstances related to entering and exiting care, and the outcomes for youth aging out of care. The second section provides excerpts from a variety of government documents pertaining to the child welfare system, including congressional testimony, speeches, court briefs, and executive orders, organized in chronological order.

---

A foster brother and sister show their love for each other while playing outside. Family relationships are essential to children's healthy growth, development, and overall well-being. (Jennifer Russell/Dreamstime.com)

## Data

### Figure 5.1. Number of Children in Foster Care, Fiscal Years 2015–2019

This figure shows the number of children who were in foster care on September 30 of fiscal years (FY) 2015 through 2019. FY refers to the federal fiscal year, which extends from October 1 through September 30.

**Figure 5.1    Number of Children in Foster Care, Fiscal Years 2015–2019**

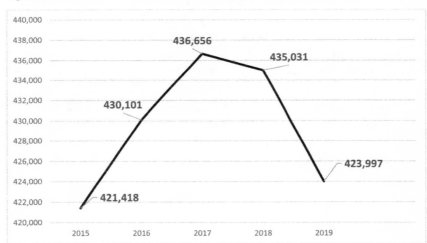

*Source*: Children's Bureau. 2020. "The AFCARS Report: Preliminary FY 2019 Estimates as of June 23, 2020—No. 27." U.S. Department of Health and Human Services, Administration for Children and Families. https://www.acf.hhs.gov /sites/default/files/documents/cb/afcarsreport27.pdf

## Figure 5.2. Number of Children in Foster Care on September 30, 2019, by Sex and by Race/Ethnicity

This figure breaks down the number of children in foster care by sex and race on the last day of the federal fiscal year (FY) 2019. There are slightly more males than females in foster care, and the number of Black or African American children currently in foster care far exceeds their percentage in the general population.

**Figure 5.2   Number of Children in Foster Care on September 30, 2019, by Sex and by Race/Ethnicity**

|  | Percent | Number |
|---|---|---|
| **Sex** | | |
| Male | 52 | 218,415 |
| Female | 48 | 205,523 |
| **Race/Ethnicity** | | |
| American Indian/Alaska Native | 2 | 10,152 |
| Asian | 1 | 2,179 |
| Black or African American | 23 | 97,142 |
| Hispanic (of any race) | 21 | 87,625 |
| White | 44 | 185,825 |
| Unknown/unable to determine | 1 | 6,148 |
| Two or more races | 8 | 32,284 |

Source: Children's Bureau. 2020. "The AFCARS Report: Preliminary FY 2019 Estimates as of June 23, 2020 — No. 27." U.S. Department of Health and Human Services, Administration for Children and Families. https://www.acf.hhs.gov/sites/default/files/documents/cb/afcarsreport27.pdf

## Figure 5.3. Race and Ethnicity of Children Entering Foster Care in FY 2008 and FY 2018

This figure shows the races and ethnicities of the children in foster care on September 30, 2008, and September 30, 2018. The percentage of Black or African American children in care decreased between FY 2008 and FY 2018, while the percentages of white children, Hispanic children, and children of other races increased.

Figure 5.3   Race and Ethnicity of Children Entering Foster Care in FY 2008 and FY 2018

*Source*: Children's Bureau. 2020. "Foster Care Statistics 2018: Numbers and Trends, May 2020." U.S. Department of Health and Human Services, Administration for Children and Families. https://www.childwelfare.gov/pubPDFs/foster.pdf

## Figure 5.4. Circumstances Associated with Child's Removal for Children Entering Foster Care, FY 2019

This figure demonstrates the circumstances that led to the removal and placement in foster care for the children currently in foster care on September 30, 2019.

Figure 5.4   Circumstances Associated with Child's Removal for Children Entering Foster Care, FY 2019

| Reason for Removal | Percent | Number |
|---|---|---|
| Neglect | 63 | 158,258 |
| Drug abuse (parent) | 34 | 86,694 |
| Caretaker inability to cope | 14 | 34,594 |
| Physical abuse | 13 | 32,008 |
| Housing | 10 | 25,658 |
| Child behavior problem | 8 | 20,871 |
| Parent incarceration | 7 | 17,669 |
| Alcohol abuse (parent) | 5 | 13,637 |
| Abandonment | 5 | 11,424 |
| Sexual abuse | 4 | 9,782 |

**Table 5.4**   *(continued)*

| Reason for Removal | Percent | Number |
|---|---|---|
| Drug abuse (child) | 2 | 5,500 |
| Child disability | 2 | 3,969 |
| Relinquishment | 1 | 2,350 |
| Parent death | 1 | 2,141 |
| Alcohol abuse (child) | 0 | 991 |

*Source*: Children's Bureau. 2020. "The AFCARS Report: Preliminary FY 2019 Estimates as of June 23, 2020 — No. 27." U.S. Department of Health and Human Services, Administration for Children and Families. https://www.acf.hhs.gov /sites/default/files/documents/cb/afcarsreport27.pdf

## Figure 5.5. Children Exiting Foster Care during FY 2019 Broken Down by Reason for Discharge

This figure identifies the reasons for discharge for children who exited foster care between October 1, 2018, and September 30, 2019.

**Figure 5.5   Children Exiting Foster Care during FY 2019 Broken Down by Reason for Discharge**

| Reason for Discharge | Percent | Number |
|---|---|---|
| Reunification with parent(s) or primary caretaker(s) | 47 | 117,010 |
| Living with other relatives | 6 | 15,422 |
| Adoption | 26 | 64,415 |
| Emancipation | 8 | 20,445 |
| Guardianship | 11 | 26,103 |
| Transfer to another agency | 1 | 2,726 |
| Runaway | 0 | 608 |
| Death of child | 0 | 385 |

*Source*: Children's Bureau. 2020. "The AFCARS Report: Preliminary FY 2019 Estimates as of June 23, 2020 — No. 27." U.S. Department of Health and Human Services, Administration for Children and Families. https://www.acf.hhs.gov /sites/default/files/documents/cb/afcarsreport27.pdf

## Figure 5.6. Youth Outcomes Reported at Ages 17, 19, and 21

This figure reveals the disparate outcomes of transition-age youth based on whether they continue to remain in care or have aged out of care.

Figure 5.6   Youth Outcomes Reported at Ages 17, 19, and 21

| Outcomes | Age 17 In Care (n = 16,480) | Age 19 In Care (n = 3,550) | Age 19 Not in Care (n = 5,348) | Age 21 In Care (n = 1,399) | Age 21 Not in Care (n = 6,440) |
|---|---|---|---|---|---|
| Employed full-time | 2% | 15% | 17% | 35% | 33% |
| Employed part-time | 13% | 29% | 25% | 32% | 25% |
| Employment-related skills | 20% | 32% | 29% | 37% | 31% |
| Social Security | 12% | 11% | 12% | 8% | 11% |
| Educational aid | 3% | 30% | 17% | 31% | 16% |
| Receiving public assistance (food, housing, or financial) | N/A | N/A | 30% | N/A | 31% |
| Other financial support | 8% | 17% | 12% | 18% | 9% |
| High School degree or GED | 5% | 60% | 53% | 77% | 68% |
| Attending school | 93% | 66% | 43% | 43% | 23% |
| Referred for substance abuse treatment | 27% (in lifetime) | 11% (in past 2 years) | 15% (in past 2 years) | 6% (in past 2 years) | 11% (in past 2 years) |
| Incarcerated | 33% (in lifetime) | 11% (in past 2 years) | 25% (in past 2 years) | 7% (in past 2 years) | 23% (in past 2 years) |
| Given birth to or fathered a child | 5% (in lifetime) | 8% (in past 2 years) | 11% (in past 2 years) | 14% (in past 2 years) | 24% (in past 2 years) |
| Homelessness | 17% (in lifetime) | 11% (in past 2 years) | 26% (in past 2 years) | 15% (in past 2 years) | 30% (in past 2 years) |
| Connection to an adult | 93% | 92% | 88% | 93% | 85% |
| Medicaid | 85% | 89% | 69% | 90% | 64% |
| Other health insurance | 15% | 13% | 17% | 13% | 18% |

Source: Administration for Children & Families. 2020. "National Youth in Transition Database Report to Congress." February 18. https://www.acf.hhs.gov/sites /default/files/documents/cb/nytd_report_to_congress.pdf

## Documents

### President Ronald Reagan's Presidential Proclamation for National Foster Care Month (1988)

*In May 1988, President Ronald Reagan issued the first presidential proclamation for National Foster Care Month. Every year since, the current president of the United States has issued an annual proclamation in recognition of National Foster Care Month. National Foster Care Month is now an initiative of the Children's Bureau. Each May, the Children's Bureau takes the time to acknowledge foster parents, family members, volunteers, mentors, policy makers, child welfare professionals, and other members of the community who help children and youth in foster care find permanent homes and connections.*

*The original focus of National Foster Care Month was to recognize foster parents for the contributions they make in opening their homes to children in need, but the theme has since changed every year based on the needs of the time. The theme of 2020 was "Foster Care as a Support to Families, Not a Substitute for Parents." The Children's Bureau, along with several partners, hosts a dedicated National Foster Care Month website developed with Child Welfare Information Gateway. The website provides resources, real-life stories, and outreach tools related to each year's theme.*

May 10, 1988

By the President of the United States of America

A Proclamation

The family is the indispensable foundation of society; at its best, it performs tasks that no other entity can hope to duplicate. The family has the primary responsibility for nurturing children, transmitting our culture, and building the character traits that make for healthy adults and good citizens. Upon the strength of the family rests the future of our Nation.

For a variety of reasons, however, some parents are unable to provide a minimally acceptable level of care for their children, and temporary or permanent alternative placement is necessary. National Foster Care Month presents an appropriate opportunity for all of us—public officials, business, religious, and community leaders, and parents alike—to reflect on the pressures facing families today and on the need for increased efforts to ensure that abandoned or abused children have the opportunity to live in healthy, loving homes.

The emphasis in foster care must be on the well-being of the child, and public policy must serve to promote alternative placement that represents actual care and not mere custody. Because the tasks facing foster parents often include special challenges, such as care of a child who is physically or mentally handicapped or who has been emotionally or physically abused, the mothers and fathers whom society qualifies to accept this added responsibility must be held to a high standard. To accomplish this goal, many more happy and successful families must be willing to step forward and to offer to share heart and home with children desperately longing for both. The aim of all foster care must be the establishment for the child of a sense of permanence and belonging.

National Foster Care Month also provides an opportunity to offer public thanks for the sacrifices and dedication of the many foster parents and concerned professionals working in the field of foster care. Their jobs require extraordinary patience and love, and their rewards are often reaped only years after their primary labor is done—when the child is grown and fully appreciates what has been done for him or her, or when society pauses from its hectic rush forward to recognize the good they have accomplished.

Finally, this month-long observance calls us to deeper thought on the role of values and ideas in the very formation of families. For if the goal of child care is the creation of a warm, stable environment, it is self-evident that the best place to start is in the pursuit of strong and stable marriages. If the need for foster care is not to outstrip our society's capacity for remedial action, it is critical to focus more efforts on policies that promote and protect the triad of mother, father, and child as the harmonious chord God intended for them to be.

To demonstrate our esteem and appreciation for those who devotedly and selflessly share their lives with foster children, the Congress, by Senate Joint Resolution 59, has designated the month of May 1988 as "National Foster Care Month" and has requested the President to issue a proclamation in its observance.

*Now, Therefore, I, Ronald Reagan,* President of the United States of America, do hereby proclaim the month of May 1988 as National Foster Care Month. I call upon all educators, churches, health care providers, the media, public and private organizations, and the people of the United States to observe this month with appropriate ceremonies and activities.

*In Witness Whereof,* I have hereunto set my hand this tenth day of May, in the year of our Lord nineteen hundred and eighty-eight, and of the Independence of the United States of America the two hundred and twelfth.

Ronald Reagan

**Source:** Reagan, Ronald. "Proclamation 5820—National Foster Care Month, 1988." May 10, 1988. Ronald Reagan Library. https://www.reaganlibrary.gov/archives/speech/proclamation -5820-national-foster-care-month-1988

## Senator John H. Chafee's Remarks in Defense of the Adoption and Safe Families Act (1997)

*On November 19, 1997, President Bill Clinton signed into law the Adoption and Safe Families Act (ASFA). The law introduced a sweeping reform to the nation's adoption and foster care system and represented a fundamental shift in child welfare policy away from the previous single-minded focus on reunification toward giving more weight to children's health, safety, and overall well-being. Significant reforms into the foster care system included shortening decision-making timelines for assessment and intervention services to children, moving children to permanency, and encouraging the practice of adoption through a new adoption incentive payment program.*

*Although AFSA reaffirmed the importance of making reasonable efforts to preserve and reunify families, it outlined specific instances in which reunification efforts were not necessary. It additionally required the Department of Health and Human Services to establish new state performance standards and a state accountability system, whereby states could face financial penalties for failure to demonstrate improvements in child outcomes. The following is a speech given in defense of the act's passage by its primary sponsor in the Senate, Senator John H. Chafee.*

Mr. CHAFEE. Mr. President, I would like to express my strong support for legislation that will be considered by the Senate and has been considered by the House this morning. This legislation is the Adoption and Safe Families Act of 1997. This bill, which is a compromise version of legislation that I introduced originally now has as supporters and sponsors: Senator Rockefeller, Senator Craig, Senator Bond, Senator DeWine, Senator Coats, Senator Jeffords, Senator Landrieu, Senator Levin, Senator Kerrey, Senator Dorgan, Senator Moynihan, Senator Moseley-Braun, and Senator Johnson. Mr. President, this legislation will make some critical changes to the child welfare system—changes that will vastly improve the lives of hundreds of thousands of children currently in foster care and waiting for adoptive homes. I am very hopeful that the President, who has indicated his support for this legislation, will sign this measure promptly.

Mr. President, just yesterday, there was yet another story in the newspapers about a young girl, 9 years old, who was found dead from severe abuse in her sister's Bronx apartment. The tragic story of young Sabrina Green's short life is harrowing, and it is all too reminiscent of the cases we read and hear about, unfortunately, every single day. Each time I read about a case like Sabrina Green's, I feel outrage and frustration with a system that cannot take care of the most vulnerable members of our society. Now, Mr. President, we cannot bring Sabrina Green back to life, nor can we bring back any of the hundreds of children who have died under similar circumstances; but we can take action to prevent such deaths in the future, and that is what we are doing today.

The bill that will come over to us shortly, Mr. President, will put the safety and health of the child first. That is a significant change in the law. Under this legislation, the safety and health of the child will come first. We will not continue the current system of always putting the needs and rights of the biological parents first. While we still believe that family reunification is a worthy goal, it's time we recognize that some families simply cannot and should not be kept together. Children who have suffered severe abuse or whose parents have committed violent crimes should be moved out of those homes rapidly and into adoptive homes. Our bill does that. Children who are in foster care for over 15 months deserve to have a decision made about their future. Our legislation does both of those things.

It is also time we put a stop to children lingering in foster care for years. There are currently half a million children in this country—500,000 children in the United States of America—who have been removed from their abusive or neglectful parents and are living in foster care. In my State, there are 1,500 of these children in foster care. Nationally, each of these children in foster care will remain so for an average of 3 years before a decision is made about their future, and many of them will wait much longer. The average is 3 years. Some have stayed for years and years in foster care. Today, we are sending those half a million children a message of hope. Under this legislation, their time in foster care will be shortened. States will be required to make a permanent plan for these children after a year, and if a child has been in foster care for more than

15 months—1 year and 3 months—the State will be required to take the first steps toward terminating parental rights and finding an adoptive home.

Terminating parental rights is the critical first step in moving children into permanent placements, but it is not enough. We also must promote adoption of these children, and our bill does that. Our bill removes geographic barriers to adoption. There are no limitations under this bill about children in one State having to be adopted in that State. We remove these geographic barriers to adoption and require States to document efforts to move children into safe adoptive homes. We also provide financial bonuses to States that increase their adoption rights. There is money here for States that increase the rate of adoption in their States.

There are legal and procedural barriers to adoption, and there are also financial barriers. Lack of medical coverage is one such barrier to families who want to adopt special needs children. What is a special needs child? It is a child who has medical problems or physical problems, or a child of such an age, maybe 15 or 16, in a foster home. Adoptive parents are very reluctant to take on a child of that age. Many of these children have significant physical and mental health problems due to years of abuse and neglect and foster care. Many of these children have been shuttled from foster parent to foster parent. So the adoptive parents are taking a huge financial risk in adopting these children if the parents are not guaranteed that there will be health insurance for these special needs children. Our bill ensures that special needs children who are going to be adopted will have medical coverage. We also ensure that children whose adoptive parents die or whose adoptions disrupt or terminate for some reason, they will continue to receive Federal subsidies when they are adopted by new parents.

Mr. President, I am very proud of this legislation. The Senate and House sponsors have worked tirelessly for many months to come to an agreement. Our shared commitment to improving the lives of these children brought us together. In closing, I want to especially thank my good friend, Senator Jay Rockefeller, who has spent years devoting his time and attention to these children. I also thank Senator Craig, who brought his own personal experiences and dedication to this effort, and Senator DeWine, who brought so much expertise and professional experience to this initiative. I also want to thank the other members of the coalition, those Senators that I mentioned earlier, and I will repeat their names—Senator Bond, Senator Coats, Senator Jeffords, Senator Landrieu, Senator Levin, Senator Kerrey, Senator Dorgan, Senator Moynihan, Senator Moseley-Braun, and Senator Johnson.

I also want to congratulate the House sponsors who worked so hard on this—Congressman Camp and Congresswoman Kennelly.

I thank our staffs for the extraordinary efforts they devoted to achieving passage of this legislation. Particularly, I salute Laurie Rubiner, of my staff, and Barbara Pryor, of Senator Rockefeller's staff. All of these individuals that are mentioned, and others, have been so helpful in achieving passage of this legislation, which I think has just now passed the House and will be coming here. We look for rapid action here.

**Source:** Chafee, John H. Speaking on the *Adoption and Safe Families Act of 1997. Congressional Record* 143, No. 160 (November 13, 1997): S12526–S12527. United States Government Printing Office. https://www.govinfo.gov/content/pkg/CREC-1997-11-13/html/CREC-1997-11-13-pt1-PgS12526-2.htm

### Testimony of Youth Aging Out of Foster Care (2007)

*When youth in foster care cannot be reunified with their families of origin, the goal of the child welfare system is to find them an alternative permanent home. As time passes and youth grow older in care, however, it becomes harder and harder to secure them in a permanent, safe, and loving home. Each year, more than 20,000* youth "age out" of the system when they reach the maximum age that the state will support them. Such youth often have few skills or resources to make it on their own and lack family members or other supportive adults to assist them as they navigate the challenges of transitioning to independent living.

Youth who age out of foster care fare poorly compared to their counterparts in the general population. They are far less likely to graduate high school, to attend college, and to obtain gainful employment. They are more likely to fall into criminal activity, early pregnancy, poverty, and mental illness. A large percentage of them become homeless the day they age out.

In 1999, Congress permanently authorized the John H. Chafee Foster Care Independence Program (CFCIP), which was designed to enhance resources and strengthen state accountability for helping older youth leaving foster care to achieve self-sufficiency. Nearly a decade later, however, its impact on outcomes for former foster youth was still uncertain because the Department of Health and Human Services had not yet established an assessment and data collection system for the program.

On July 12, 2007, the U.S. House of Representatives' Committee on Ways and Means' Subcommittee on Income Security and Family Support held a hearing exploring the challenges faced by children who age out of the foster care system at age 18 and the effectiveness of the assistance available to them. The hearing further examined what policies and support systems could be implemented to ensure better outcomes for foster youth who age out. A little over a year after the hearing, Congress passed and President George W. Bush signed the Foster Connections to Success and Increasing Adoptions Act.

One important provision of the law allowed states to receive reimbursement under Title IV-E of the Social Security Act for costs associated with supporting youth to remain in foster care up to age 21. Thanks in part to this provision, over 25 states and the District of Columbia have now extended foster care beyond age 18.

*The following includes the testimony of two foster youth who aged out of care.*

## Statement of Tyler Bacon, Florida

Mr. BACON. Thank you. Mr. Chairman, Ranking Member Weller, and Members of the Subcommittee, thank you for allowing me to come speak to you and share my experience of the foster care system, my knowledge and expertise on foster care.

My name is Tyler Bacon and I am 22 years old. I entered the foster care system at the age of 13. I remember the day I entered as if it were yesterday. I was in a court because we were going through some family therapy. I remember the judge asking my mother what she wanted to do with me. My mother responded this is not my child, I do not want anything to do with him and I do not care what happens.

He paused, looked over at my father and asked my father what he wanted to do. I turned and looked at my father as he said nothing, no response, not standing up for his own son and not knowing what to say or how to respond.

That day, I was placed in the foster care system.

While in the foster care system, I grew up in several group homes, attended several high schools and educational programs to try to succeed. While in the group homes, I was with 20 to 60 other young men at one home with staff, five per home. Understaffed and not able to ask questions or get the proper assistance that I needed to be able to learn how to be a successful adult, I struggled through the group homes.

I did not know what to ask. I did not know how to ask, how to become a man, how to become an adult, what I needed to know when I turned 18. I thought when I turned 18 that I was going to be prepared. I thought I was going to be ready. I was looking forward to my 18th birthday, because I was finally going to be on my own and I was finally going to be a man.

My 18th birthday was the scariest day of my life. On my 18th birthday, I thought I was going to have a good birthday. I woke up to see my bags packed and told I was too old to be in the foster care system. I was an adult in the State's eyes, that I had to go.

I had nowhere to turn. No family. No friends. Nothing. While in the foster care system, I was not able to connect with a family. I was told I was unadoptable. No family wanted me because I was too old and I had too many family issues.

On my 18th birthday, instead of a cake, I was walking to a homeless shelter so I had somewhere to live. I struggled but I was determined to be successful and get back on my feet. While I was homeless, I was still in high school, afraid to tell someone I was homeless because I was afraid they would kick me out of school and I would not finish my education. I was determined to succeed and graduate.

I finally graduated in 2004 in the top 5 percent of my high school. Determined. I was finally able to get back on my feet and achieve my own apartment and have a house to call my own. I still struggled, still had obstacles that I had to face.

I did not know how to do anything. I did not know how to pay bills, how to budget, basic stuff that normal everyday people take advantage of. I did not know how to be a man and how to be a successful independent civilian in society.

Again, because of financial issues, I needed someone to turn to. This caused me to want to turn back to my bio family, the family who gave me up. I thought everybody is talking about if you ever need help, you can turn back to your family. I tried to reconnect with my family but nothing changed.

They still did not want me. In an altercation and a confrontation with my family, I was stabbed, ended up in the hospital having immediate surgery. Given that situation, I was unable to work. I was unable to pay for my bills, and I ended up once again homeless, evicted from my apartment because I was not able to pay my bills and I had no one to help me.

I had no family to turn to. I had no one to go home to. I had no one to help me get back on my feet. Again, I was homeless.

I struggled for a year, bouncing from friend to friend, whoever would let me stay, ending up in a hotel. I had nowhere else to go. I had to pay for my own hotel so I had a roof over my head while I was working at minimum wage at a part time job. The hotel cost me $1,200 a month, unable to save up some money to find my own apartment or fix the eviction notice that I had, to be able to pay off that.

I had nowhere else to go. Fortunately, I had family and friends within the foster care system. My brothers and sisters that I looked to that are foster youth, I looked to them as brothers and sisters.

They financially helped me and gave the opportunity to get back on my feet. They gave me financial support a family would give me and helped me get my own apartment. Again, I am thankful for them.

There are a lot of issues. No foster youth should have to go through the struggles that I went through in life. No one should have to go through these struggles.

People in a family setting take advantage because they are able to go back to their family in times of economic need. If something were to come up, people who grew up in a family setting would be able to go back to them and live in that home.

Foster youth do not have that family to turn back to. Instead, we fall back on homeless shelters, jail systems, or potentially if you are able to financially afford it, hotels.

I ask and I push for Congress to take action now. I ask for simple things. I ask that we look into extending foster care up to the age of 21.

I ask that because when you are 18, you are still struggling to learn how to be an adult, how to financially support yourself and take care of yourself. Most people who are 18 are still struggling through high school, not yet graduated, and we look at our success, the foster youth success of graduating and it is very, very low.

This is because we are forced out at the age of 18 and struggling to maintain our own lives. Education is not our first priority. Our life and our shelter is our first priority.

I can say that from experience. I have yet to attend college because my main priority was to get on my feet and find shelter for myself.

I also ask that we help provide health insurance up to the age of 21. Most youth who live in a family setting still receive health insurance through their parents' medical insurance up to the age of 21. I ask just because we are foster youth, why should we not receive the same?

I also ask that we push for permanency for all youth in the foster care system. I ask that we try our best to set foster youth up with family. Family is a very, very important thing. I ask if we cannot find a family for them, we find a successful mentor to help them through the obstacles that everybody faces in life.

Permanency is having someone to talk to and you do not need an appointment to talk to them.

I ask Congress, when you look into the issues that foster youth face and look at what we need to change, I ask you to look at yourselves and ask what would you do if we were your child? If we were your child, would you help us and provide us with medical insurance, financial stability, and opportunities for us to be able to succeed in life?

We do not ask for much. We just ask to be treated like every other kid.

Thank you.


### Statement of Nicole Dobbins, Oregon

Ms. DOBBINS. Chairman McDermott, thank you for making us so welcome. Ranking Member Weller and Members of the Subcommittee, I thank you for hearing my testimony on behalf of the 24,000 teens aging out of the foster care system each year.

Good morning. My name is Nicole Marie Dobbins. Like Chairman McDermott said, I am 24 years old. I am a former foster youth and a lifelong resident of Portland, Oregon.

I spent a total of 6 years on and off in the State foster care system, entering at the age of two with my younger sister, due to my mother's drug addiction and inability to care for us.

My sister and I were reunited after a couple of years with my bio mom, but only to be put back in foster care at the age of 14 due to other issues, and again, drug abuse on my mother's behalf.

Foster care is where I remained for the next 4 years until only 1 day after graduating high school, I was kicked out of my foster home, a place I had been living in for 2 years prior. I was forced to hand over my key with no explanation of what was going on other than now I was 18, graduated, and not allowed to stay any longer.

I did not attend any closing court hearing nor did I receive any farewell from my caseworker. I recall having a meeting a week or so later in which they asked me what I planned to do, as if I were to have all the answers at that time.

This is how I exited the foster care system, and on that note, I was expected to be an adult. Sadly, the State played no active role in my transition. I was 18 years old and homeless, without any permanent connections to adults in my life, I had no one and there was no one to understand my struggle. I was forced to find a way all on my own.

The difficult part was not that I was homeless or that I was kicked out. The difficult part was I thought I had found some-one in my foster mother that would be there for me beyond foster care and be there for me in the long run through trials and tribulations.

I was wrong, and now I had to figure it out on my own. At 18, I was not prepared for the loss of adult support.

Growing up in and out of the system provided me with little stability and poor connections to people who cared about me. I left foster care hurt and angry. I longed for someone to be that person I could rely on. I longed for a healthy family. I longed for what every child longs for. I longed to be loved.

I found hope and stability in education because when I had nothing else, I always turned to that for an escape.

When I was only 10 years old, I was in the fourth grade. I knew I wanted to go to college, not because I wanted to be anything special or because of any one particular thing fascinated me. I wanted to go to college so that I could support my family and be a role model to my younger sister. Mostly, because I did not want to end up like my mother.

I knew I had to take a path my mother did not. She never graduated from high school, which made me the first in my family to get a high school diploma.

At the age of 18, I made the transition from foster care to what caseworkers call "independence." With the plan in mind to attend college, I was accepted into Oregon State University.

However, there was one huge problem. I was now a graduate of high school and homeless.

It was only June and school did not start until September. Before I would ever see college, I had to get through the Summer. It was a struggle that I managed to tackle.

In some ways, education saved my life. I felt very blessed to have my financial needs for school met. I am thankful for the resources such as Chafee educational training vouchers, which was a huge help to me and lessened my stress in receiving that each year.

However, these resources were not given to me at the time of transition. I had to seek them out after my sophomore year in college.

Education alone was never enough. I was a freshman in dorms with many new friends and excited about the opportunity to start a new life. Externally, I appeared to be happy, but what I kept from everyone was how I felt inside.

I was sad and lonely and hurting and often cried myself to sleep. I was too scared to ask for help and too proud to say I needed any. My peers did not understand me. They had family visiting and care packages arriving when I barely had people calling and checking in on me.

It was not long before I was diagnosed with depression. I dealt with depression without any medication because I had no health coverage. I was diagnosed by the Student Health Services and allotted five free counseling visits based on the student health fees that I paid to go to Oregon State.

I purchased a month's worth of medication but chose not to take them based on knowing that I would not have the financial commitment to continue the education, so I did not want to cause more harm to the depression than already was there.

I am one of the youth that could have benefited from Representative Cardoza's bill for health insurance to be used in foster care. That is something I would like to see put in place so that youth like myself will not have to struggle as much as I did.

Take this journey with me, as I recall one of the hardest times in college. Being kicked out of the dorms for the holidays. Thanksgiving came around and I did not realize I was going to have to leave until a week beforehand. My new friends all had family plans and I was not about to be anyone's burden by asking to join.

On holidays, I waited. I waited to be asked over to friends' houses. Looking back, I was thankful that I always was asked. Now I cannot help but wonder and I hope you do, too, where do youth go when they do not get asked?

I owe great gratitude to organizations such as FosterClub and the National Foster Care Coalition for offering an outlet for me to make change in the child welfare system.

Before my work with FosterClub, I never heard of permanency. I have now learned what permanency means and because of that, I have been given the chance to establish it in my own life.

Permanency just does not appear. It is nurtured. As foster youth, we do not know what healthy relationships look like. It is up to someone to teach us.

I have been given the divine opportunity to change child welfare professionals around the importance of permanency, as well as share my own experience with thousands of foster youth around the Nation because of these organizations.

Now I have acquired a huge network of supportive people in my life and I can honestly say that today, I would not be sitting here a college graduate, an educated professional, without the support and love from adults currently in my life.

I pose this question or these questions. What about the youth currently in care scheduled to transition without permanent families, without support, without health care, without education, and without a plan or worse, without anyone at all?

What will we do for them? I want to remind you this is only my story.

I want to thank you for listening to my testimony and I want to thank you on behalf of all the foster youth transitioning. You have the chance to make a difference. I just want to thank you again for hearing us.

**Source:** U.S. House of Representatives. Hearing before the Subcommittee on Income Security and Family Support of the Committee on Ways and Means. "Statement of Tyler Bacon" and "Statement of Nicole Dobbins." *Children Who Age out of the Foster Care System.* 110th Cong., 1st Sess. (July 12, 2007). https://www.govinfo.gov/content/pkg/CHRG-110hhrg43505/html/CHRG-110hhrg43505.htm

## Testimony of Former Foster Youth Dawna Zender Hovenier and Celebrity Psychologist Dr. Phil McGraw on the Overmedication of Youth in Foster Care (2014)

*In 2011, the Government Accountability Office released a report revealing that 20–39 percent of children in state foster care were prescribed psychotropic medication compared to 5–10 percent of children on Medicaid that were not in foster care. The report also found that children in foster care were also prescribed much higher dosages than their peers served by Medicaid—often in amounts that exceeded U.S. Food and Drug Administration guidelines. In some states, the difference was astronomical. In Texas, for example, foster children were 53 times more likely to be prescribed five or more psychiatric medications at the same time than nonfoster children, and in Massachusetts, they were 19 times more likely to be so prescribed.*

*In response to growing concern about the ongoing overprescribing of psychotropic drugs to foster youth, President Barack Obama proposed in his 2015 budget a $750 million five-year initiative to improve the capacity of the states and tribes to address mental health challenges among foster youth by providing funding and incentives for evidence-based, trauma-informed services and treatments that either do not involve or are less reliant on psychotropic drugs. More than 100 advocacy groups, including the Dr. Phil Foundation, signed a letter urging lawmakers to fund the initiative.*

*On May 29, 2014, The House Ways and Means Subcommittee on Human Resources heard testimony on the disproportionate use of psychotropic medications on foster youth and the president's proposal to address the issue. Included here are statements from 21-year-old Dawna Zender Hovenier, a former foster youth who had spent seven months locked in a psychiatric hospital after being diagnosed with borderline personality disorder, and celebrity psychologist Dr. Phil McGraw, founder of the Dr. Phil Foundation and a spokesman for Court Appointed Special Advocates (CASA).*

## Statement of Dawna Zender Hovenier, the Mockingbird Society

Ms. HOVENIER. Thank you, Chairman Reichert, Ranking Member Doggett, and committee members for giving me the opportunity to speak.

My name is Dawna Zender Hovenier. I am 21 years old and have spent 7 years in foster care in Washington State. On my 18th birthday, I aged out of foster care and was released after spending 7 months in an adolescent psychiatric hospital.

My hope is that the government will quit spending millions of dollars forcing kids like me to take drugs they do not need and give them things they do need, such as a volunteer CASA who believes in them, skilled mental health professionals who they can talk to and, most of all a loving, compassionate family that believes in them.

I was ordered into the psychiatric hospital after my social worker told the court I had borderline personality disorder, major depressive disorder, and suicidal ideation. I was forced to take strong doses of psychotropic medication and told I could probably never live on my own. Only my CASA and the man who became my father agreed with me that I did not need the drugs.

The 7 months I was locked up and forced to take these drugs felt like being in jail. After reviewing my records, I discovered that the foster care system paid $15,000 a month, about $120,000 total, to lock me up and take these drugs.

Last year, I earned my certified nurses aide certificate after successfully completing 2 years of classes at Bellingham Technical College. My GPA? It was a 3.92. I am currently enrolled at Whatcom Community College in Bellingham, Washington. Thanks to Federal and State funding for former foster youth, I was able to complete all my prerequisites required for a nursing degree. I am hoping to be accepted into an RN program to pursue my dreams of becoming a nurse.

I have lived independently for more than 2 years. I have been off all psychiatric medications for more than 3 years. I have never felt better or happier.

What happened? How did I transition from being diagnosed a mentally disabled foster youth to a model student and productive member of society? I don't have time to tell my whole story. Despite everything I experienced growing up, I know I was lucky. When I was 16, the man who recently became my father and is here with me today adopted my then 10-year-old brother from foster care. My younger brother was also forced to take strong doses of psychiatric drugs. He has been off them since his adoption more than 5 years ago.

My dad hired an attorney to fight the State's plan to transfer me to an adult psychiatric facility. He picked me up on my 18th birthday and sent me to live with his friends. They are now my family, too. So today it feels like I have two dads and a mom.

The next 6 months were among the most difficult in my life. Because of my diagnosis in foster care, we could not find a psychiatrist willing to take me off the medications, so we had to do it ourselves. This meant battling many intense withdrawal symptoms. One of the medications I was on can cause seizures, resulting in death if not carefully discontinued. My dad wrote a book about adopting my brother from foster care, and some of the professionals who read it advised him on how to get me off these medications.

Six months after aging out of foster care I managed to graduate from Mount Baker High School with my class. A few months later, I moved into my own apartment. My new family helped me find an excellent therapist, who supported me in my decision to get off these medications

Today I am able to talk about my feelings, but when I was in the psychiatric hospital, I was so drugged up, I didn't even know how I felt. My twin sister said I was like a zombie. I know some of the kids I was locked up with needed medication. They heard voices that weren't there and got violent sometimes, but I believe many of the foster kids were like me and needed loving parents to guide them.

When I think about the government spending over $120,000 locking me up and forcing me to take these drugs, it makes me very angry. I wish that the money could have been spent helping foster youth.

Despite all of this, I have been so lucky. A few months ago, on the same day as my brother's adoption 5 years ago, my dad adopted my twin sister and me. What really helped me get off the medication was being surrounded by people who loved me and wanted to help me. I believe what most foster youth need is love, not drugs.

Although I can never get back the 7 months that I was locked up and forced to take these drugs, I hope that telling my story here today and continuing to work with the Mockingbird Society will help other youth like me and encourage change.

In closing, I want to thank the Mockingbird Society for making it possible for me to come from Seattle to be here today. They are an awesome youth advocacy organization that helps young people share our experiences about foster care and gives us a chance to be heard.

Thank you, Chairman Reichert, for inviting me here today. I want to thank you for all the work you do for foster youth.

Dr. Phil, I also want to thank you for everything you have done.

And I am grateful to my CASA for being the person who knew me and told the court that I did not need these drugs, and for all my family, my twin sister, and my therapist for supporting me to get off these medications. Thank you.

## Statement of Phil McGraw, PhD, Talk Show Host, "Dr. Phil"

Mr. MCGRAW. Chairman Reichert, Ranking Member Doggett, and distinguished Members of the Committee, I wish I didn't have to follow this young lady. That is a tough act, to say the least.

I am honored to be invited here to talk about the possible misuse of these psychotropic drugs. They are all too often prescribed to America's foster children. Look, these drugs can change and even save lives, there is no question about it, but when it comes to these vulnerable children, these drugs are just too often misused as chemical straitjackets. It is just a haphazard attempt to simply control and suppress undesirable behavior rather than treat it, nurture it, and develop these treasured young people, and simply put, it just makes them less inconvenient. It just makes them less inconvenient so they don't take as much energy to manage.

And you have my written statement, and I kind of want to begin where it leaves off because I believe that 80 percent of all questions are really statements in disguise. And I think everybody here already agrees, these drugs are flowing too much; there is just no question about that. You know the numbers.

The real question is why? You know, why is this happening? I mean, three times as many foster children as their counterparts are getting these drugs; 40 percent of them are on three classes of drugs, some are on five classes of drugs. This is polypharmacy. Is there more psychopathology with these foster children? Of course, there is. They have more abuse and neglect that they have had to go through. Eighty percent are diagnosed with mental illness as opposed to 20 percent in the general population, but this is no justification.

I have been working with this population for 5 years, for five decades. Robin and I have been national spokespersons for CASA for a number of years. Their budget has been cut, which just broke my heart to see. These kids face problems that you are not going to fix by throwing drugs at them. And a lot of them don't even take the drugs; they sell them. Dr. Charles Sophy is with me here today. He is the chief medical director for the L.A. County DCFS, the largest in the country. He told me within the last month, near a shelter in L.A., some of those children tried to sell him their psychotropic drugs, not knowing he was the medical director, and more than once in an hour trying to sell the drugs. If they do take them, are they less inconvenient? Maybe. But it is not convenience without consequences.

They should never be used without evidence-based research. There should be proper diagnostics done and appropriate monitoring done, and it should always be in conjunction with evidence-based therapies, and anything less, we just have to be honest, we are sabotaging these kids, we are just flat out sabotaging them. And in my view, this is like pulling a thread. The entire system is flawed. It is not just the drugs. The entire system is flawed. Do we need to turn off the flood of drugs? Yes. But the problem is we have got a reverse incentive system here. It is a system where the government continues to pay for the drugs. We say you shouldn't give them, but yet they continue to be compensated for them, and these foster children, the more labels they get, the more drugs they are on, the more money they get to take care of that child. So they are actually paid for pathology. The more scripts, the less treatment, the more scripts, the less energy, and so it just becomes an assembly line, high volume, move them in, move them out process, and these children deserve better than that.

Real treatment takes high energy, it takes—it is low volume. I mean, you have got to have more people, it takes more time, but we have got too many doctors with insufficient training in these drugs. They don't know what the drugs do. We don't—most of us, if we are honest, we have to tell you, we don't know why the drugs work when they do work. We don't know the agent of action, the agent of change, but we have too many doctors with insufficient training about these drugs that are prescribing them, and there is no follow up because the foster parents change. So there is no long-term follow on this, and then the therapists they do get, they change. You have got children with detachment problems, attachment disorders, detachment problems, and we rotate their therapist in and out.

As soon as they bond with one, then they are faced with another one. So it just becomes a serious problem.

I have been in this situation, hopefully, fortunately not as bad as some of these children, but I was homeless when I was 15 years old. I was living on the streets in Kansas City. I was living in a car. We finally got a room at the YMCA, my dad and I, and then ultimately an apartment where we got an apartment, but we had no utilities because we didn't have money for the deposit. So we froze to death in the dark from 4:30 on, but I tell you what happened to me. Nobody ran at me with a handful of drugs. I fortunately had a football coach and some others who taught me about responsibility, taught me about the things to do that were important, and that is what CASAs do with these children. That is what therapists involved with evidence-based treatments would do with these children. But we have got to stop the flow of drugs and we have got to focus on reunification. We have just got to try to get these children back home.

This system is broken, and it is flawed, and psychology has made great strides. We truly do have alternatives to offer these children, and without the side effects that the drugs have, but it takes time and it takes money, and it takes a completely different model than what we have right now, and so I am obviously very passionate about this.

I just feel so strongly that these children need somebody to put an arm around their shoulder, somebody to help them, rather than just throw drugs at them, and there is nothing better for these children than to be able to look themselves in the mirror and say, I did this, I found my way, I got my coping skills.

So I will stop. I want to thank the committee for inviting me to participate. A wise man once said—well, actually it was me that said it, you can't change what you don't acknowledge. And this committee is making a bold acknowledgment of this problem, and so I am happy to answer any questions.

**Source:** U.S. House of Representatives. Hearing before the Subcommittee on Human Resources of the Committee on Ways and Means. "Statement of Dawna Zender Hovenier" and "Statement of Dr. Phil McGraw." *Caring for Our Kids: Are We Overmedicating Children in Foster Care?* 113th Cong., 2nd Sess. (May 29, 2014). https://www.govinfo.gov/content/pkg/CHRG-113hhrg94399/html/CHRG-113hhrg94399.htm

### Dr. William C. Bell's Testimony on the Importance of Fathers in Reducing the Need for Foster Care (2019)

*On February 9, 2018, the Family First Prevention Services Act was signed into law as part of the Bipartisan Budget Act of 2018. Among various other provisions, the law prioritized keeping families together and children out of foster care by putting federal money toward evidence-based prevention services, such as at-home parenting classes, mental health counseling, and substance abuse treatment. Nearly a year and a half after the law's passage, Dr. William C. Bell, president and CEO of Casey Family Programs, testified before the House Ways and Means Subcommittee on Worker and Family Support about the critical role that fathers play in the lives of their children and the opportunities to support fathers under the Family First Prevention Services Act. A portion of Dr. Bell's written testimony is included here.*

Good afternoon Chairman Davis, Ranking Member Walorski and members of the committee. My name is William C. Bell and I am the president and CEO of Casey Family Programs. Casey Family Programs is the nation's largest operating foundation focused on safely reducing the need for foster care and building communities of hope for children and families across America. . . .

I thank you for the opportunity to be here today to talk about the resilience of families and the critical role that fathers play in the lives of their children. . . .

Casey Family Programs has learned from research—and from providing direct service for over five decades—that most children grow up to have better outcomes in life when they are nurtured and cared for by their own families.

We have also learned that fathers and their engagement is critical to achieving this result. Fathers have a significant role to play in children's physical, emotional, and social development and they are essential partners in the prevention of maltreatment and achievement of timely permanence for children involved in the child welfare system.

Studies have highlighted myriad benefits of father involvement for child safety and well-being:

- Non-resident fathers may play a role in ameliorating the circumstances that led to abuse.
- Non-resident fathers' involvement with their children is associated with a higher likelihood of a reunification outcome and a lower likelihood of an adoption outcome.
- Children with highly involved non-resident fathers are discharged from foster care more quickly than those whose fathers have less or no involvement.

For children who are reunited with a parent, usually their mother, higher levels of non-resident father involvement are associated with a substantially lower likelihood of subsequent maltreatment allegations. Data show that outcomes for children improve through high quality relationships and engagement between fathers and their children. We know from our work, from research, but most important from talking with youth directly, that having an involved father confirms to a child that they are loved, provides a child with emotional support and enhanced self-esteem, increases a child's intellectual and moral development, and provides increased opportunities for academic success.

According to a 2013 analysis on the influence of father involvement on child welfare permanency outcomes, children have a higher risk for poor psychosocial outcomes when their fathers are absent or not involved. Unfortunately, these children are more likely to live in poverty, drop out of school, and engage in risky behaviors like using alcohol, tobacco, and illicit drugs.

Unfortunately, child-serving systems often discount the importance of a father's involvement in the lives of their children. Only 54% of the approximately 400,000 children in foster care had contact with their fathers in the year leading up to the analysis, compared to 72% of children from the general population. While data on the involvement of fathers whose children are in out-of-home placements is scarce, the study documented that when fathers are involved, their children have shorter lengths of stay in foster care and they are more likely to be reunited with birth parents or placed with relatives after foster care.

Too often many government systems focus on payment of child support as the non-custodial fathers' only critical responsibility and method of connection with supporting the rearing of their children. Even as initiatives and investments designed to build protective factors among children have grown, father-specific programs and resources have continued to be developed at the margins, if at all. One example of effective programming in this area is parent partner programs. This type of program has been continuously identified by parents as providing critical support and assistance to them when navigating the child welfare system. Having fathers with first-hand experience serving as peer/parent mentors to fathers currently navigating the system can be an effective approach to help identify and address challenges, build on family strengths, provide a vital social connection, and contribute to positive outcomes for children and families.

While financial support is important, data shows that outcomes for children improve not by virtue of financial support alone, but also through high-quality relationships and safe and healthy interactions between fathers and children. Engaging fathers and connecting them with the right kinds of services and supports can directly impact the way fathers contribute to their child's development, yet there are a number of issues that impact the experiences that fathers have across multiple systems and influence their ability and capacity to engage in meaningful and consistent ways.

These potential barriers include:

1. Significant systemic bias against father engagement in child welfare (e.g., case names reflect mother);
2. Insufficient efforts to locate and involve non-custodial fathers;
3. Gate-keeping actions that reduce access between fathers and their children;
4. Circumstances that result in non-custodial fathers being less accessible (i.e., incarceration, homelessness, impairment by substance abuse, military enlistment, etc.);
5. Lack of father-specific services and supports;
6. Dynamics around domestic violence and fathers who have committed acts of abuse towards involving their children.

In spite of these potential barriers, many jurisdictions have high-lighted and implemented numerous strategies to strengthen father engagement.

These include:

- Organizational assessment and planning for enhanced father involvement to help guide the development of fatherhood approaches and initiatives in child-serving systems.
- Dedicated staff to support fathers. One example is the father engagement specialists employed at the Allegheny County (Pennsylvania) Department of Human Services' Office of Children, Youth and Families.
- An effective process for locating and engaging fathers, such as the development and implementation of a robust family search and engagement framework, that includes identification, making initial contact, family group conferencing, assessment, safety planning and permanency planning.
- Development of a network of providers in the communities focused on fathers as well as a network of support to

fathers whose children are involved with the child welfare system.

- Home visiting programs that include fathers. Home visiting programs tend to focus on pregnant women and mothers of young children, however, some home visiting programs are implementing strategies to better engage fathers in these important services. . . .

Casey Family Programs relies on alumni of foster care, birth parents and foster parents alike to inform its work with the authentic voice of those who have lived experience with the child protection system. Birth parent and foster parent partnerships that are inclusive and supportive of all parents of children in out-of-home care, including fathers, can improve relationships and communication between fathers and their children; between fathers and co-parents of their children; and between fathers and child welfare agency staff. Strengthening and supporting families to be resilient and to have sources of support is a proactive approach to prevent child abuse and neglect. . . .

Casey Family Programs also works directly with children and families to develop and demonstrate effective, practical solutions to safely reduce the need for foster care, improve child well-being, and secure safe and lifelong families for every child in our care. We operate nine field offices in five states—Arizona, California, Idaho, Texas, and Washington—that provide direct services to urban, suburban and rural communities.

We know from our own direct work with children and families how critical it is to involve fathers—and paternal family members—in the lives of their children through case planning, family finding efforts and permanency conversations. At the core of our Case Practice Model is a philosophy built on the belief that children thrive when they are an integral part of their families and communities.

Children have a profound need to know who they are and where they came from. They also have a need to feel connected to people who look like them, share the same history, and enjoy the same traditions and cultures. For these reasons, our Case Practice Model prioritizes family-based and family-focused work that serves the whole family, including fathers, paternal relatives, and maternal relatives.

In child welfare cases, too many non-custodial fathers are often not sought out or included in case planning efforts. Their absence can be assumed as an expression of disinterest or detachment.

For fathers who may not have been involved in a child's life there is critical work that must be done to build relationships between the child and their father, and to support the father not only in getting to know his child, but also to support him in learning how to navigate an often complicated web of systems: child welfare, probation, child support, behavioral and mental health, etc.

Practices like family group conferencing, family connections meetings, and responsible parenting are successful tools Casey Family Programs has used to support strengthening the functioning of families to include fathers and other paternal relatives. Even when it is challenging to locate a father, there are technologies available, such as Skype and Facebook that can offer connections. In addition, involving the paternal side of the family offers a whole extended family to a child, providing opportunities for meaningful relationships, new family connections, relational permanency, and increased options for legal permanency, including guardianship.

At today's hearing we have experts with us who have talked about specific Fatherhood programs and interventions that have been shown to be effective, and I also want to highlight a few promising programs that Casey Family Programs is aware of across the country.

At the Allegheny County (Pennsylvania) Department of Human Services Office of Children, Youth and Families, father engagement specialists are able to work with fathers one-on-one to help support closer relationships with their children, families, and communities. Father engagement specialists are not caseworkers, but work alongside the caseworker. They have the flexibility to meet fathers at times and locations that are convenient for them and to work on specific issues deemed important to the father. Allegheny County also offers fatherhood programming through its network of Family Support Centers and the Father Collaborative Council of Western Pennsylvania.

In 2016, the Indiana Department of Child Services (DCS) issued a request for proposal to build its network of providers to implement fatherhood programming that offers assistance and support to fathers whose children are involved with DCS. Following provider selection, fatherhood service standards were implemented to support the providers in working with DCS to successfully engage fathers in services to improve their child's safety, stability, well-being, permanency, and to assist fathers in strengthening their relationships with their children. These standards included an understanding of male learning styles and help-seeking behaviors for effective engagement. The standards also included the provision of supportive services in the home or community environment, and promotion of community awareness regarding the value of engaging fathers.

Casey Family Programs has also worked with the Paternal Opportunities, Programs and Services Organization (POPS) in San Diego, CA. This organization advocates for fathers and helps manage cases, with the goal of family reunification by assisting fathers in developing parenting skills in tandem with a step-by-step reunification plan. POPS also provides fathers with moral support, counseling, case strategy, parenting education, self-growth through support groups, legal clinics, individual counseling, and group counseling. . . .

We commend Congress for its leadership and work to pass into law the Family First Prevention Services Act (Family First). There should be nothing more important to us as a nation than ensuring the safety of our children and ensuring that they have the opportunity to grow up surrounded by a Community of Hope.

This legislation makes it clear that our national child and family well-being response systems will always seek to fully address the well-being of children while also addressing the well-being of their families and their communities. We have always known that it is vitally important that we intervene as early as possible to ensure the safety of children. . . .

There is tremendous opportunity in Family First to enable states and tribes to support and strengthen their families who are in need and improve the safety of their child. Beginning as early as October 1, 2019, states and eligible tribes will have the ability to access new federal funding to provide prevention services and programs for up to 12 months for children at imminent risk of entering foster care, any parenting or pregnant youth in foster care, parents—biological or adopted—and kin caregivers.

The new Title IV-E prevention services, as well as training and administrative costs associated with developing these services, would have no income test ("delinked" from the AFDC income eligibility requirement). Eligible services are evidence-based mental health and substance abuse prevention and treatment services and in-home parent skill-based services.

Family First also allows states, for the first time, the opportunity to use Title IV-E funding to offer evidence based parenting skills education to both mothers and fathers. Parent education programs focus on enhancing parenting practices and behaviors; such as developing and practicing positive discipline techniques; learning age-appropriate child development skills and milestones; promoting positive play and interaction between parents and children; and locating and accessing community services and supports. These programs can be incredibly helpful to first-time parents, including teen parents, non-custodial fathers, and fathers needing support and guidance in understanding and fulfilling their role. . . .

As we look ahead to the implementation of Family First, there are some evidence-based programs that are already supporting fathers within the context of their families, such as Nurse Family Partnership, which works with both mothers and fathers who are expecting a first child. Nurse Family Partnerships is currently being reviewed by the Clearinghouse created under Family First to identify promising, supported or well supported evidence-based programs that states can use to provide families with prevention services that are outcomes-based.

In 2016, the Texas Department of Family and Protective Services contracted with the Child and Family Research Partnership to conduct the Father Participation and Retention Evaluation which examined home visiting programs in Texas. The findings revealed that families where fathers participated in at least one home visit were enrolled in the home visiting program for an average of 17.2 months. This was nearly 7 months longer than the average 10.6 months of enrollment for families where fathers did not participate in any home visits.

While promising fatherhood engagement programs currently exist—and we have heard about additional approaches today—states and communities must continue to promote, expand, and develop these types of programs that initiate and strengthen the connection between fathers and their children. Using the tools provided by Congress, like Family First, we believe that these programs will have a significant impact on improving life outcomes for children and their families.

**Source:** U.S. House of Representatives. Committee on Ways and Means, Subcommittee on Worker and Family Support. "Written Testimony of William C. Bell." *Celebrating Fathers and Families: Federal Support for Responsible Fatherhood.* 116th Cong., 1st Sess. (June 11, 2019). https://www.congress .gov/116/meeting/house/109611/witnesses/HHRG-116 -WM03-Wstate-BellW-20190611.pdf

### *Sharonell Fulton, et al. v. City of Philadelphia*, Petition for Writ of Certiorari and City Respondents Brief in Opposition (2019) (Excerpts)

*Catholic Social Services (CSS) has served vulnerable families and pioneered foster care in Philadelphia since it was founded over 200 years ago to help mothers, children, and families in need. For the past 50 years, the agency has had a contractual relationship with the city to place foster children. During that time, CSS recruited, licensed, and supervised over 1,000 foster families. In 2018, however, the agency came under intense scrutiny for its policy of not placing foster children with same-sex or unmarried couples. This policy was based on the Catholic Church's opposition to gay marriage. Although no same-sex couples had ever approached CSS, its stated policy was that if a same-sex or unmarried couple did seek services, the organization would help them find a match from among the 29 nearby foster agencies willing to partner with LGBTQ and unmarried foster parents.*

*A few days after a Philadelphia newspaper first drew widespread attention to CSS's placement policy, the Philadelphia City Council passed a resolution that condemned "discrimination that occurs under the guise of religious freedom" and instructed the Department of Human Services (DHS) to change its contracting practices on these grounds. DHS responded by launching an investigation into CSS and blocking all future foster placement referrals to the agency.*

*In May 2018, foster mother Sharonell Fulton and social worker, child advocate, and foster mother Toni Simms-Busch joined CSS in filing a lawsuit asking a court to order DHS to resume referring foster care cases to CSS. Represented by Becket Law, the petitioners argued that the city's actions violated both the First Amendment's free exercise clause, which protects religious belief and expression, and the establishment clause, which among other things prohibits government from favoring nonreligion over religion.*

*A Philadelphia district court denied the petitioners' request, arguing that the city's policy was acceptable under the Supreme*

*Court's 1990 decision in* Employment Division v. Smith, *which held that government actions do not violate the Constitution's free exercise clause if they are neutral and generally applicable. Becket Law immediately appealed to the Third Circuit Court of Appeals. On April 22, 2019, in a split decision, the Third Circuit Court of Appeals denied CSS's request to continue providing foster care services while litigation proceeded.*

*In July 2019, the petitioners filed a writ of certiorari asking the Supreme Court to hear the case. The Supreme Court agreed to grant certiorari in February 2020 and heard oral arguments in November 2020. The Supreme Court unanimously ruled in June 2021 that the City of Philadelphia's decision to cancel CSS's contract to provide foster care services on account of their religious beliefs violated their First Amendment right to free exercise of religion. The majority opinion featured an unusual coalition of three of the court's conservatives alongside its three most liberal members. Court observers speculated that the three liberal justices joined the majority opinion, written by Chief Justice John Roberts, because they saw it as a ruling decided on narrow legal grounds that did not threaten most other LGBTQ antidiscrimination laws.*

*The first excerpted document is from the petition for writ of certiorari filed on behalf of Sharonell Fulton, et al. The second selection provides excerpts from the brief in opposition presented by the City of Philadelphia.*

## Petition for Writ of Certiorari

Catholic Social Services ("CSS") is a religious foster care agency and ministry of the Archdiocese of Philadelphia. CSS has been serving Philadelphia foster children for more than a century. But its foster care services are being shut down by the City of Philadelphia because the City disagrees with the Archdiocese about marriage. As a Catholic agency, CSS cannot provide written endorsements for same-sex couples which contradict its religious teachings on marriage. The mayor, city council,

Department of Human Services, and other city officials have targeted CSS and attempted to coerce it into changing its religious practices in order to make such endorsements. The City's actions are a direct and open violation of the First Amendment. Yet the lower courts have upheld them.

CSS's beliefs about marriage haven't prevented anyone from fostering. Philadelphia has a diverse array of foster agencies, and not a single same-sex couple approached CSS about becoming a foster parent between its opening in 1917 and the start of this case in 2018. Despite this history, after learning through a newspaper article that CSS wouldn't perform home studies for same-sex couples if asked, the City stopped allowing foster children to be placed with any family endorsed by CSS. This means that even though no same-sex couples had asked to work with the Catholic Church, the foster families that actually chose to work with the Church cannot welcome new children into their homes at a time when Philadelphia has an admittedly "urgent" need for more foster parents.

It is no mystery why Philadelphia has punished CSS. Having worked in harmony with CSS for decades, Philadelphia is shutting down CSS because, it said, it wants to prohibit "discrimination that occurs under the guise of religious freedom." But well aware that it can't target religious exercise, Philadelphia started looking for a rationale to justify this predetermined result.

In its search for a rationale, Philadelphia first cited its Fair Practices Ordinance, even though that law has never been applied to foster care. Philadelphia then relied on a contractual provision, but that provision turned out to be inapplicable and permitted discretionary exemptions. So the City decided to revise its contracts to specifically prohibit CSS's religious practice. It later argued that this change was required by the City charter, but that turned out to be inapplicable, too. Yet Philadelphia still claimed to be acting pursuant to a neutral, generally applicable law.

Despite ample evidence that Philadelphia's policies were neither neutral nor generally applicable, the Third Circuit upheld those policies under *Employment Division v. Smith*, holding that both *Smith* and the nation's civil rights laws would be a "dead letter" if the First Amendment protected CSS. In doing so, the court joined the wrong side of a 6–2 circuit split over what a free exercise plaintiff must prove to prevail under *Smith* and *Lukumi*. Properly understood, *Smith* does not support the decision below, which turns the Free Exercise Clause upside down. But the propensity of lower courts to read *Smith* so narrowly is powerful evidence that *Smith* has confused rather than clarified the law and should be reconsidered.

The Third Circuit also distorted this Court's caselaw on unconstitutional conditions, holding that Philadelphia's exclusion of CSS because of the agency's religious speech and actions could be treated as a mere limitation on the use of government funds. That claim fails where, as here, the government acts as the gatekeeper to determine who may engage in a particular activity.

In *Obergefell v. Hodges*, Chief Justice Roberts wrote that "[h]ard questions arise when people of faith exercise religion in ways that may be seen to conflict with the new right to same-sex marriage," giving as an example "a religious adoption agency declin[ing] to place children with same-sex married couples." 135 S. Ct. 2584, 2625-2626 (2015) (Roberts, C.J., dissenting). He predicted that "[t]here is little doubt" such a case "will soon be before this Court." *Id.* at 2626. That prediction has now come true.

Here and in cities across the country, religious foster and adoption agencies have repeatedly been forced to close their doors, and many more are under threat. These questions are unavoidable, they raise issues of great consequence for children and families nationwide, and the problem will only continue to grow until these questions are resolved by this Court. . . .

## Statement of the Case

## I. The foster care crisis and Catholic Social Services

Fueled in part by the opioid epidemic, the United States faces a foster care crisis, with a significant and growing shortage of foster families. In Philadelphia alone, more than 6,000 children are in foster care. In March 2018, Philadelphia's Department of Human Services (DHS) made an "urgent" plea for 300 new foster homes.

Faith-based foster agencies like CSS have long played a crucial role helping to find loving homes for these children. CSS helps connect children with parents like petitioner Sharonell Fulton, who has lovingly fostered 40 children in over 25 years; petitioner Toni Simms-Busch, a longtime social worker who decided to foster and adopt two children; and plaintiff Cecelia Paul, who used her training as a pediatric nurse to foster infants born with drug addictions. Philadelphia even named Mrs. Paul a foster parent of the year. After fostering 133 children over 46 years, Mrs. Paul passed away in October 2018, so her rights can no longer be vindicated by this petition. Due to Philadelphia's policies, Mrs. Paul spent her last months prevented from engaging in the loving ministry to which she had devoted so much of her life.

A. CSS's long history serving at-risk children.

CSS is a nonprofit charitable organization operating under the auspices of the Archdiocese of Philadelphia. It seeks to "continue the work of Jesus by affirming, assisting and advocating for individuals, families, and communities." CSS serves the people of Philadelphia through immigration assistance, providing homes for unaccompanied minors, running residential homes for at-risk teens, providing food and shelter for the homeless, and other ministries. Finding and working with families to provide foster care for Philadelphia children has always been a crucial part of CSS's religious ministry, dating back to at least 1917—long before the City became involved in foster care.

In the 1950s, the City (through its Department of Human Services) began partnering with private agencies to facilitate foster care. Because foster care placements are now controlled by the City, today "you would be breaking the law if you tried to provide foster care services without a contract." CSS therefore cares for foster children through its annually renewed contract with the City. This relationship has been in place for decades.

B. Philadelphia's foster care system.

The City places no limit on the number of agencies that can obtain contracts to provide foster services. CSS is one of thirty foster agencies that contract with the City. Having this broad array of agencies helps serve Philadelphia's diverse population. Some agencies specialize in serving the Latino community, some focus on serving those with developmental disabilities, and several specialize in caring for children with special needs. Four agencies have the Human Rights Campaign's (HRC) "Seal of Approval," recognizing their excellence in serving the LGBT community.

When families are ready to foster, they can reach out to any of these agencies. Philadelphia tells families they should research agencies to "feel confident and comfortable with the agency" and to "find the best fit for you."

If an agency is unable to partner with a potential foster family, the standard practice is to refer that family to another agency. Such referrals "are made all the time."

If an agency believes it can partner with a potential foster family, the agency will then conduct a detailed assessment of the applicant and the relationships of those living in her home. This process is called a home study. The minimum requirements for home studies and foster parent certifications are set by state law.

Philadelphia acknowledges it has "ha[s] nothing to do" with home studies. They are "not expressly funded under the contract" between the City and the agency, because "compensation is based on the number of children in [an agency's] care rather than on the number of home studies performed."

At the conclusion of a home study, the foster agency determines whether it can certify the family to work with that agency to care for foster children. If so, the City then decides whether to place children in that family's home. Philadelphia pays CSS a *per diem* for each foster child placed in one of its certified homes; most of these funds go directly to foster parents to defray the costs of caring for children. CSS also raises private funds to cover costs that the *per diem* does not.

C. CSS's religious exercise.

CSS exercises its religion by caring for foster children and acting in accordance with its Catholic beliefs in the process. This means that CSS cannot make foster certifications inconsistent with its religious beliefs about sex and marriage. CSS sincerely believes that the home study certification endorses the relationships in the home, and therefore it cannot provide home studies or endorsements for unmarried heterosexual couples or same-sex couples. CSS would refer those couples to another agency, but as the Third Circuit noted, the record shows that no same-sex couple ever approached CSS seeking a foster certification.

## II. Philadelphia targets CSS.

In March 2018, a reporter from the *Philadelphia Inquirer* asked the Archdiocese about CSS's policy regarding same-sex couples. The Archdiocese's spokesperson confirmed CSS's longstanding religious beliefs.

Three days after the article was published, the City Council passed a resolution calling for an investigation into "discrimination" occurring "under the guise of" religion; the Mayor (who had previously called the Archbishop "not Christian" and said he "could care less about the people at the Archdiocese") prompted inquiries by both the Commission on Human Relations and DHS; and the Commission opened an inquiry into CSS, forgoing its required complaint and formal notice procedures. The head of DHS, Commissioner Cynthia Figueroa, investigated whether *religious* agencies certified same-sex couples. She did not investigate secular agencies, and later acknowledged that she had not informed secular agencies of any policy against such referrals.

The Commissioner summoned CSS for a meeting. There, she told CSS that it should follow "the teachings of Pope Francis," and told CSS "times have changed," "attitudes have changed," and it is "not 100 years ago."

Minutes after this meeting, Philadelphia cut off CSS's foster care referrals. This meant that no new foster children could be placed with any foster parents certified by CSS.

Philadelphia informed CSS of its rationales in two letters. The first letter claimed CSS had violated the Fair Practices Ordinance (FPO). The second informed CSS that, unless it changed its religious practices, its annual contracts would no longer be renewed, meaning it could no longer provide foster care to Philadelphia children.

Shortly after receiving this second letter, CSS, together with Sharonell Fulton, Cecelia Paul, and Toni Simms-Busch, sued Philadelphia and sought a preliminary injunction. The district court denied that injunction after a hearing, and the Third Circuit affirmed. . . .

Current status of CSS's program.

Today, CSS's foster care program continues to dwindle as foster children are adopted, age out of care, or return to their birth homes. Since last fall, delays in the family courts have caused a dramatic slowdown in adoptions from foster care. This unexpected delay has meant that more children have remained in CSS's foster homes than originally anticipated, but the program is still less than half its prior size, and is still being wound down by the City.

CSS was caring for more than 120 children when this lawsuit was filed, and is now caring for fewer than 60. Of an original staff of seven workers devoted full time to foster care, CSS has retained just three foster care employees who now split time with another program. This has allowed CSS to keep its program open, but it is only a temporary solution. Without the ability to care for any more children, CSS's numbers will continue to dwindle until its foster program must close.

## Reasons for Granting the Petition

Philadelphia's actions here were baseless, discriminatory, and entirely unnecessary. CSS has been successfully providing foster care services to Philadelphia children for far longer than the City, and this religious ministry has never prevented a single LGBT couple from fostering. Yet the City is trying to exclude CSS from foster care because CSS refuses to embrace the City's beliefs about marriage. The City's shifting rationales prove that its actions were a result in search of a rule. In upholding those actions, the Third Circuit made it nearly impossible to prove a Free Exercise Clause violation in the circuit and contributed to a deepening split among the Courts of Appeals over how plaintiffs prove free exercise claims. It also departed from this Court's decisions in *Smith*, *Lukumi*, and *Masterpiece*. The lower courts' confusion over *Smith*, in this case and others, demonstrates that *Smith* should be reconsidered.

Free speech rights are also imperiled by the decision below, which allows governments to exclude religious foster and adoption agencies unless they speak the government's preferred message regarding marriage.

The Court should grant certiorari to resolve the confusion over *Smith* and to clarify that the First Amendment provides real protection for religious charities serving those in need.

**Source:** *Sharonell Fulton, et al. v. City of Philadelphia, et al.* "Petition for a Writ of Certiorari." July 2019. https://

www.supremecourt.gov/DocketPDF/19/19-123/108931
/20190722174037071_Cert%20Petition%20FINAL.pdf

## City Respondents Brief in Opposition

### Introduction

The City of Philadelphia contracts with private agencies to help it fulfill its obligations to care for abused and neglected children—including, among other things, the recruiting, screening, and certification of eligible foster parents. Private foster-care agencies that choose to contract with the City are paid with taxpayer funds to perform this public function. This case concerns just one obligation of Catholic Social Services in just one of its contracts with the City: the obligation to give a fair look to every prospective foster parent who walks in the door.

For many years, the City's standard foster-care contracts have prohibited discrimination based on characteristics enumerated in the Philadelphia Fair Practices Ordinance, including race and sexual orientation. The City has never allowed contractors to turn away potential foster parents based on a protected characteristic. Although this longstanding policy applies to all City contractors—and although the City has long contracted with Catholic Social Services, and continues to do so for a range of other child-welfare services—CSS contends that the City's decision to enforce this policy against it reflects religious hostility. On that basis, CSS seeks a "highly unusual" remedy: "an injunction forcing the City to renew a public services contract with a particular private party," free of the nondiscrimination policy. . . .

### Factual and Legal Background
***Philadelphia's obligations to abused and neglected children.***
Pennsylvania law requires local agencies—including the city of Philadelphia, through its Department of Human Services

(DHS)—to accept and assume custodial responsibility for children who have been abused or neglected. It also charges these agencies with advancing the well-being of children within their care, consistent with the best interest of each child. The Commonwealth of Pennsylvania, DHS, and a number of private foster-care agencies each play a role in the city's foster-care system.

The city has protective custody of roughly five thousand children who cannot live with their legal parents. Many of these children are placed in homes with foster parents, though some are also in "congregate care," such as group homes, institutional placements, or residential-treatment facilities. The City also provides foster care to this population partly by using taxpayer funds to contract with private community-umbrella agencies and private foster-care agencies, each of which must be licensed by Pennsylvania and is subject to child-welfare laws and regulations.

The City's Department of Human Services has long contracted with Catholic Social Services (CSS)—and other religious organizations—to provide public child-welfare services. To this day, the Department works closely with CSS to provide a range of services and values its ongoing relationship with CSS. CSS serves Philadelphia's at-risk children through congregate care, as a community-umbrella agency, and through private foster care. This case concerns only CSS's obligations as a family foster-care agency. When this litigation began, the City was paying CSS to perform that role—which encompasses, among other things, identifying and recruiting potential foster parents, as well as training and certifying them on a continuing basis. This relationship, like the City's relationships with other private foster-care agencies performing the same function, was structured through one-year contracts renewable on an annual basis. Agencies certifying their continuing compliance with applicable state regulations and other terms set by the City.

***Catholic Social Services' now-expired contract with the City of Philadelphia.*** When a prospective foster parent walks into a private foster-care agency to apply to be a foster parent, the City contract requires the agency to evaluate and assess that person for certification. The contract between the Department and CSS for FY 2018—which was substantially similar to the City's FY 2018 contracts with all other private foster-care agencies—included a provision obligating CSS "to recruit, screen, and provide certified resource care homes" for dependent children or youth, consistent with state law. The contract further required that CSS "obtain Certifications as required by law and by DHS policy," including for "all prospective foster parent applicants [and] all prospective adoptive parent applicants."

The Department expects each agency with whom it contracts to evaluate and assess for certification each and every prospective foster parent that wishes to work with it. To that end, its contract with CSS, like its contracts with other agencies, expressly prohibited discrimination on certain specified grounds and required compliance with the City's Fair Practices Ordinance. This ordinance precludes discrimination based, among other things, on race and sexual orientation. DHS has *never* authorized providers to refuse to certify, let alone refuse to establish fostering relationships with, prospective parents because of their membership in any protected category, including sexual orientation. And long before this dispute arose, DHS believed that each of its foster-care providers would consider every prospective parent who requested to work with that agency.

***Catholic Social Services' policy on same-sex couples.*** On March 9, 2018, the Department learned from a *Philadelphia Inquirer* reporter that two of the Department's contractor foster-care agencies—Catholic Social Services and Bethany Christian Services—had policies of categorically refusing service to same-sex couples seeking to become foster parents. This was the first that DHS had heard about such policies.

Commissioner Figueroa was immediately concerned that CSS and Bethany were at risk of violating their City contracts with DHS, and contacted the City's Law Department. She also called both CSS and Bethany to determine the accuracy of the *Inquirer* report and learned from both that they refused, on religious grounds, to consider same-sex couples for certification as foster parents. Commissioner Figueroa also called other foster-care agencies to inquire about their practices, focusing on religious agencies because she understood the particular objections at issue to arise from religious belief, but also calling at least one agency that was not religiously affiliated to determine its policy. None of the other agencies she contacted had a similar policy.

Commissioner Figueroa consulted with the City's lawyers, who told her that CSS's policy would, in practice, violate the City's Fair Practices Ordinance and the services provision of their contract with the Department. Because this raised a serious legal issue that could affect CSS's ability to enter into the upcoming year's contract, DHS and CSS convened a meeting. There, CSS Secretary James Amato stated that, for religious reasons, CSS "would not move forward with a home study for a same-sex couple." He added that CSS had provided services to the City for over one hundred years.

Commissioner Figueroa responded by emphasizing that this history was not conclusive: She observed that times had changed over the course of that relationship, that women and African-Americans did not have the same rights when it started, and that she herself would likely not have been in her position a century earlier. Commissioner Figueroa—herself a lifelong Catholic—also said something like, "it would be great if we followed the teachings of Pope Francis."

Ultimately, CSS made clear that it would not comply with its contractual requirement to evaluate and consider certifying same-sex couples. CSS would therefore be unable to renew its contract for providing these services. As a result, Commissioner

Figueroa decided to stop placing new children with CSS while discussions over the status of the contract continued. This decision was consistent with the parties' contract, which does not require the City to make any placement referrals with particular providers. It is also consistent with Commissioner Figueroa's past practice, which has been to close intake to an agency whenever it is at risk of no longer providing services, regardless of the reason, to minimize the number of children's replacements that might need to be changed or transferred if the relationship ends. Commissioner Figueroa's intake closure went into effect on March 15, 2018, though the City allowed exceptions where a child had siblings in a CSS home or where a CSS foster family had a prior relationship with the child. The district court credited Commissioner Figureroa's testimony that DHS was solely responsible for this decision.

The intake freeze had limited consequences. It did not affect children already placed with CSS. Nor did it affect the overwhelming majority of DHS's contractual relationships with CSS—namely, CSS's congregate-care and community-umbrella-agency services, which remain fully active to this day under a new, multimillion-dollar contract. As the City's Law Department made clear in a letter to CSS, the City has "respect [for CSS's] sincere religious beliefs" and does not "want to see [its] valuable relationship with CSS . . . . come to an end." It hoped that CSS might agree to comply with the City's Fair Practices Ordinance so the parties could enter into a new contract. In the meantime, the City emphasized its willingness to enter into an interim maintenance contract "to continue to supervise the foster children in its care properly with the least amount of disruption for them."

**Source:** *Sharonell Fulton, et al. v. City of Philadelphia, et al.* "City Respondents' Brief in Opposition." October 10, 2019: 1, 4–9. https://www.supremecourt.gov/DocketPDF/19/19-123 /118736/20191010161858525_19-123%20BIO--PDFA.pdf

### Donald Trump's Executive Order on Strengthening the Child Welfare System (2020)

*On June 24, 2020, amid the coronavirus pandemic, President Donald Trump issued an executive order with the stated goal of promoting a child welfare system that "reduces the need to place children in foster care [and] achieves safe permanency for those children who must come into foster care . . . more quickly and effectively." Among other things, the order aims to increase collaboration between public, private, faith-based, and other community groups to help keep families together or to find children forever families; it instructs the Department of Health and Human Services (HHS) to develop a plan for addressing the barriers that kin and youth aging out of foster care may face in accessing existing federal assistance and benefits; and it requires HHS to improve data collection on the demographics of children waiting for adoption, the number and demographics of currently available foster families, the average foster parent retention rate, the targeted number of foster homes needed to meet the needs of foster children, and the average length of time required to complete foster and adoptive home certifications.*

**By the authority vested in me as President by the Constitution and the laws of the United States of America, it is hereby ordered as follows:**

Section 1. Purpose. Every child deserves a family. Our States and communities have both a legal obligation, and the privilege, to care for our Nation's most vulnerable children.

The best foster care system is one that is not needed in the first place. My Administration has been focused on prevention strategies that keep children safe while strengthening families so that children do not enter foster care unnecessarily. Last year, and for only the second time since 2011, the number of children in the foster care system declined, and for the third year in a row, the number of children entering foster care has declined.

But challenges remain. Too many young people who are in our foster care system wait years before finding the permanency of family. More than 400,000 children are currently in foster care. Of those, more than 124,000 children are waiting for adoption, with nearly 6 out of 10 (58.4 percent) having already become legally eligible for adoption.

More than 50 percent of the children waiting for adoption have been in foster care—without the security and constancy of a permanent family—for 2 years or more. The need for stability and timely permanency is particularly acute for children 9 years and older, children in sibling groups, and those with intellectual or physical disabilities.

Even worse, too many young men and women age out of foster care having never found a permanent, stable family. In recent years, approximately 20,000 young people have aged out of foster care each year in the United States. Research has shown that young people who age out of the foster care system are likely to experience significant, and significantly increased, life challenges—40 percent of such young people studied experienced homelessness; 50 percent were unemployed at age 24; 25 percent experienced post-traumatic stress disorder; and 71 percent became pregnant by age 21. These are unacceptable outcomes.

Several factors have contributed to the number of children who wait in foster care for extended periods. First, State and local child welfare agencies often do not have robust partnerships with private community organizations, including faith-based organizations. Second, those who step up to be resource families for children in foster care—including kin, guardians, foster parents, and adoptive parents—may lack adequate support. Third, too often the processes and systems meant to help children and families in crisis have instead created bureaucratic barriers that make it more difficult for these children and families to get the help they need.

It is the goal of the United States to promote a child welfare system that reduces the need to place children into foster care;

achieves safe permanency for those children who must come into foster care, and does so more quickly and more effectively; places appropriate focus on children who are waiting for adoption, especially those who are 9 years and older, are in sibling groups, or have disabilities; and decreases the proportion of young adults who age out of the foster care system.

Children from all backgrounds have the potential to become successful and thriving adults. Yet without a committed, loving family that can provide encouragement, stability, and a life-long connection, some children may never receive the support needed to realize that potential.

This order will help to empower families who answer the call to open their hearts and homes to children who need them. My Administration is committed to helping give as many children as possible the stability and support that family provides by dramatically improving our child welfare system.

Sec. 2. Encouraging Robust Partnerships Between State Agencies and Public, Private, Faith-based, and Community Organizations. (a) In order to facilitate close partnerships between State agencies and nongovernmental organizations, including public, private, faith-based, and community groups, the Secretary of Health and Human Services (the "Secretary") shall provide increased public access to accurate, up-to-date information relevant to strengthening the child welfare system, including by:

(i) Publishing data to aid in the recruitment of community support. Within 1 year of the date of this order and each year thereafter, the Secretary shall submit to the President, through the Assistant to the President for Domestic Policy, a report that provides information about typical patterns of entry, recent available counts of children in foster care, and counts of children waiting for adoption. To the extent appropriate and consistent with applicable law, including all privacy laws, this data will be disaggregated by county or other sub-State level, child age, placement type, and prior time in care.

(ii) Collecting needed data to preserve sibling connections.

(A) Within 2 years of the date of this order, the Secretary shall collect information from appropriate State and local agencies on the number of children in foster care who have siblings in foster care and who are not currently placed with their siblings.

(B) Within 3 years of the date of this order, to support the goal of keeping siblings together (42 U.S.C. 671(a)(31)(A)), the Secretary shall develop data analysis methods to report on the experience of children entering care in sibling groups, and the extent to which they are placed together. The Secretary's analysis shall also assess the extent to which siblings who are legally eligible for adoption achieve permanency together.

(iii) Expanding the number of homes for children and youth.

(A) Within 2 years of the date of this order, the Secretary shall develop a more rigorous and systematic approach to collecting State administrative data as part of the Child and Family Services Review required by section 1123A of the Social Security Act (the "Act") (42 U.S.C. 1320a–2a). Data collected shall include:

(1) demographic information for children in foster care and waiting for adoption;

(2) the number of currently available foster families and their demographic information;

(3) the average foster parent retention rate and average length of time foster parents remain certified;

(4) a target number of foster homes needed to meet the needs of children in foster care; and

(5) the average length of time it takes to complete foster and adoptive home certification.

(B) The Secretary shall ensure, to the extent consistent with applicable law, that States report to the Secretary regarding strategies for coordinating with nongovernmental organizations, including faith-based and community organizations, to recruit and support foster and adoptive families.

(b) Within 1 year of the date of this order, the Secretary shall issue guidance to Federal, State, and local agencies on partnering with nongovernmental organizations. This guidance shall include best practices for information sharing, providing needed services to families to support prevention of children entering foster care, family preservation, foster and adoptive home recruitment and retention, respite care, post-placement family support, and support for older youth. This guidance shall also make clear that faith-based organizations are eligible for partnerships under title IV-E of the Act (42 U.S.C. 670 et seq.), on an equal basis, consistent with the First Amendment to the Constitution.

Sec. 3. Improving Access to Adequate Resources for Caregivers and Youth. While many public, private, faith based, and community resources and other sources of support exist, many American caregivers still lack connection with and access to adequate resources. Within 1 year of the date of this order, the Secretary shall equip caregivers and those in care to meet their unique challenges, by:

(a) Expanding educational options. To the extent practicable, the Secretary shall use all existing technical assistance resources to promote dissemination and State implementation of the National Training and Development Curriculum, including, when appropriate, in non-classroom environments.

(b) Increasing the availability of trauma-informed training. The Secretary shall provide an enhanced, web-based, learning-management platform to house the information generated by the National Adoption Competency Mental Health Training Initiative. Access to this web-based training material will be provided free of charge for all child welfare and mental health practitioners.

(c) Supporting guardianship. The Secretary shall provide information to States regarding the importance and availability of funds to increase guardianship through the title IV-E Guardianship Assistance Program (42 U.S.C. 673), which provides Federal reimbursement for payments to guardians and for associated administrative costs. This information shall include which States have already opted into the program.

(d) Enhancing support for kinship care and youth exiting foster care. The Secretary shall establish a plan to address barriers to accessing existing Federal assistance and benefits for eligible individuals.

Sec. 4. Ensuring Equality of Treatment and Access for all Families. The Howard M. Metzenbaum Multiethnic Placement Act of 1994 (the "Multiethnic Placement Act") (Public Law 103-382), as amended, prohibits agencies from denying to any person the opportunity to become an adoptive or a foster parent on the basis of race, color, or national origin (42 U.S.C. 671(a)(18)(A)); prohibits agencies from delaying or denying the placement of a child for adoption or into foster care on the basis of race, color, or national origin (id. 671(a)(18)(B)); and requires agencies to diligently recruit a diverse base of foster and adoptive parents to better reflect the racial and ethnic makeup of children in out-of-home care (id. 662(b)(7)). To further the goals of the Multiethnic Placement Act, the Secretary shall:

(a) within 6 months of the date of this order, initiate a study regarding the implementation of these requirements nationwide;

(b) within 1 year of the date of this order, update guidance, as necessary, regarding implementation of the Multiethnic Placement Act; and

(c) within 1 year of the date of this order, publish guidance regarding the rights of parents, prospective parents, and children with disabilities (including intellectual, developmental, or physical disabilities).

Sec. 5. Improving Processes to Prevent Unnecessary Removal and Secure Permanency for Children. (a) Federal Review of Reasonable Effort Determinations and Timeliness Requirements.

(i) Within 2 years of the date of this order, the Secretary shall require that both the title IV-E reviews conducted pursuant to 45 CFR 1356.71 and the Child and Family Services Reviews conducted pursuant to 45 CFR 1355.31–1355.36 specifically and adequately assess the following requirements:

(A) reasonable efforts to prevent removal;

(B) filing a petition for Termination of Parental Rights within established statutory timelines and court processing of such petition, unless statutory exemptions apply;

(C) reasonable efforts to finalize permanency plans; and

(D) completion of relevant required family search and notifications and how such efforts are reviewed by courts.

(ii) In cases in which it is determined that statutorily required timelines and efforts have not been satisfied, the Secretary shall make use of existing authority in making eligibility determinations and disallowances consistent with section 1123A(b)(3)(4) of the Act (42 U.S.C. 1320a-2a(b)(3)(4)).

(iii) Within 2 years of the date of this order, the Secretary shall develop metrics to track permanency outcomes in each State and measure State performance over time.

(iv) Within 6 months of the date of this order, the Secretary shall provide guidance to States regarding flexibility in the use of Federal funds to support and encourage high-quality legal representation for parents and children, including pre-petition representation, in their efforts to prevent the removal of children from their families, safely reunify children and parents, finalize permanency, and ensure that their voices are heard and their rights are protected. The Secretary shall also ensure collection of data regarding State use of Federal funds for this purpose.

(b) Risk and Safety Assessments.

(i) Within 18 months of the date of this order, the Secretary shall collect States' individual standards for conducting risk and safety assessments required under section 106(b)(2)(B)(iv) of the Child Abuse Prevention and Treatment Act (42 U.S.C. 5106(b)(2)(B)(iv)).

(ii) Within 2 years of the date of this order, the Secretary shall outline reasonable best practice standards for risk and safety assessments, including how to address domestic violence and substance abuse.

Sec. 6. Indian Child Welfare Act. Nothing in this order shall alter the implementation of the Indian Child Welfare Act or replace the tribal consultation process.

Sec. 7. General Provisions. (a) Nothing in this order shall be construed to impair or otherwise affect:

(i) the authority granted by law to an executive department or agency, or the head thereof; or

(ii) the functions of the Director of the Office of Management and Budget relating to budgetary, administrative, or legislative proposals.

(b) This order shall be implemented consistent with applicable law and subject to the availability of appropriations.

(c) This order is not intended to, and does not, create any right or benefit, substantive or procedural, enforceable at law or in equity by any party against the United States, its departments, agencies, or entities, its officers, employees, or agents, or any other person.

DONALD J. TRUMP
THE WHITE HOUSE,
June 24, 2020.

**Source:** Trump, Donald J. "Presidential Executive Order Strengthening the Child Welfare System for America's Children." June 24, 2020. The White House. https://www.presidency.ucsb.edu/documents/executive-order-13930-strengthening-the-child-welfare-system-for-americas-children

## Introduction

This chapter provides an annotated list of selected books, articles, and reports on a variety of topics related to foster care in the United States, which offers readers a starting point for further research. Several magazines, journals, online forums, and nonprint sources are listed and annotated as well.

## Books

Aguirre, Lisa. 2018. *Faces of Foster Care: Messages of Hope, Hurt and Truth*. Grand Rapids, MI: WestBow Press.

> In this collection of 20 mini-memoirs, Lisa Aguirre, a longtime volunteer at the Washington, DC, Family & Youth Initiative, strives to make readers more aware of older youth in foster care. Aguirre provides firsthand accounts of people from around the country, including former foster youth, social workers, adoptive parents, and a child welfare administrator, all of whom were involved in some way with the foster care system. Through their stories, readers learn about the nearly insurmountable odds foster youth face in terms of quality of care and trying to establish a life beyond the system and how child welfare in this country can improve through a shift in focus and allocation of funds.

---

A foster child jumps rope at her new home as her mother looks on. Permanency and predictability of care are essential for improving life outcomes for foster youth. (Rmarmion/Dreamstime.com)

Berry, Kristin. 2020. *Keep the Doors Open: Lessons Learned from a Year of Foster Parenting.* Eugene, OR: Harvest House Publishers.

> In this autobiography, Kristin Berry, an adoptive mother of 8 children, recounts her experiences as a foster parent of 23 children over the course of nine years. Berry provides personal experiences to help readers gain an understanding of the heartache and pain sometimes involved in foster parenting, but she also highlights the adventures and unexpected joys and triumphs of foster parenting. She encourages readers to consider opening their doors to children in need of temporary loving homes.

Brown, Waln K., John R. Sieta, and Carle O'Neil. 2009–2020. *Foster Care* (5 book series). Tallahassee, FL: William Gladden Foundation Press.

> *Foster Care* is a five-book series edited and published between 2009 and 2020 by child welfare professionals Waln K. Brown, John R. Sieta, and Carle O'Neil. The first book, *Growing Up in the Care of Strangers: The Experiences, Insights and Recommendations of Eleven Former Foster Youth*, provides child welfare and social work professionals with insightful feedback from former foster youth who grew up in a variety of placement settings and went on to become college-educated professionals. The second book, *A Foster Care Manifesto: Defining the Alumni Movement*, is written by foster care alumni for current and former foster youth. It outlines how they can use their experiences to transform the foster care system for the better. The third book, *Best Interests of the Child? A Brief History of Foster Care in America*, provides a critical examination of the American child welfare system, arguing that it has not always been dedicated or designed to serve the best interest of children. The fourth book, *Adoption in America: What You Need to Know before You Adopt*, is a concise handbook and compilation

of resources for prospective adoptive parents. The fifth and final book in the series, *Emancipating from the Care of Strangers: The Experiences, Insights, and Recommendations of Ten Former Foster Kids*, highlights the stories of youth who emancipated directly from placement with no family support or preparation for life outside of care. The book uses the actual experiences of emancipated youth to provide insight into what is required to better prepare foster youth for life after foster care.

Ecke, Leigh. 2009. *Flux*. Alexandria, VA: Foster Care Alumni of America.

Published by Foster Care Alumni of America, *Flux* features contributions from a diverse group of more than 100 foster care alumni who explore their emotional journeys from foster care to adulthood. The authors provide advice to foster youth transitioning out of the system based on their own experiences on topics such as finding and developing a unique identity, creating and strengthening a support system, handling biological family relationships, developing intimacy with others, and navigating parenting issues.

Fahlberg, Vera I. 2012. *A Child's Journey through Placement*. Philadelphia: Jessica Kingsley Publishers.

In this authoritative text, Vera I. Fahlberg, MD, shares information and advice garnered from years of experience working with children. Her goal is to help child welfare workers, foster and adoptive parents, educators, and mental health professionals better understand and become more effective in their relationships with individual children who are cared for in an out-of-home placement. Fahlberg provides a wealth of expertise on topics ranging from the significance of attachment and separation to the developmental stages specific to adoption children. She also offers practical advice on case planning, managing behavior, and minimizing trauma caused by moves. Themes present throughout the book include the significance of interpersonal relationships, the necessity of building alliances with children and adults by enhancing communication skills, and the importance of development plans for the continuity of relationships throughout a lifetime.

Gelles, Richard. 2017. *Out of Harm's Way: Creating an Effective Child Welfare System*. New York: Oxford University Press.

This book, written by Richard Gelles, a prominent researcher and former dean of the University of Pennsylvania School of Social Policy and Practice, calls attention to the many ways that the child welfare system fails to ensure the safety and well-being of maltreated children. The book is divided into two parts. Part I, *Tragedy and Its Aftermath*, provides examples of dysfunction in the system. Gelles specifically focuses on four critical deficient aspects of the system. The first is the need to decide who is the client. He argues that child welfare systems attempt to balance the needs of the child and those of the parents, often failing both. The second is that child welfare practitioners often do not have effective tools at their disposal when making pivotal decisions regarding child abuse and neglect, case goals, and placement. Third, Gelles argues that federal funding creates perverse incentives that keep children in out-of-home placements. Finally, Gelles maintains that the more than 20,000 youth aging out of the system each year—who are suddenly thrust into homelessness, unemployment, welfare, and oppressive disadvantage—are indicative of child neglect within the system itself.

In part II, *Centers of Gravity*, Gelles provides solutions for each of these dysfunctional aspects of the system and introduces empirical research as a blueprint for reform. Gelles ultimately concludes that the child welfare system will only operate effectively if it first and foremost begins to prioritize the interests and needs of children over and above those of their parents.

Mooney, Robert P. K. 2020. *A Foster Kid's Road to Success*. Salt Lake City: RPKM Publishing.

In this inspiring memoir, Robert Mooney tells the story of his youth in foster care from age 6 until he aged out at 18, during which time he changed homes 20 times. He recounts how athletics, music, and his imagination helped him cope with the trauma of abuse, neglect, loss of family members, and the lack of a stable home. Determined to lead a fulfilling life despite his troubled past, Mooney eventually got married, started a family, and became a very successful lawyer. Mooney wrote this book to inspire teens who are likely to age out of foster care and to teach them important lessons needed to succeed in life after aging out.

Rymph, Catherine E. 2017. *Raising Government Children: A History of Foster Care and the American Welfare State*. Chapel Hill: University of North Carolina Press.

In this detailed volume, Catherine E. Rymph, an associate professor of history at the University of Missouri, traces the evolution of the modern American foster care system from its inception in the 1930s through the 1970s. Her coverage specifically focuses on the ideas, debates, and policies surrounding foster care and foster parents' relationship to public welfare. She begins by surveying how modern foster care originated in programs to support dependent children dating back to the colonial period. She then addresses the significance of the New Deal to the development of publicly funded foster care and its relationship to the nascent welfare state. From there, she examines the impact that World War II had on increasing the need for foster care and exacerbating the tensions over women's roles as workers, mothers, and caregivers. Rymph next addresses the ambiguity of foster parents' roles as both parents and workers in the postwar period and the emergence of the pernicious idea that foster children were inherently damaged. She concludes with an examination of policy changes of the 1960s, which she argues made foster care a more punitive system firmly linked to public assistance, in which children of color were overrepresented.

## Articles and Reports

Davis, Noy, Amy Harfield, and Elisa Weichel. 2019. *A Child's Right to Counsel: A National Report Card on Legal Representation for Abused and Neglected Children*. 4th ed. First Star Institute and the Children's Advocacy Institute. Accessed January 15, 2021. http://www.caichildlaw.org/Misc/RTC4.pdf

In 1974, Congress passed the Child Abuse Prevention and Treatment Act (CAPTA), which first addressed the representation of abused and neglected children in dependency proceedings by requiring these children to be represented by a guardian ad litem (GAL), an individual appointed by the court to represent the best interests of a minor child in legal proceedings. CAPTA has since been amended to clarify that lawyers may be appointed and that GAL's must have appropriate training in early children and adolescent development and must obtain a clear understanding of the child's situation and needs so they can advocate in the best interest of the child. Building upon CAPTA mandates, individual states have passed laws to improve the legal representation of children in dependency proceedings.

In 2007, the First Star Institute published the first edition of *A Child's Right to Counsel*, a report evaluating state laws related to the legal representation of children in civil child abuse and neglect proceedings. The report assigned

each of the 50 states and Washington, DC, with a letter grade based on the following criteria: whether state
law mandates that attorneys be appointed for children
in dependency proceedings; whether state law defines
the duration of an attorney's appointment; the extent
to which children receive client-directed representation
and to which state law requires specialized education and
training for a child's counsel; whether state law expressly
gives the child the legal status and rights of an adult
party; and whether a state applies rules of professional
conduct regarding immunity from liability and confidentiality to attorneys representing children in dependency
proceedings.

This fourth edition of the report further documents
how states are implementing laws to promote the effective
representation of children and confirms that states continue to move in the direction of quality representation
of children. It encourages those states that are still receiving a poor or failing grade to make use of existing federal
support to help their courts achieve better outcomes for
abused and neglected children.

Denby, Romona, Efren Gomez, and Richard Reeves. 2017.
*Care and Connections: Bridging Relational Gaps for Foster Youths.*
Washington, DC: Center for Children and Families at Brook-
ings. Accessed February 1, 2021. https://www.brookings.edu
/wp-content/uploads/2017/09/09-14-2017_fostercarereport2.pdf
Youth aging out of foster care face poor life outcomes in
terms of emotional well-being, educational and occu-
pational attainment, and housing stability compared to
their peers in the general population and those who have
achieved permanency while in care. Many of these disadvantages are perpetuated due to the lack of supportive,
healthy, and consistent relationships with adults. Although
research suggests that these types of relationships improve
the life chances of foster youth, there have been relatively

few major attempts to incorporate this insight into programs and practice.

In 2011, the Administration for Children and Families, Children's Bureau, funded four projects in different parts of the United States with the goal of helping increase relationship-building skills for youth transitioning out of care: the DREAMR Project in Clark County, Nevada; the Connections Project in San Diego, California; Adult Connections in Chicago, Illinois; and Work Wonders in Providence, Rhode Island. This report analyzes the mixed results and promising outcomes of these projects and explores the challenges of implementing and evaluating relationship-based interventions in child welfare. The report concludes with recommendations for practitioners and researchers interested in increasing relational capacities for foster youth.

Dworsky, Amy, Mark E. Courtney, Jennifer Hook, Adam Brown, Colleen Cary, Kara Love, Vanessa Vorhies, et al. 2011. *Midwest Evaluation of the Adult Functioning of Former Foster Youth*. Chicago: Chapin Hall at the University of Chicago. Accessed October 12, 2020. https://www.chapinhall.org /research/midwest-evaluation-of-the-adult-functioning-of -former-foster-youth/#

The Midwest Evaluation of the Adult Function of Former Foster Youth (Midwest Study) is a longitudinal study that has been following a sample of young people from Iowa, Wisconsin, and Illinois as they transition out of foster care into adulthood. It is a collaborative effort involving Chapin Hall at the University of Chicago, the University of Wisconsin Survey Center, and the public child welfare agencies in Illinois, Iowa, and Wisconsin. Foster youth in the three participating states were eligible to participate in the study if they had entered care before their 16th birthday, were still in care at age 17, and had been removed from home for reasons other than delinquency.

Baseline survey data were collected from 732 participants when they were 17 or 18 years old. Participants were then reinterviewed at ages 19, 21, 23 or 24, and 26. The goal of the study was to demonstrate how former foster care youth are faring in several areas after they age out, ranging from employment records, living arrangements, and academic experiences to criminal justice system involvement, physical health, familial relationships, and pregnancy rates. The findings reveal that young people are aging out of foster care without the knowledge, skills, and resources to thrive on their own. The data also suggests that extending foster care until age 21 may be associated with better outcomes, at least in some domains.

Dworsky, Amy, Cheryl Smithgall, and Mark E. Courtney. 2014. "Supporting Youth Transitioning out of Foster Care: Issue Brief 1: Education Programs." OPRE Report #2014-66. Washington, DC: Office of Planning, Research and Evaluation, Administration for Children and Families, U.S. Department of Health and Human Services. Accessed February 16, 2021. https://www.acf.hhs.gov/sites/default/files/documents/opre/chafee_education_brief_final_to_opre_012015.pdf

In 1999, Congress passed, and President Clinton signed into law the Foster Care Independence Act, which amended Title IV-E of the Social Security Act to establish the Chafee Foster Care Independence Program (the Chafee Program). This program doubled the maximum amount of funds potentially available to states for independent living services for transition-age foster youth and gave states greater discretion over how they use those funds. In addition to other independent living services, states were authorized to provide a wide range of services aimed at promoting educational attainment and economic self-sufficiency. The Foster Care Independence Act additionally required that a small percentage of Chafee Program funding be set aside for rigorous evaluation of state programs and an assessment of their effects on employment, education, and personal development. In 2003, the Administration for Children and Families (ACF) contracted with the Urban Institute, Chapin Hall at the University of Chicago, and the National Opinion Research Center to conduct a Multi-Site Evaluation of Foster Youth Programs.

In 2014, ACF again contracted with the Urban Institute and Chapin Hall to plan for the next generation of evaluation activities funded by the Chafee Program. As part of that process, the research team developed 10 categories of independent living programs for youth transitioning out of foster care into adulthood. This brief is one of three that focus on evaluating programs providing services to youth transitioning out of care in the areas of education, employment, and financial literacy and asset building. This first brief in the series concentrates attention on the category of programs that aim to improve educational outcomes. It highlights why education services are important to youth currently or formally in care, what we know about the current types of programs and services offered, and the degree to which these services are effective. The brief additionally addresses research gaps and how the available evidence should inform planning for future evaluation.

Edelstein, Sara, and Christopher Lowenstein. 2014. "Supporting Youth Transitioning out of Foster Care: Issue Brief 3: Employment Programs." OPRE Report #2014-70. Washington, DC: Office of Planning, Research and Evaluation, Administration for Children and Families, U.S. Department of Health and Human Services. Accessed February 16, 2021. https://www.urban.org/sites/default/files/publication/43271/2000128-Supporting-Youth-Transitioning-out-of-Foster-Care-2000128-Supporting-Youth-Transitioning-out-of-Foster-Care-Employment-Programs.pdf

This is the third brief in a three-part series produced by the Urban Institute in partnership with Chapin Hall under contract with the Administration for Children and Families (ACF) that focus on evaluating state programs funded by the Chafee Foster Care Independence Program that provide services to youth transitioning out of care in the areas of education, employment, and financial literacy and asset building. This final brief focuses on the category of programs and initiatives aimed at improving employment prospects for transition-age youth. It highlights the importance of programs that help foster youth develop the skills necessary to succeed in the workplace and connect them to employment. It reviews what we know about the current types of programs and services offered and the degree to which these services are effective. The brief additionally addresses research gaps and how the available evidence should inform planning for future evaluation.

Edelstein, Sara, and Christopher Lowenstein. 2014. "Supporting Youth Transitioning out of Foster Care: Issue Brief 2: Financial Literacy and Asset Building Programs." OPRE Report #2014-69. Washington, DC: Office of Planning, Research and Evaluation, Administration for Children and Families, U.S. Department of Health and Human Services. Accessed February 16, 2021. https://www.urban.org/sites /default/files/publication/43276/2000129-Supporting-Youth -Transitioning-out-of-Foster-Care-Financial-Literacy-and -Asset-Building-Programs.pdf

This brief is the second of three produced by the Urban Institute in partnership with Chapin Hall under contract with the Administration for Children and Families (ACF) that focus on evaluating state programs funded by the Chafee Foster Care Independence Program that provide services to youth transitioning out of care in the areas of education, employment, and financial literacy and asset building. This brief evaluates programs designed to improve financial literacy and asset building among transition-age youth. It highlights why financial literacy and asset building are important to youth currently or formally in care, what we know about the current types of programs and services offered, and the degree to which these services are effective. The brief additionally addresses research gaps and how the available evidence should inform planning for future evaluation.

Fernandes-Alcantara, Adrienne L., Sarah W. Caldwell, and Emilie Stoltzfus. 2017. "Child Welfare: Oversight of Psychotropic Medication for Children in Foster Care." *Congressional Research Service* R42466. February. Accessed January 20, 2021. https://crsreports.congress.gov/product/pdf/R/R43466

Because of their history of abuse, neglect, and other forms of trauma, children in foster care often experience mental health issues requiring treatment and care. Data compiled over the past decade, however, demonstrates that children in foster care are far more likely than their peers in the general population to be prescribed psychotropic medication and in higher doses. The overuse of psychotropics by children in foster care has come under intense scrutiny by policy makers and stakeholders in the child welfare field. The U.S. Congress has taken a strong interest in oversight of prescription medications used by children in care, and members have sponsored various hearings and fact-finding forums.

This report provides a background on the mental health needs of children in foster care and the prevalence of psychotropic medication use among these children. It then discusses congressional oversight and efforts by the U.S. Department of Health and Human Services (HHS) to aid states in ensuring appropriate use of psychotropic medications for children in care. The report concludes with a discussion of state efforts to monitor the use of these medications for foster children.

Font, Sara A., and Kathryn Maguire-Jack. 2020. "It's Not 'Just Poverty': Educational, Social, and Economic Functioning among Young Adults Exposed to Childhood Neglect, Abuse, and Poverty." *Child Abuse and Neglect* 101.

An overwhelming majority of cases in the U.S. Child Protective Services (CPS) system involve some form of neglect, which is generally defined as a failure to meet the basic needs of a child. These typically include the child's need for food, shelter, clothing, medical care, and supervision. Because definitions of neglect encompass the deprivation of material goods, some researchers and journalists have questioned whether neglect is distinguishable from economic hardship and poverty and whether labeling parents as perpetrators of neglect punishes poverty.

In this article, Sarah Font of Pennsylvania State University and Katherine Maguire Jack of the University of Michigan examine 29,154 individuals born between 1993 and 1996 in Milwaukee County who either received food assistance or were reported to CPS before age 16. They specifically compare outcomes for those who were investigated by CPS for neglect or abuse in early childhood and adolescence to those who experienced poverty but not CPS involvement. Font and Maguire-Jack's findings demonstrate that there is a statistically significant difference in outcomes for children who grew up in poverty but did not experience CPS involvement and those whose parents were investigated by CPS for abuse and neglect. CPS allegations of neglect are an important risk factor distinct from poverty alone for adverse adult outcomes in all domains. Consequently, targeted efforts to prevent and treat the specific effects of neglect warrant greater priority than those that merely seek to alleviate financial constraints.

Munson, Michelle R., Susan E. Smalling, Renée Spencer, Lionel D. Scott Jr., and Elizabeth M. Tracy. 2010. "A Steady

Presence in the Midst of Change: Non-Kin Natural Mentors in the Lives of Older Youth Existing Foster Care." *Children and Youth Services Review* 32:527–535.

The importance of supportive relationships with adults in the lives of youth, particularly those who are aging out of foster care, has been well documented. While various programs exist to pair foster youth with adult mentors, another form of mentorship known as natural mentorship exists when youth identify with someone as a mentor whom they have encountered in their community but have not been formally matched with, such as a neighbor, teacher, coach, or service provider. The authors of this study explore the nature of nonkin natural mentoring relationships among 19-year-old youth in the process of aging out of the foster care system with the goal of illuminating the qualities of natural mentoring relationships and the kinds of support they offer to youth transitioning out of care.

Participating youth who reported having a natural mentoring relationship were asked a series of qualitative questions about their reported relationship. These youth described the qualities of their natural mentors that were important to them, the specific features of their natural mentoring relationships that they perceived to be especially helpful, and the various kinds of support these relationships had offered to them. The authors conclude by discussing implications for social work policy, practice, and research.

Schaefer Riley, Naomi. 2019. "Honor Your (Foster) Mothers and Fathers." American Enterprise Institute. September. Accessed November 9, 2020. https://www.aei.org/research-products/report/honor-your-foster-mothers-and-fathers/

Over the past decade, the number of youth in foster care has reached historic levels due in large part to the opioid crisis. At the same time, many states are experiencing a shortage and even a decline of eligible foster homes to take children in.

In this brief report, Naomi Schaefer Riley discusses the challenge of attracting and retaining good foster families. She explores policy proposals that offer greater financial incentives to foster families and determines that while there are certain benefits to increased compensation for care, there are reasons to fear that offering more money could backfire and result in worse care for children. She concludes that that best way to attract and retain high-quality foster families is to treat them with greater respect. Riley asserts that foster parents need more information to properly care for children in their homes and to have a greater voice in the system.

Sheffield, Rachel. 2020. "A Place to Call Home: Improving Foster Care and Adoption Policy to Give More Children a Stable Family." U.S. Congress, Joint Economic Committee, Social Capital Project Report No. 4-20 (August). Accessed December 10, 2020. https://www.jec.senate.gov/public/index .cfm/republicans/2020/9/a-place-to-call-home-improving -foster-care-and-adoption-policy-to-give-more-children-a -stable-family

The Joint Economic Committee (JEC) was created as a congressional committee under the Employment Act of 1946. Chairmanship alternates between the Senate and the House every Congress, and the primary task of the committee is to review economic conditions and recommend improvements in economic policy. Within the JEC, the Social Capital Project is a multiyear research effort that investigates the evolving nature, quality, and importance of social relationships, which includes families, communities, workplaces, and religious congregations. In this report, Rachel Sheffield, a senior policy advisor for the Social Capital Project, investigates the issues that stand in the way of connecting adoptive children with loving homes. According to the report, these include a child welfare system that is often unsupportive of foster parents, government actions that are pushing faith-based foster care and adoption providers out of service, child welfare systems that keep foster children languishing in temporary placements when they would benefit from permanent adoptive placements, and policies that fail to support infant adoption when expectant parents do not desire a child or when it is unlikely expectant parents will be able to provide safe care. The report provides suggestions for how government and civil society can work together to ensure better outcomes in these areas.

Wulczyn, Fred, Britany Orlebeke, Kristen Hislop, Florie Schmits, Jamie McClanahan, and Lilian Huang. 2018. *The Dynamics of Foster Home Recruitment and Retention*. Center for State Child Welfare Data. September. Accessed February 16, 2021. https://fcda.chapinhall.org/wp-content/uploads/2018/10/Foster-Home-Report-Final_FCDA_October2018.pdf

This study uses longitudinal administrative data to answer questions about the number of foster homes that open and close each year and the characteristics of the homes and the foster parents; the reasons for home closures; the length of service of foster homes (the continuous period during which a foster home was eligible to receive foster children); and the occupancy of foster homes (the time a home actually received placements). Through an analysis of the underlying dynamics of this data, the study highlights insights that can help public agencies more effectively approach the issue of foster home recruitment and retention.

## Journals, Magazines, and Online Forums

The Center for Child Welfare Data

The Center for Child Welfare Data was established in 2004 as part of the University of Chicago's Chapin Hall research center with the goal of providing states, policy makers, child welfare agencies, and staff with actionable research that can be used to make evidence-based decisions that will improve outcomes for children and families. The Data Center works with child welfare agencies to nail down mission-critical questions about system performances. One example is the mission to keep children in foster care for as little time as possible.

To properly assess system performance in this area, the following questions must be examined: How long do children typically stay in foster care? Do some children stay longer than others? Has the length of stay in care changed over time? How effective are our efforts to reduce duration in foster care? The Data Center works with child welfare agencies to nail down essential performance questions and then uses state-of-the-art analyses and best practices in performance measurement to ensure that the answers to those questions are accurate, representative, and free of bias.

The Data Center also pursues its own research program focused on the effects of child welfare policy and research evidence use among child agencies. Foundation- and government-supported research has included using technology for assessing young people's mental health, adolescents leaving care to permanency, understanding complexity in the foster care system, and research evidence used by child welfare agencies.

Child Welfare Information Gateway

Child Welfare Information Gateway is a service of the Administration for Children and Families, Children's Bureau, that aims to promote the safety, permanency, and well-being of children, youth, and families by connecting child welfare, adoption, and related professionals as well as the public to valuable information, research, statistics, and other resources and tools. Child Welfare Information Gateway provides access to print and electronic publications, websites, databases, and online learning tools on the following topics: family-centered practice, child abuse and neglect, supporting and preserving families, out-of-home care, achieving and maintaining permanency, adoption, child welfare agency administration and management, and systemwide issues.

### Child Welfare Journal

Launched in 1922, the *Child Welfare Journal* is a bimonthly peer-reviewed journal published by the Child Welfare League of American with the goal of keeping readers abreast of the special problems facing millions of America's children and youth, including those who are homeless, abused, new to this country, or severely disabled. The journal links the latest findings in child welfare and related research with best practice, policy, and program development into one innovative resource for child welfare and associated professionals. Typically, two issues per year are special issues on specific topics. Recent special issues have focused on topics such as the challenges facing older teens and young adults as they navigate the foster care system, age out, and prepare for adulthood; empirical research on kinship care; and parental substance abuse among families involved with dependency courts.

### Child Welfare Monitor

The *Child Welfare Monitor* is the blog of child advocate, research, and policy analyst Marie K. Cohen. In January 2015, Cohen left her job as a social worker in the District of Columbia's child welfare system, expressing despair that the system did not prioritize the welfare of children in its policies. She became a member of both the District of Columbia Citizen Review Panel for child welfare and Child Fatality Review Commission and founded the *Child Welfare Monitor* to provide science-based articles that advocate for a system that prioritizes the needs of the child over and above other values.

*Children's Voice*

   *Children's Voice* is a seasonal magazine published by the Child Welfare League of America (CWLA), a coalition of hundreds of public and private agencies that serve vulnerable children and families. The magazine features a diverse range of views on a wide array of topics with the goal of encouraging discussion and debate among CWLA members and the general public about how to best ensure the well-being of children and families. Recent issues have covered topics such as the legacy and current practice of the Indian Child Welfare Act, best practices for LGBT Youth and Families, supporting sibling relationships for children in care, and transforming responsible fatherhood practice and policy.

*Foster Focus*

   *Foster Focus* is the nation's only monthly magazine dealing exclusively with the foster care industry and is one of the leading sources of foster care news. Creator, owner, and editor Chris Chmielewski spent five years in foster care before aging out of the system. He created the magazine as a resource on foster care news and developments for judges, lawyers, caseworkers, advocates, foster parents, adoptive parents, foster care alumni, and guidance counselors, among others.

*Fostering Families Today*

   *Fostering Families Today* is a comprehensive bimonthly magazine for foster families navigating the complexities of the foster care system, whether they are kinship caregivers or other types of foster or adoptive parents. Published monthly by the nonprofit journalism organization Fostering Media Connections, *Fostering Families Today* includes articles highlighting resources, expert opinions, personal stories from foster families and youth in care, and practical advice and information on the latest evidence-based practices for supporting children and youth who come from traumatic backgrounds. Recent issues have covered topics such as understanding child welfare policy, childhood trauma and attachment, navigating relationships with birth families, foster reunification, and challenges unique to kinship care.

### The Imprint

*The Imprint* is a leading daily online news publication dedicated to rigorous, in-depth journalism focused on the nation's child welfare and juvenile justice systems as well as the housing, economic, mental health, and educational issues faced by vulnerable children and families. It is a publication of Fostering Media Connections (FMC), a nonprofit organization that uses the power of media and journalism to lead the conversation about children, youth, and families in the United States.

### Journal of Foster Care

The *Journal of Foster Care* (*JFC*) is a newly established, peer-reviewed, open-access, online publication dedicated to the dissemination of quality scholarly works encompassing all areas of foster care, kinship care, and other nonparental custodial environments in the United States. It is the only U.S.-based peer-reviewed journal focused solely on foster care. *JFC*'s first issue included essays on educational outcomes for foster youth in congregate care, trauma-informed approaches to students in foster care, and an autoethnographic tale of a Louisiana mother's personal journey of fostering and adopting.

### Journal of Public Child Welfare

The *Journal of Public Child Welfare* is a peer-reviewed journal that is released five times a year. The journal aims to help social workers, psychologists, counselors, juvenile court judges, attorneys, and other child welfare professionals stay informed about the latest findings and important issues in public child welfare by publishing quantitative, qualitative, and mixed-methods theory-based or applied research, cogent reviews of the literature, policy analyses, and program evaluation articles. Recent articles have focused on topics such as the effects of neighborhood factors on social-behavioral outcomes of children involved in the child welfare system, foster parent perspectives and experiences with public child welfare, predicting substance use treatment completion and reunification among family treatment court-involved parent-child dyads, and a review of the literature on policies and practices designed to identify and care for children prenatally exposed to alcohol and other drugs.

*Represent*

*Represent*, formerly *Foster Care Youth United*, is a quarterly magazine written by and for youth in foster care. It is published by Youth Communication, a nonprofit organization that helps marginalized youth strengthen the social, emotional, and literacy skills that contribute to success in school, work, and life. The core writing staff consists of teens who work one-on-one with adult editors in the New York City newsroom. Teen readers can also submit poems and letters to the editor and can publish stories by working with editors through email. Many of the stories included in the magazine come with lessons and activities for independent living staff, social workers, and teachers. Topics covered include dealing with anger, addiction, juvenile justice, aging out, LGBTQ, college, mental health, dating, sex and pregnancy, work and money, friends, incarcerated parents, adoption, and the foster care system generally.

*Rise*

*Rise* is a newsletter written by parents who are receiving reunification or preventative services from child welfare agencies or who have had their children removed by the child welfare system. It is a sister program to *Represent* magazine, which is published by Youth Communication and is written by and for foster youth.

## Nonprint Sources

*The Children's Bureau, 1912–2012: A Passionate Commitment. A Legacy of Leadership.* 2012. Directed by the Children's Bureau. Accessed December 7, 2020. https://www.childwelfare.gov /more-tools-resources/resources-from-childrens-bureau/cb -videos/

In this video series, produced by the U.S. Department of Health and Human Services' Children's Bureau (CB), past and present CB leaders and staff speak about their commitment to the CB's work and how that passion translates into better outcomes for children, families, and communities. The series includes seven spotlight videos on the key topics of "Assistance to States and Tribes," "Child Welfare Leadership," "Collaboration in Child Welfare," "Data and Technology," "Office on Child Abuse and Neglect," "Working with American Indian Tribes," and "Working with Grantees."

*Different Stories.* 2018. Produced by Zimabwe Davies and directed by Alan Kimara Dixon. Accessed February 15, 2021. https://vimeo.com/287031130

*Different Stories* is a short documentary produced by Zimbabwe Davies and directed by Alan Kimara Dixon that demonstrates the complex stories and powerful artistic creations of youth who have experienced foster care. The film is a follow-up to Davies's and Dixon's first film, *Enter a Challenger, Exit a Champion*, which tells the story of Davies's own life during and after foster care. *Different Stories* showcases the artistic talents of three former foster youth, now in their twenties, and tells the story of their journey navigating the challenges of the foster care system. The film premiered at a September 2018 screening in Oakland, California, by nonprofit foster youth service provider Beyond Emancipation, where producer Zimbabwe Davies has served as a residential counselor for more than 10 years.

*Foster.* 2018. Directed by Mark Jonathan Harris. Los Angeles: HBO.

*Foster* is an HBO documentary that highlights the inner workings of the Los Angeles County Department of Children and Family Services, the largest child protection agency in the United States, and tracks the stories of several individuals involved in the system. Among the people the show follows is a 60-year-old woman, a veteran foster parent, who is currently mothering four at home; a foster child turned social worker; a 16-year-old who winds up under court supervision after an alleged fight in his group home and a positive test for marijuana; a couple trying to win their newborn daughter back after the mother tested positive for cocaine during labor; and a former foster youth struggling to stay in college.

*The Trials of Gabriel Fernandez.* 2020. Directed by Brian Knappenberger. Los Angeles: Luminant Media. Netflix.

*The Trials of Gabriel Fernandez* is a six-part documentary miniseries that first aired on Netflix. It recounts the heart-wrenching true story of the abuse and murder of an eight-year-old boy from Palmdale, California, by his mother and her boyfriend and the ways that the system failed to protect him. Through court transcripts and interviews with members of Gabriel's family, journalists, attorneys, and others, the series details the systemic failures that left a young child in such a terrible situation despite ample warning signs and tangible evidence of dangerous levels of abuse and torture in his home. The film raises the issue of systemic failures in child welfare agencies, including overloaded caseworkers, that allow severe child abuse to continue and contribute to the failure to remove children from abusive situations when necessary.

*Unadopted*. 2020. Directed by Noel Anaya. Oakland, CA: YR Media. Accessed October 4, 2020. https://unadoptedfilm.com/
  *Unadopted* is a short documentary produced by YR Media and 22-year-old former foster youth Noel Anaya that draws attention to the large number of foster youth who age out of the system without ever being adopted. Anaya himself entered foster care at age one and was never adopted after 20 years in the system. The film follows Anaya as he investigates court records and interviews social workers to find answers about his identity and upbringing and to discover why he was never adopted. Anaya interweaves his own story with the stories of three other teens who are confronted with the question of whether to emancipate from foster care, to opt into extended care, or to pursue a forever family.

*Unwanted*. 2017. Directed by Joey Papa. Accessed February 15, 2021. https://www.youtube.com/watch?v=RV9xZW3ghP4
  *Unwanted* is a short documentary film that aims to raise awareness of the foster care crisis in southeastern Wisconsin and throughout the nation. The film highlights the inadequate number of foster homes for children in Milwaukee County and the fact the system is not growing at the same rate that children are coming into the system. Because children are harder to place the older they get, the crisis is particularly acute for children eight years old and above. When a foster home is not available, these children may be temporarily placed in a group home or a hotel or may even be transported to another county hours away from their home.
  Through personal narratives of individuals who have suffered because of a shortage of care, the film enlightens

viewers to the reality of the crisis and makes a plea for individuals and communities to take action to rescue children from a life of chaos and abuse. The film also highlights the work of Safe Homes for Children, an organization that seeks to intervene in the lives of families facing addiction or other crises and to provide temporary care for children so that their parents can get the help they need before their children are forcibly removed and placed in state care.

Below is a chronological list of some of the defining moments and major events impacting the development of foster care in America.

**1562**   English Poor Laws allow the placement of poor children in indentured service until they come of age. This practice is eventually imported into the United States and becomes the basis for placing orphaned, abused, and neglected children in homes.

**1600s**   Many localities throughout the American colonies begin to codify the English Poor Law tradition, which provides for children to be placed with a family and indentured to protect them from extreme neglect and poverty.

**1636**   Benjamin Eaton, who lived in the nation's first colony of Jamestown, becomes the nation's first recorded foster child when he is apprenticed out by his widowed mother.

**1729**   Ursuline nuns establish the first orphan asylum in North America for the surviving children of the Natchez Indian attack on the French settlement at Natchez, Mississippi.

---

A foster child draws a sun and house on asphalt in a park. Once children are placed in foster care, the primary goal of state social service agencies is to make every attempt to reunify them with their families—and when reunification is not possible, to find them a permanent, safe, and loving home. (Deyangeorgiev/Dreamstime.com)

**1800**    In the early 1800s, growing poverty in America's developing cities increases the need for out-of-home care for children. Many poor children and orphans who lacked a suitable caretaker are housed in almshouses, insane asylums, and even adult prisons. During this period, religious communities begin to establish orphanages throughout the country. Later in the century, as state legislatures start to outlaw the placement of children in almshouses, public funding contributes to the expansion of orphanages.

**1851**    Massachusetts passes the first modern adoption law, the Adoption of Children Act. By requiring judges to determine whether the adoptive parents had "sufficient ability to bring up the child" and whether "it is fit and proper that such adoption should take effect," the law represents a turning point for children's rights by focusing on the well-being of the child in addition to the interests of adults.

**1853**    Concerned by the large number of abused and homeless children living in squalid slums on the streets of New York City, Congregational minister Charles Loring Brace founds the Children's Aid Society, which establishes lodging houses and industrial schools for children. A year later, Brace begins a "placing-out" program, known as the *orphan train movement*, in which approximately 200,000 orphaned or abandoned children from Eastern cities are sent to live with families in small towns and rural areas, primarily on farms in the Midwest.

**1860s**    The State of Massachusetts begins paying board to families who take care of children too young to be indentured.

**1874**    The New York chapter of the American Society for the Prevention of Cruelty to Animals takes on the case of eight-year-old orphan Mary Ellen Wilson, who received severe beatings from her caretakers. Her foster mother is convicted of assault and battery and given a one-year sentence. This case leads to the establishment of the New York Society for the Prevention of Cruelty to Children (NYSPCC) and other similar organizations.

**1885**    Pennsylvania passes the first licensing law making it a misdemeanor to care for two or more unrelated children without a license.

**1893**    South Dakota begins providing subsidies to the Children's Home Society.

**1899**    The first juvenile court system in the world is established by the Illinois General Assembly in Cook County, Illinois.

**1900**    State social service agencies begin to consider children's individual needs when making placements and to inspect foster homes and supervise foster parents.

**1909**    President Theodore Roosevelt calls the first White Conference on the Care of Dependent Children in response to concerns about the institutional placement of children. The conferees recommend that measures be taken to prevent the removal of children from their homes and to place those that do have to be removed due to exceptional circumstances with families instead of institutions.

**1912**    On April 9, President William Howard Taft signs the law establishing the Children's Bureau in response to recommendations of the White House Conference of 1909. The Children's Bureau, the first federal government department devoted to the welfare of children, is given the responsibility to investigate and report on all matters pertaining to infant mortality, the birth rate, orphanages, juvenile courts, dangerous occupations, accidents and diseases of children, and employment. Originally part of the Department of Labor, the Children's Bureau is eventually moved to the Department of Health and Human Services' Administration on Youth and Families. The Children's Bureau remains the agency primarily responsible for implementing federal child welfare initiatives.

**1923**    The Children's Bureau publishes *Foster-Home Care for Dependent Children*, signifying the growing preference for foster family care over institutional care.

**1935** The Social Security Act of 1935 authorizes the first federal grants for child welfare services. Though initially minimal, these grants prompt the states to establish child welfare agencies and to develop programs for facilitating child welfare services.

**1944** The U.S. Supreme Court rules in the case of *Prince v. Massachusetts* that the state has broad authority to regulate the actions and treatment of children and that parental authority can be lawfully restricted if such restrictions are made for the child's welfare.

**1960** The U.S. Department of Health, Education, and Welfare (DHEW), which is charged with administering Aid to Dependent Children (ADC), implements the Flemming Rule. This rule, named for current DHEW secretary Arthur Flemming, is passed in response to the "Louisiana Incident," in which Louisiana purged more than 20,000 children from its welfare rolls because their mothers had birthed them out of wedlock. The ruling declares that states cannot deny funding to children simply because they are living in households deemed "unsuitable." Under the ruling, states are required to either provide appropriate services to make the homes suitable or to move children to a suitable placement while continuing to provide financial support for such children.

**1961** Amendments to the Social Security Act codify the Flemming Rule and create the Foster Care component to ADC. Under ADC-Foster Care, the states receive federal matching funds for foster care payments made on behalf of children who had received ADC payments prior to removal from an unsuitable home.

**1962** Public Welfare Amendments to the Social Security Act expand funding for children removed from homes deemed unsuitable and require state agencies to report families whose children are identified as candidates for removal to the court system.

**1972** The Children's Bureau sponsors and President Richard Nixon proclaims National Action for Foster Children Week to raise awareness of the needs of children in foster care and to recruit more foster parents.

**1974**   President Richard Nixon signs the Child Abuse Prevention and Treatment Act (CAPTA) into law on January 31. The act, which marks the beginning of a new national response to the problem of child abuse and neglect, provides funding for states that meet certain legislative benchmarks to engage in child abuse prevention, identification, prosecution, and treatment activities and demonstration project grants for public and private agencies. The act also creates the National Center on Child Abuse and Neglect (now known as the Office on Child Abuse and Neglect) within the Children's Bureau to serve as a focal point for CAPTA activities. Today, CAPTA continues to provide minimum standards for child maltreatment definitions and support state-level prevention and intervention efforts.

**1975**   In an effort to increase adoptions for children with special needs and circumstances, the Children's Bureau bestowed a grant to the Child Welfare League of America to develop a Model State Subsidized Adoption Act. The act provides that when efforts to achieve placement without subsidy have failed, a child can be certified as eligible for subsidized adoption under the following conditions: physical or mental disability, emotional disturbance, recognized high risk of physical or mental disease, age disadvantage, sibling relationship, racial or ethnic factors, or any combination of these factors.

**1977**   Seattle juvenile court judge David W. Soukup develops the Court Appointed Special Advocate (CASA) model after he realizes that he had insufficient information to make life-changing decisions for children who had suffered from child abuse and neglect because the only information available was that provided by the state Child Protective Services. Under the CASA model, now used throughout the country, courts assign a trained volunteer to a child in foster care. This volunteer stays with the child throughout their placement changes as long as they are in foster care, providing a consistent advocate and detailed court reports on behalf of the child.

**1977**    The Administration on Children, Youth and Families (ACYF) is created within the Department of Health and Human Services to administer the programs of the former Office of Child Development. The Children's Bureau becomes one of three major divisions of this new agency.

**1977**    The U.S. Supreme Court rules in the case of *Smith v. Organization of Foster Families for Equality and Reform et al.*, overturning a district court ruling that New York's procedures governing the removal of foster children from foster homes were an unconstitutional deprivation of due process because they denied a foster child a hearing before transferring the child to another foster home or returning the child to his or her natural parents. The Supreme Court concludes that because foster parents provide care under a contractual agreement with an agency and are compensated for their services, they do not have the full authority of a legal custodian; therefore, the city did not engage in an unconstitutional deprivation of due process rights.

**1978**    In recognition of the high number of Native American children being removed from their families and placed in care outside of Native American communities, Congress enacts the Indian Child Welfare Act (ICWA) of 1978. The act grants tribal courts jurisdiction over Native American children living on and off reservations who were wards of the state and gives tribal governments the right to intervene in state court proceedings. In effect, the ICWA makes it extremely difficult for nonnative people to adopt Native American children. The act additionally establishes the Indian Child Welfare Act grant program, which provides funding to a wide array of tribal child welfare services.

**1980**    In response to increasing concerns that many children were being removed from their homes unnecessarily and that inadequate efforts were being made to reunify children in care with their biological families or to place them with adoptive families, Congress passes and President Jimmy Carter signs the Adoption Assistance and Child Welfare Act. The law reflects a growing emphasis on achieving timely permanence for children and establishes a major federal role in the administration and oversight of child welfare services. Among its provisions are federal adoption assistance for children with special needs and a mandate for the states to make "reasonable efforts" to prevent children from having to be removed from their homes or to reunify children with their families as quickly as possible. The act also requires that each child in foster care have a plan for achieving a permanency goal (e.g., reunification, relative placement, or adoption) and periodic court and administrative hearings to review progress toward the goal.

**1982**   The U.S. Supreme Court rules in the case of *Santosky v. Kramer* that a statute permitting the permanent termination of parental rights based on a preponderance of the evidence standard violated the due process clause of the 14th Amendment. The court holds that the permanent termination of parental rights requires clear and convincing evidence.

**1985**   After several surveys conducted in the early to mid-1980s reveal that a growing number of older youth are aging out of the foster care system with little support or preparation for adulthood—and that a significant number of homeless shelter users had been recently discharged from foster care—Congress creates the first federal Independent Living Program. The program authorizes an annual entitlement of $45 million for the next two years to provide states with resources to create and implement independent living services for AFDC-eligible children aged 16 and over. In 1988, the program is expanded to permit states to provide services to all youth in foster care aged 16 to 18, not just those who are AFDC eligible. The program's authorization is made permanent in 1993 and is later expanded through the Foster Care Independence Act of 1999.

**1988** President Ronald Reagan issues the first presidential proclamation for National Foster Care Month in May.

**1989** The U.S. Supreme Court rules in the case of *Mississippi Band of Choctaw Indians v. Holyfield* that the Indian Child Welfare Act governs adoptions of Indian children and that tribal courts have jurisdiction over state courts, regardless of where the child was born or whether the parents lived on a reservation.

**1989** The U.S. Supreme Court rules in the case of *DeShaney v. Winnebago County Department of Social Services* that state child welfare agencies are not liable under the 14th Amendment to the U.S. Constitution for failing to prevent child abuse when the child is in parental custody and when the state did not create the danger of abuse or increase the risk of abuse.

**1993** President Clinton signs the Family Preservation and Support Services Program Act into law. The act authorizes funding for services—such as various forms of counseling and therapy—to help preserve, support, and reunify families in crisis. The act also provides funding for states to develop statewide automated child welfare information systems and establishes the Court Improvement Program, which allocates grants to improve the court's role in achieving stable, permanent homes for children in foster care.

**1994** The Child Waiver Demonstration Program is authorized as part of the Social Security Amendments of 1994. This program permits certain states greater flexibility in how they use child welfare funding to test innovative approaches to delivery and services.

**1994** President Bill Clinton signs into law the Multiethnic Placement Act (MEPA). The act prohibits state agencies and other entities involved in foster care or adoptive placements that receive federal financial assistance from delaying or denying a child's foster care or adoptive placement solely based on the child's or the prospective parent's race, color, or national origin. It also requires states to diligently recruit foster and adoptive parents who reflect the racial and ethnic diversity of the children in the state who need foster and adoptive homes.

**1996** Following testimony that provisions of the Multiethnic Placement Act (MEPA) harmed African American and other minority children by implicitly condoning avoidance of transracial placements, Congress passes and President Clinton signs the Interethnic Provisions of 1996. Among other things, these amendments repeal a provision that had allowed states to consider the child's ethnic or cultural background and the prospective parents' ability to meet the child's related needs in placement decisions. In 1997 and 1998, the Department of Health and Human Services issues guidance documents suggesting that under the law "a child's race, color, or national origin cannot be routinely considered as a relevant factor in assessing the child's best interest." In practice, however, state and local governments have increasingly passed kinship care policies designed to keep children in families with their same racial and ethnic makeup.

**1996** President Bill Clinton signs into law the Personal Responsibility and Work Opportunity Reconciliation Act. In addition to implementing broad changes to federal welfare policy generally, the act limits eligibility for federal foster care and adoption assistance payments to children in families that would have been eligible for AFDC. The act also requires states to consider giving preference to adult relatives over nonrelative caregivers when choosing a placement.

**1997** President Bill Clinton signs into law the Adoption and Safe Families Act (ASFA). The law introduces significant reforms into the foster care system, including shortening decision-making timelines for assessment and interventions services to children and moving children to permanency. Although AFSA reaffirms the importance of making reasonable efforts to preserve and reunify families, it outlines specific instances in which reunification efforts are not necessary. It also encourages the practice of adoption through a new adoption incentive payment program. ASFA additionally requires the Department of Health and Human Services to establish new state performance standards and a state accountability system, whereby states could face financial penalties for failure to demonstrate improvements in child outcomes.

**1999**   President Bill Clinton signs into law the Foster Care Independence Act, which creates the permanently authorized John H. Chafee Foster Care Independence Program (CFCIP). This program is designed to enhance resources and strengthen state accountability for helping older youth leaving foster care to achieve self-sufficiency. The law doubles annual funds available to the states and expands the population of youth eligible to receive independent living services, including youth who have left care, through the age of 21. It additionally grants greater flexibility to the states and tribes in designing independent living programs and allows them to support young adults in a variety of ways, including help with education, employment, financial management, housing, and making connections with mentors.

**2000**   President Bill Clinton signs into law the Strengthening Abuse and Neglect Courts Act. The act strives to improve administrative efficiency and effectiveness of abuse and neglect courts by funding efforts to reduce the backlog of abuse and neglect cases and to automate case-tracking and data collection systems.

**2001**   Congress reauthorizes the Promoting Safe and Stable Families Act. The reauthorization amends the John H. Chafee Independent Living Program to provide specific funding for education and training vouchers for foster youth and to create new funding for mentoring children of incarcerated parents.

**2002**   The Children's Bureau joins with corporate and nonprofit partners to launch the AdoptUSKids national photo listing website. The website is the first national online photo listing site to feature photographs and biographies of children in the foster care system.

**2006**    President George W. Bush signs the Safe and Timely Interstate Placement of Foster Children Act. This legislation requires states to institute and maintain procedures for orderly and timely interstate placements of children in foster care.

**2006**    President George W. Bush signs the Child and Family Services Act. The act reauthorizes the Promoting Safe and Stable Families program, specifically providing funding to help states improve caseworker retention, recruitment, and training and to support monthly caseworker visits to children in foster care.

**2008**    President George W. Bush signs the Fostering Connections to Success and Increasing Adoptions Act. The act specifically amends various provisions of the Social Security Act to create new funding and programs for supporting relative caregivers, increasing incentives for adoption, improving health and education outcomes for children and youth in foster care, and enhancing services to youth aging out of foster care. The act also gives states the ability to extend eligibility for Title IV-E funding for foster care youth to remain in foster care beyond age 18 until age 21. In addition, it permits tribal governments to begin directly operating their own programs through funding under provisions of the Social Security Act.

**2010**    President Barack Obama signs the Affordable Care Act into law. The act contains a provision extending Medicaid coverage to all youth who exit out of foster care as young adults up to age 26.

**2010**    Congress reauthorizes the Child Abuse Prevention and Treatment Act (CAPTA). Updates include provisions to strengthen collaboration between service providers and to improve data collection and systems training for individuals charged with identifying, preventing, and responding to incidents of child maltreatment.

**2016**   President Obama adds "sexual orientation" as a protected trait under antidiscrimination rules governing federal funds to adoption and foster agencies, effectively restricting the allocation of funding to any agency that engages in discrimination against same-sex couples in their placement decisions.

**2018**   President Donald Trump signs the Family First Prevention Services Act into law on February 9. The law aims to prioritize keeping families together by putting federal money toward evidence-based prevention services, such as at-home parenting classes and mental health counseling and substance abuse treatment. It additionally limits placing children in institutional settings by capping federal funding for group homes, also known as "congregate care."

**2019**   President Donald Trump issues an executive order reversing Obama era restrictions prohibiting the allocation of federal funding to faith-based groups who only place children with married mothers and fathers.

**2020**   President Donald Trump issues an executive order titled Strengthening the Child Welfare System for America's Children with the stated goal of reducing the need to place children in foster care and achieving safe and timely permanency for children who are placed in care. Among other things, the order aims to increase collaboration between public, private, faith-based, and other community groups to help keep families together or to find children forever families, it instructs the Department of Health and Human Services (HHS) to develop a plan for addressing the barriers that kin and youth aging out of foster care may face in accessing existing federal assistance and benefits, and it requires HHS to improve data collection on the demographics of children waiting for adoption, the number and demographics of currently available foster families, the average foster parent retention rate, the targeted number of foster homes needed to meet the needs of foster children, and the average length of time required to complete foster and adoptive home certification.

**2020**    The U.S. Supreme Court hears oral arguments in the case of *Sharonell Fulton, et al. v. City of Philadelphia*. The case centers on the question of whether the City of Philadelphia violated the First Amendment's free exercise clause when it canceled Catholic Social Service's contract to provide foster care services because the agency does not provide service to unmarried and same-sex couples on religious grounds.

**2020**    The Supporting Foster Youth and Families through the Pandemic Act is passed as part of the federal stimulus bill signed into law on December 27. Among other things, the act provides $400 million in new funding for states to use for housing, education, transportation, and financial assistance for older youth, including those in extended foster care as well as young adults up to age 27 who have aged out of the system. The act also places a pandemic-driven pause on aging out of the system by requiring states to allow youth to remain in foster care past the standard age cutoff.

**2021**    The U.S. Supreme Court rules in the case of *Sharonell Fulton, et al. v. City of Philadelphia* that Philadelphia's decision to cancel Catholic Social Service's contract to provide foster care services on account of its religious beliefs violated the agency's First Amendment right to free exercise of religion.

**abandonment**   Occurs when a parent or guardian deserts a child without any regard for the child's health, safety, and welfare; fails to maintain contact with a child; or fails to provide supervision or reasonable support for a child.

**adjudicatory hearing**   A hearing held by a juvenile or family court to determine whether there is enough evidence of abuse, neglect, or abandonment for the state to intervene to remove a child. Also referred to as a fact-finding hearing.

**adoption**   A procedure by which a person or persons legally assume the role of parents, with all the rights and responsibilities of that role, in respect to a person who is not their biological child. There are three types of adoption. A closed adoption occurs when birth parents and adoptive parents have no contact with one another. A semi-open adoption occurs when personal contact between birth parents and adoptive parents may or may not occur during the adoptive process, depending on the preferences of the various parties. An open adoption occurs when the contact information for both the birth mother and the adoptive parents is shared and no barriers are put up to prevent contact between the parties, either before the adoption is finalized or after.

**adoption assistance**   Federal funding (allocated under Title IV-E of the Social Security Act) or state benefits granted to adoptive families to help offset the short- and long-term costs associated with adopting special needs children. Benefits may include monthly cash payments, medical assistance, social services, and nonrecurring adoption expenses.

**adoption placement**   The placement of a child or children with prospective adoptive parents with the intent of legally finalizing an adoption.

**advocate**   A person who acts or who speaks on behalf of another person with the goal of promoting his or her well-being, best interest, and personal wishes.

**aging out**   When foster youth emancipate or leave foster care because they have turned a certain age, usually 18 or 21 (depending on state law). Aging out usually results in the loss of financial and other support from the state for foster care payments, health care, housing, and other costs.

**almshouses**   A house supported by a church or private charity to house and support aged, infirmed, or extremely poor individuals.

**attachment**   The formation of a significant and stable emotional connection between a child and his or her parent(s) or caregiver(s). The process of attachment begins in infancy as a child bonds with one or more primary caregivers. A failure by a child to develop stable and healthy attachments early in life can result in a wide range of attachment disorders and relational difficulties later in the child's life.

**birth or biological parent(s)**   Refers to the person who gave birth to or who biologically fathered a child. Also known as the birth mother or birth father.

**caregiver**   Anyone who provides for the physical, emotional, and social needs of a dependent person. Examples include parents or parental surrogates, childcare workers, and health care specialists.

**case plan**   The document created by a juvenile court judge or a foster care agency, along with the foster youth and family, identifying expectations, outcomes, goals and services provided to ensure child safety, well-being, and permanency.

**child abuse**    Occurs when a parent or caregiver, whether through intentional action or failing to act, causes injury, death, emotional harm, or risk of serious harm to a child. The various forms of abuse include neglect, physical abuse, sexual abuse, exploitation, and emotional abuse.

**child exploitation**    The use of a child for someone else's advantage, gratification, or profit, often resulting in unjust, cruel, and harmful treatment of the child. Examples include child labor and commercial sexual exploitation.

**child labor trafficking**    The act of recruiting, harboring, transporting, or obtaining through force, fraud, or coercion an individual who is 18 years old or younger for labor or services.

**Child Protective Services (CPS)**    The social services agency responsible in most states for investigating reports of child abuse and neglect and for providing services that include foster care to families in crisis.

**child sex trafficking**    The act of recruiting, harboring, transporting, providing, obtaining, patronizing, or soliciting an individual who is 18 years old or younger for sex, including prostitution and the production of child pornography.

**closed adoption**    Form of adoption in which birth parents and adoptive parents have no contact with one another.

**commercial sexual exploitation of children (CSEC)**    The commercial sexual exploitation of a person under the age of 18, for the purpose of child pornography, prostitution, or child sex tourism.

**concurrent planning**    The process of providing services with the primary goal of reunifying a child with their family of origin while simultaneously ensuring that a child is with a family who would be willing to provide a permanent home through adoption or guardianship if reunification does not occur. Concurrent planning aims to eliminate delays in attaining permanency for children in foster care.

**congregate care**   Placement that consists of 24-hour supervision in a highly structured setting, such as a group home or residential treatment facility.

**Court Appointed Special Advocate (CASA)**   An adult volunteer assigned by a juvenile court judge to advocate for the best interest of a child living in foster care because of abuse and neglect.

**due process**   The principle that the state must respect each person's legal rights, including the rights to a court hearing, representation by an attorney, and speedy, fair, and impartial legal proceedings.

**emancipation**   The legal process through which a youth is legally declared an adult by a court prior to the age of 18; can also refers to a youth in foster care who is no longer a ward of the court or eligible for foster care services.

**emotional abuse**   A consistent pattern of using emotions to criticize, embarrass, shame, blame, or otherwise manipulate another person.

**English Poor Laws**   The body of laws first developed in 16th-century England that governed the provision of relief for the poor.

**faith-based organization (FBO)**   A nonprofit organization or service provider affiliated with or inspired by a certain religion or religious beliefs.

**family preservation services**   Programs designed to keep families safely together and avoid foster placement through the provision of support and intervention services aimed at helping families address major challenges and enhance family functioning.

**fictive kin**   People not related by birth or marriage who have an emotionally significant relationship with a child.

**finalization**   The act of establishing a legal family connection between the adopted person and the adoptive parent or parents. This act grants the rights and responsibilities to adoptive parents that are equivalent to those granted to families created by birth.

**foster care adoption** The adoption of a child from the foster care system after a court has (1) determined that the child cannot safely reunite with his or her birth family and (2) terminated the birth parents' rights to the child.

**foster care agency** A private agency that certifies and supervises foster homes.

**foster care placement** An approved family home, group home, or residential treatment facility where a child will receive care, nurturing, and support.

**foster care system** A system intended to serve dependent, neglected, and abused children who need to be either temporarily or permanently removed from their families of origin.

**foster child** A child who has been placed in legal custody of a state or county because the child's custodial parents/guardians are unable to provide a safe home due to abuse, neglect, or inability to care for the child.

**foster parent** A relative or nonrelative adult who has been approved by a local social services agency to provide a temporary home for and to educate, care for, and nurture children in foster care.

**group homes** A licensed home or facility intended to serve as an alternative to a family foster home. Group homes normally house 4 to 12 unrelated youth with house parents or a rotating staff of caregivers. More specialized therapeutic or treatment group homes employ specially trained staff to assist residents with emotional or behavioral concerns. Also known as congregate care homes.

**guardian** A person who fulfills the custodial and parenting responsibilities of a child with respect to care, education, and decision-making.

**guardian ad litem** An individual appointed by court order to represent the best interests of infants, minors, or mentally incompetent persons in legal proceedings, such as divorce, child custody, child abuse and neglect, and parental rights and responsibility cases.

**home study**  The process through which a state or private agency gathers information about and evaluates the fitness of prospective foster, kinship, and adoptive parents with the primary purpose of ensuring that each child is placed with a family or caretaker that can best meet his or her needs.

**independent living program**  A program designed to provide support and services to youth who are preparing to transition out of foster care because they have reached a certain age. Services often include training for employment, education, housing, relationships, health, and other life skills.

**juvenile and family court**  A court of law that deals with dependent children and has jurisdiction over issues involving child maltreatment, domestic violence, juvenile delinquency, divorce, child custody, and child support.

**kinship adoption**  An adoption of a child by someone related by family ties or a prior relationship.

**kinship care**  When foster children are placed in the home of a relative or person who had an established relationship with the child before he or she was removed from the parental home.

**legal guardianship**  A judicially created relationship granting a caretaker legal responsibility for the care of a child. A legal guardian remains under the supervision of the court.

**licensing**  Regulations in each state that ensure children are cared for in physically and developmentally safe environments. Some states do not require licensing for kinship or relative care homes.

**mandated reporter**  Groups or individuals who are required by state law to report suspected child abuse and neglect to the appropriate authorities. Mandated reporters typically include educators, health care and mental health professionals, social workers, childcare providers, and law enforcement.

**Medicaid** A joint federal and state program that provides medical insurance for low-income families and foster children.

**mentor** An individual who serves as a role model and who listens to, encourages, and provides other forms of support to another individual.

**methamphetamine** A highly addictive stimulant associated with serious health and psychiatric conditions, including heart and brain damage, impaired thinking and memory problems, aggression, violence, and psychotic behavior.

**natural mentor** Someone who a young person identifies as a mentor—such as a coach, teacher, neighbor, club leader, etc.—rather than someone they are formally matched with through a youth mentoring program.

**neglect** A form of child abuse in which a parent or caregiver fails to provide needed food, shelter, clothing, medical care, or supervision to the degree that a child's health, safety, and well-being are threatened with imminent risk or serious harm.

**nongovernmental organization (NGO)** Legally recognized, independent not-for-profit organization that operates independently from government entities. NGOs include charities, nonprofits, voluntary groups, trade unions, professional associations, and human rights advocacy groups.

**nonprofit** Legally recognized, independent not-for-profit organization that operates independently from government entities. Nonprofits include charities, voluntary groups, trade unions, professional associations, and human rights advocacy groups.

**open adoption** For of adoption in which contact information for both the birth mother and the adoptive parents is shared, and no barriers are put up to prevent contact between the parties, either before the adoption is finalized or after.

**opioids** A class of drugs naturally found in the opium poppy plant that work in the brain to produce a variety of effects, including the relief of pain. Opioids include the illegal drug heroin, synthetic opioids such as fentanyl, and pain relievers legally available by prescription, such as oxycodone, hydrocodone, codeine, morphine, and others.

**orphan**    A child who has separated from or lost both of his or her parents due to death, disappearance, abandonment, or desertion.

**orphanage**    An institution that houses children who are orphaned, abandoned, or whose parents are unable to care for them.

**parental rights**    The legal rights—and corresponding legal obligations—that come from being a parent of a child. Among other rights and responsibilities, this legal relationship includes a parent's responsibility to financially support, supervise, and provide a safe living environment for the child and a parent's rights to custody and to visit with and make educational, religious, or medical decisions for the child.

**permanency**    The achievement of permanent care, or a "forever home," for a child. Children are determined to have achieved permanency when they have been discharged from foster care because they have reunited with a parent or other family member, when they have been legally adopted, or when they have been discharged to the care of a legal guardian.

**permanency planning**    The services and interventions, individually designed for each child, that have the goal of achieving a "forever home" for the child in the shortest possible time. The plan could include reunification with the birth parents, placement with relatives, adoption, or independent living. Long-term or permanent foster care is not considered a permanent plan.

**physical abuse**    Any intentional act causing injury or trauma to another person by way of bodily contact.

**relinquishment**    When a birth parent voluntarily gives up his or her legal parental rights and responsibilities so that a child can be adopted.

**residential facility**   A structured 24-hour care facility with a professionally trained staff that provides a range of therapeutic, educational, recreational, and support services to young people to help them overcome behavioral, emotional, mental, or psychological issues.

**respite care**   Short-term childcare services offered to provide parents and other caregivers a break or temporary relief from the care of children. Respite care can be planned or offered during emergencies or times of crisis.

**reunification**   Refers to the process of returning children in out-of-home care to their families of origin.

**semi-open adoption**   Form of adoption in which personal contact between the birth parents and the adoptive parents may or may not occur during the adoptive process, depending on the preferences of the various parties.

**sexual abuse**   Unwanted sexual activity, with perpetrators using force, making threats, or taking advantage of victims not able to give consent. Child sexual abuse, also called child molestation, is a form of child abuse that includes sexual activity of any kind with a minor.

**special needs**   Children that are more difficult to place in foster care because they are older, are part of a sibling group, are multiethnic or biracial, or have medical, behavioral, emotional, or developmental issues.

**substance abuse**   A pattern of harmful use or dependence on an addictive substance, especially alcohol or drugs.

**Temporary Assistance for Needy Families (TANF)**   Federal program that aids needy families by granting states the funds and flexibility to implement their own welfare programs. TANF Replaced Aid to Families with Dependent Children (AFDC) with the intent of making welfare temporary and helping recipients move into work.

**termination of parental rights**   The legal severance of the rights of a parent or parents to the care, custody, and control of a child and to any benefits that, by law, would flow to the parent from the child.

**therapeutic foster care**    Care provided by foster parents who have received special training to care for a wide variety of children and adolescents with significant emotional or behavioral concerns.

**transition-age youth**    Youth between the ages of 16 and 24 who are in transition from state custody or foster care to independent living.

**transitional living program**    A program that usually includes housing to aid youth in the process of aging out of or emancipating from foster care.

**trauma**    A psychological emotional response to an event or experience that is deeply distressing or disturbing and that overwhelms an individual's ability to cope or causes feelings of helplessness. Trauma can be acute, chronic, or complex. Acute trauma results from a single stressful or dangerous event. Chronic trauma results from repeated and prolonged exposure to highly stressful events. Complex trauma results from multiple traumatic events.

**trauma-informed practice**    A policy, procedure, and treatment framework that involves understanding, recognizing, and responding to the widespread impact and effects of trauma.

**tribe, tribal**    An American Indian or Alaska Native tribal entity that is federally recognized as having a government-to-government relationship with the United States, with the responsibilities, powers, limitations, and obligations attached to that designation.

**visitation**    Planned face-to-face contact between a child or children in out-of-home care and their biological family members. The purpose of visitation is to maintain family attachment during the process of placement and permanency planning.

**voluntary placement**    When a child's parent or guardian temporarily places the child in foster care by signing a voluntary placement agreement with the local department of social services instead of going to court.

**WIC (Women, Infants, and Children)**    A federally funded supplemental nutrition program for children. Caretakers of certified children are provided monthly vouchers to purchase specific food items and other essentials.

Page numbers followed by *f* indicate figures.

## About the Author

**Christina Villegas**, PhD, is an associate professor of political science at California State University, San Bernardino. She has written a variety of articles and books on topics related to the American founding, the U.S. Constitution, and public policy.